The Linen Goddess

The Linen Goddess

*Travels from
the Red Sea to Prizren*

Sheila Paine

PALLAS ATHENE

CONTENTS

Waiting for a ferry by the Blue Nile, Tissasat, Ethiopia

Rashaida girls, Massawa environs, Eritrea
Next page: Statue of a woman in traditional costume, Pogradec, Albania

Preface

T he dust of winter lay opaque over the shuttered waterfront cafés. In the low Lenten sun the words 'feta salad', 'moussaka', daubed on their windows, shone white in the grime. Only the small bar, where Anna made strong coffee for the locals, was open. The old men sat around at rickety tables outside, the young swung their legs from the low whitewashed wall that separated the bar from the stony littered beach. The port notices, painted on wooden boards, had faded now that the new harbour had been built a little further round the island. 'Boat Services,' they said. 'Regular departures from Diafani to Rhodes, Heraklion, Piraeus, Alexandria.'

I had begun many thousands of miles away to the east, and quite a few years before, intrigued by a talismanic triangle with three tassels, either worn as an amulet to ward off evil spirits and illness, or embroidered as a pattern on clothing with the same purpose. I had searched for it westward from Afghanistan and the mountains of the Hindu Kush, until my wanderings had led me to this island of Karpathos. And, though I had found the amulet both worn and embroidered throughout my journeys, I had come no closer to discovering its origins. I had had to conclude that these might be too far removed in time to be traceable, but it did seem that its dissemination westward had been in the hands of Turkic peoples.

Now, kicking stones along the seashore by the old wooden jetty, I thought of the spider's web of links that tied the travels I had already made, to the way my search for the amulet should take me next. They were links that tangled unhelpfully in my mind: narcotic hemp, the triangular skirts of fertility goddesses, quotes from Ezekiel.

Or of men like J. Theodore Bent, and empires like that of neolithic
Old Europe and, millennia later, of Alexander and of the Ottomans.
Perhaps even fulgurite – stone struck by lightning – had some relevance.
And the most important elements in this unholy mix: the Orthodox
Church and Islam.

Confused and disorientated, I kicked another stone and decided,
rightly or wrongly, that the best way to start tackling all these themes
was to head for Alexandria.

The port officer lit a fourth cigarette, flicking the ash of the previous
one off his navy trousers, and pored over timetables sent from Piraeus.
'No boats to Alexandria,' he muttered. 'Only in summer.'

I walked across to Anna's bar, and sat down with a map. It was clear
that drawing a slightly squiggly line between Karpathos and Alexandria,
and extending it south to the Horn of Africa and north to the Balkans,
not only defined the western boundary of what had become my particular patch of the world, but marked the tectonic collision between the
Orthodox Church and Islam. There were even flash-points at each end
– civil war and starvation in the south, civil war and ethnic cleansing in
the north – and, in between, terrorist bombs, machine-gunned hostages,
and border shelling.

Why wait for summer?

In retrospect this urgency was irrelevant, for my journeys were to
take me several years. It had seemed ludicrously irresponsible to walk
around a war zone looking for embroidery and amulets, and so I had made
my way northward only gradually, waiting for the Balkan conflict to end,
though it clearly never would. I wandered, sometimes aimlessly, I dilly-
dallied, retraced my steps, zigzagged to and fro, and even pursued red
herrings like the Bents and blue beads.

Summers came and went. Ethnic cleansing came and went, and came
again. War stayed. Civil war and starvation in Sudan slipped out of the
headlines. And as for surfing the internet for information on that country when I set off, that had been an extraordinarily novel thing to do.
Now dotcom millionaires had been and gone, and the word 'surfing' had
fallen into disuse. Going on the internet had become as banal as lifting
up the phone and backpackers had their own websites where they

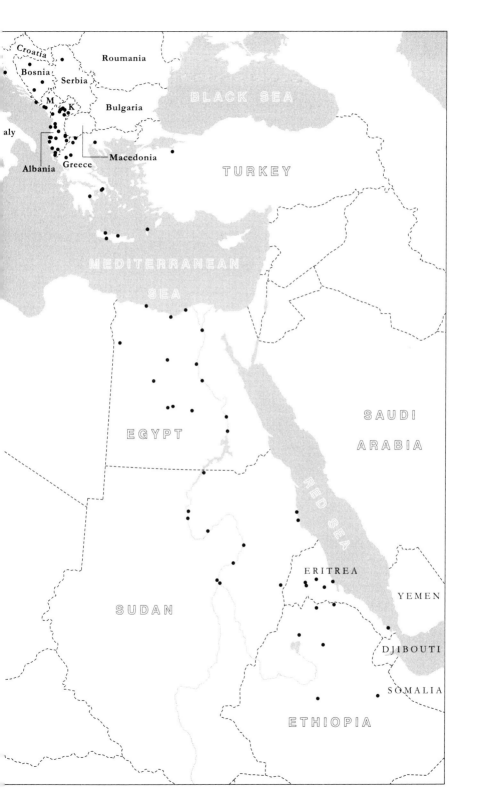

exchanged information. The era of the old Pudding Shop in Istanbul, with its pinned scraps of paper giving the low-down on bedbugs and cannabis for those heading east, had vanished for ever.

In the end, I neither began at my planned point of departure, Alexandria, nor did I ever reach my intended destination, Banja Luka, safe haven of the Bosnian war, long forgotten by the world, and diminishing in equal measure in my consciousness and in my determination to reach it. Instead, a chance meeting in Albania, and a remark about aprons, blew me sideways like summer thistledown into Kosovo.

The Quest

The task had seemed simple enough at the beginning: where had the idea first come from that a little triangle of silk embroidery, hung with three tassels, had the strength to fend off evil? And where did people still believe in it?

It was so potent an amulet in those high, isolated valleys of the Hindu Kush and the Himalaya where I had first found it, that it was known to protect against diseases that were not understood, and against evil spirits that inexplicably carried off babies, or arbitrarily pounced, bringing leprosy or fever. And if the mullahs insisted on a prayer or a quote from the Koran being stitched inside the triangle, the additional protection of Allah was thought only to be beneficial.

But what about the most westerly places where I had so far found the tasselled triangle? On my first journey, taking the southerly route from the Hindu Kush through Afghanistan, Pakistan, Iran, northern Iraq and Turkey, it had been Bulgaria: Bulgaria, with its whiffs of new entrepreneurial scams and its hordes of tourists sunning themselves at ridiculously named Black Sea resorts: 'Sunny Beach', 'Golden Sands'. There, the embroidered triangle was a talismanic motif on old marriage cushions, but I had seen no one wearing it as an amulet. Instead, people's faith appeared to lie in bobbles of red and white cotton pinned on to their clothes and worn from the first of May.

Then, on the second journey, the westernmost limit was Karpathos, where I now found myself. I had reached this Greek island by the northerly route from the western Himalaya through old Soviet Central Asia, Russia, Ukraine and the Carpathians. But Karpathos was a tourist island, overrun by earnest German hikers and French magazine photographers. What was the Asian amulet doing in such a place?

Here it was still worn for protection, still triangular in shape and made of fabric, but stuffed with pagan rather than Islamic devices – garlic, sharp

bits of broken needle, tangled fishing net, umbilical cord and fulgurite
– together with souvenirs of the Orthodox Church: candle grease, dried
flowers from the Good Friday *epitaphios*, olive branches from the altar.

Travelling westward, there had been a distinct change in the form of
the amulet. In the central and northern lands that once had been part
of the prehistoric civilization of Old Europe, which included Bulgaria
and Karpathos, the embroidered triangular amulet with three tassels had
become stylized into a goddess. She was worked in red thread on ritual
linen towels to be hung on trees, or stitched meticulously on ceremonial cushions. The triangle was her skirt, a small diamond above was her
head, and the three tassels had become her legs and a child being born.
    Where had this change occurred? Was it at some frontier of Turkic influ-
ence? Was it where silk gave way to linen? For this goddess was a
powerful symbol, counted onto the threads of linen, its potency deriving not only from the myths of the neolithic, but also from the slubs of
peasant weaving.
    My travels to the west, from Asia to Europe, had taken me across an
unseen border, from the world of silk to that of linen. I thought of silk,

slipping to the touch, cool and glazed as the surface of a winter lake, Its sybaritic sheen evolving incongruously from a warm tangle of cocoons nestling in women's armpits, then swirled in steam, unravelled and

spun into slivered filament. Dyed to blazing colours, silk is cut in swathes to make flowing oriental robes, whose excessive sleeves and dragonly decorations bespeak the ancient right to luxury that is its essence. But silk was now a world away.

Linen carries no such aura of splendour. The essence of linen is drudgery, its strong straight fibres husked and retted, bogged and broken, scutched and hackled, by bent women in boots and bonnets, and tired men in cloth caps and worn waistcoats. Its weave is direct, its texture tough, plain to the touch. Drab and ever-fading, it symbolizes the journey of peasant life.

Those long hours, spent muscles and ricked backs, make linen precious – it is meanly stitched into straight shifts that waste not an inch of cloth. The only concession made to the human form is to shape the garment by cutting small rectangles from the loom width, and dividing them again to form gussets for arms and sides.

Always, the throat is accommodated with difficulty: a neck slit is folded back into two triangles or, if a curved piece has to be cut out, it is done to incantations and spells. For linen should really never be cut, only severed by stone: linen is mystical.

And the finest linen of all was that of Ancient Egypt: *'Fine linen with broidered work from Egypt was that which thou spreadest forth to be thy sail; blue and purple from the isles of Elishah was that which covered thee.'* (Ezekiel 27:7)

Egypt and Alexandria it should be then, and perhaps straight ahead into Sudan – once another source of fine linen, and unknown amulets – but now closed territory and embroiled in civil war. Then beyond to the south and Ethiopia, turning east through Somalia and Djibouti up to the Ottoman conquests of the Red Sea, and maybe across to Yemen where, in the far north, the embroidered dresses of the town of Sa'ada were appliquéd over the breasts with the triangular motif of the amulet. In the decades of drought of the sixth millennium BC, the same motif in Old Europe had denoted rain and was incised on the breasts of the people's stone fertility goddesses. For rain and the milk that kept the new-born alive were equated.

But time seeped away and in the end it was not in Alexandria or even Egypt that I began my journeys. Nor did I go with the blessing of Ezekiel, but with the misgivings of a friend visiting Eritrea:

> *Dear Sheila*
>   *Sorry I didn't see you before I left. When are you about to take off?*
>   *Beautiful weather here and still fine atmosphere despite problems all around.*
>   *Thought you might like to know that the Horn is hotting up. Five Belgians killed here last week and several Westerners have received bullets in the back of the head down near Harar. Somalia I think would be very danger-ous. Not that this will put you off of course. Look what Burton faced! Might see you around.*
>   *Ciao, bella. Mike. x x*

I began then in the Horn of Africa, more precisely at the Red Sea port of Massawa in Eritrea. Though Eritrea had long been considered part of Ethiopia, its coast had been one of the most southerly footholds of the Ottoman empire. It had been settled too by the Italians for almost a hundred years. It looked north and east, clinging only lightly to the edges of black Africa, and finally and recently had freed itself from Ethiopia after a thirty-year war. And in the hinterland of Massawa roamed the Rashaida nomads, not African at all but originating from somewhere north and east of Arabia, and so likely to be trailing Asian and Turkic influences. Patterns and amulets perhaps.

The whole region of the Horn was a promising melting-pot of Africa and Arabia; of Turkish, Arabic and even Greek influence and a clash-point of Islam, Orthodoxy and paganism.

And Massawa was where J. Theodore Bent, after collecting in 1884 the only known linen dresses of Karpathos, had begun his journey to the 'Sacred City of the Ethiopians'. Accompanied – as always – by Mrs Bent.

Eritrea

Massawa

The island port of Massawa lies off the coast of Eritrea, a bleached huddle beyond a causeway and beyond another causeway, like some whitewashed Victorian pier set adrift.

Ancient Greeks and Egyptians traded here. Arabs and Indians too. Turks came, remained for hundreds of years, and dealt in slaves, pearls and fish. Italians grabbed it in the European scramble for Africa. Ethiopians blanket-bombed it, leaving graceful white arcades ripped with grey gashes, and stucco façades pitted by bullet holes into fragile lace.

Between the ruins – where, presumably, narrow lanes once jostled with sun-stippled houses – wide dirt spaces were home to wild, jackally dogs. Washing lay stretched on the dust, goats trod vacantly. Girls plaiting each other's black hair sat on doorsteps where doors had gone, skinny-limbed kids played around rubbled shacks plugged with corrugated iron. All looked desperately poor. A young girl hurled a stone at me. Rooks cawed.

When night fell it was warm and starlit, obscuring the scars and mellowing the streets into soft alleyways of scented sand, disturbed by vibrant oriental music and the muffled footsteps of passers-by, and by the greenly-lit signs of open-fronted stalls – 'Foodstuff Merchant & Ship Chandler', 'Red Sea Grocery' – that spilled their wares into the streets: cans of oil, bags of spices and incense, bolts of glitzy fabric, a life-size plastic mannequin in a tight blue satin dress. Everywhere was the mildewed, fetid smell of all sub-tropical seaports.

Massawa was richly Turkish, but it was the Italians who had linked it by causeway to the stepping-stone of the island of Tualad, already tied

by a wider causeway to the African coast. It was on Tualad that the
Italians built their villas, set along a sandy grid of roads: elegant Art-Deco
palaces like old Odeon cinemas, painted in colours of butterscotch and
toffee-apple and studded by oval windows outlined in tortoiseshell-like
designer glasses. The villas had been bombed, too, but still stood, roofless and pockmarked. Beautiful curved glass walls striped with green (they
reminded me of the Hoover building on the road out to Oxford) stood
sandblasted and full of rubble. Between them, a few of the older
Turkish buildings had survived, their windows cooled by slatted apple-
green shutters, their walls of honeyed woodwork latticed and slipped over
white plaster. Gentle currents of air moved through the laths.

And the Rashaida?

They were not Asian or Turkic, it transpired, but Arabic, the last
settlers on the Red Sea fringe of Africa, arriving only in the nineteenth
century. Their faces were coffee-coloured, sharper than those of the
local Tigrinya people, I was told. They kept themselves apart and spoke
only Arabic. I began by engaging Teklit, a young waiter from the smart
hotel at the water's edge of Massawa, who spoke both Tigrinya and
German, but not English. We set off on foot, picking up by the roadside a bearded man with fine face and yellow shirt, whom Teklit identified
as Rashaida and who offered to take us to someone he knew who spoke
Tigrinya as well as Arabic, a fellow called Ali. Obliged to employ this
cumbersome retinue of interpreters, I strode along the road to find the
Rashaida, but soon found myself trailing along behind my masculine staff,
as any woman must.

We stopped first at Ali's hut, a simple construction of bound twigs and
palm mats in a settlement a short distance inland from Tualad. Ali
himself – tall, hook-nosed, dressed in a grubby *jellabyya* – came out to
greet us, winding a white turban round his head. He shook hands
enthusiastically with my interpreters, nodded cursorily in my direction, and then led us inside, putting on a waistcoat machine-embroidered
with palm trees and pineapples when he learned what our interest was.

The hut was furnished simply with two iron bedsteads, a palm floor
mat, some basic cooking pans and, hanging from the ceiling, a food carrier
made of leather strips decorated with cowries. The dispersal of cowries
from their home ground of the ocean around the Maldives and their
importance as currency and talisman – even taking into account their
resemblance to the female vulva – always astounds me. Here at least they

would have come via the Red Sea, but what about the cowrie headdresses
of the Kalash valleys in northern Pakistan? Teklit, perceiving that my mind was wandering, sat himself down impor-
tantly to field questions. German to Tigrinya to Arabic and back again.
Everyone used to wear amulets, Ali said, but now some have given them
up. They are known as *kitab* and are more often rectangular than
triangular, and then only have pendants if they are for a woman. They
are usually in metal, but can be in leather or cloth for poorer people, and
are worn round the neck or the arm. Or just left in the house, Ali
added. Many that women wear are merely for decoration, but most are
to do with religion. If people are sick they buy a prayer from the priest
and then have an amulet made to put it in. But not just against sickness.
Against the devil, too – amulets keep you on the straight and narrow.
And against the evil eye (Ali used the Italian word 'malocchio'). No, he
wasn't wearing one himself.

The Rashaida are semi-nomadic, living on their camels, sheep and goats,
selling a camel if they need cash. When they're ready to move on they
just shut the doors of their huts and leave them for someone else to use,
though sometimes they might come back. The real nomads are those
Rashaida who live in the desert further north along the coast, Ali added.
And the Afar, they are true nomads, those wilder people living to the south
in the Danakil depression and formerly prone to chopping off the genitals of their enemies, or even those of just their visitors. They wore silver
amulets of the triangle standing on its apex, that is to say in its no doubt
more ancient role as symbol of the female pubic zone. But to go to
Danakil required equipment and back-up facilities befitting a real expedition. Those I did not have and felt reluctant to acquire for the sake of
a silver triangle which for me was the wrong way up.

As for the dresses of the coastal Rashaida, they were embroidered by
hand, Ali knew, whereas the two girls who had joined us at his hut, both
carrying babies protected by square leather amulets, wore long dresses
with zigzag patterns that were unmistakeably machined. To see the real
ones, we would need to go into the desert a little way north along the
coast, but there was no transport. We hijacked a minibus and bribed the
driver to take us there once he had dropped his passengers off.

The Rashaida we found lived in low Bedouin-style tents held by posts
tied with rags. There was no furniture, nor any cushions, only palm mats,
and a fire burning on the floor. Hordes of small naked girls, and boys

in filthy white shifts ran around. The minibus driver paced impatiently up and down.

The women wore the same silver-beaded face masks we had seen in Ali's village, and their dresses were embroidered in colourful bands of floral pattern. Almost all by machine. An old man stood by, a long curved sword in one hand and, on the other arm just above the elbow, two rectangular metal amulets tied with string.

They were an unpleasant, grasping bunch of people for whom the dollar each one asked for taking their photograph was never enough and who eyed my glasses, earrings and pen covetously. When I opened my bag to find the extra money they demanded, its contents vanished in a fast swirl of small bodies and dirty white cotton. The old man shouted and immediately my possessions were piled on the sand in front of me. After a surreptitious fumbling to reassure myself of the presence of my money-belt, we climbed back into our minibus to return to Massawa.

As I strolled around Tualad in the evening, a taxi pulled up: 'Did you manage to see the Rashaida this morning, Madam?' a perfect stranger asked. 'They're usually hard to find.'

As for the Afar, the closest it was possible to get by public bus was the twig-and-thorn village of Fono, where women with gold rings in their noses carried their babies slung over their backs in goatskins decorated with cowries. There was no sign of any embroidery or amulets, or of the Afar. Maybe the Rashaida would be the furthest my search would take me. On the slow journey back through desert and stony outcrops spotted with umbrella trees, the distant views were of mountains to the west, and to the east the Red Sea, where lay hidden the ruins of the ancient Axumite port of Adulis.

J. Theodore would have been there.

'Adulis?' said the man in Tualad's tourist office. 'Impossible to visit. Only a group, never one person alone.'

'Can I join a group to go there?'

'We have no groups.'

In the modern port of Massawa huge mechanical diggers were working behind the rusty iron fence separating the shoreline from the jagged façades opposite that must once have formed an elegant Italian seafront. I enquired at the small port office about boats to Yemen. 'No, we have no. No, boats are no.'

Fulgurites are natural glasses formed by lightning strikes to the ground. They can be found in many parts of the world – even possibly on Mars. They appear on exposed mountain tops; they remain in areas of 'fossil dune complexes, where they occur topographically above palaeolimnic deposits in mid-slope position of interdune depressions.' And on one occasion, when a lightning bolt hit a concrete sidewalk in Detroit, fulgurites suddenly littered the ground.

The bits of fulgurite stuffed into the amulets of Karpathos as magical elements able to avert the evil eye, I never managed to see. Simply known as 'astropeleki' – a word from ancient Greek – it was impossible to guess what they looked like. It seemed that fulgurites formed in the mountains were like glass – rocks fused by the massive electrical power of lightning – while fulgurites formed when sand was hit were known as 'petrified lightning' and thus perhaps might look more like silica blitzed into tubes, I thought.

The nightwatchman at the Hotel Savoiya in Massawa – a decrepit old Turkish building, its stairs encrusted with sand – accosted me as he came on duty early. 'Sister' he shouted, 'you British, me with army British Somaliland, now Somali people no good.'

He brought out two newspaper packets and tipped them out. They were full of amulets. 'See, sister, ancient. Kitab.' Most were the conventional silver rectangle or tube. But one was bizarre. A weird pale green circle set in dull silver with three silver bell pendants.

'Glass? Stone?' I asked.

He threw his hands in the air. 'No, sister. The gods go boom, boom, boom,' he yelled, in imitation of thunder.

'Then the gods, sister, go zoom, zoom, zoom.' He waved his hands in decisive downward strokes mimicking lightning.

Could this be a fulgurite?

'How much?' I asked.

'Tomorrow you leave, the bus driver sleeps here. I wake you 4.45.'

'I have a perfectly good alarm clock.'

'Twenty dollars,' he said.

'I'll think about it.' But I knew I would give in. It was yet another of those odd lifelines thrown just when you wonder why on earth you are here, when all threads that led and lead on, seem to be lost. But I deeply suspected that lightning striking on the earth would hardly produce a circle of cut green glass like a Woolworth's Christmas tree bauble. I went out for supper.

On my return he rushed up to me. 'Sister, sister, when the skies open crash, crash, that white stuff' – there was no doubt at all that he meant lightning – 'then it is like the sun in the light, it gives out all around.'

'Fifteen dollars,' I said.

'Sister, I wake you 4.15.'

At four he was banging on the door. 'Last bus, last bus!' He handed me a small packet wrapped in tinfoil. I thought to ask him which tribe the 'lightning stone' came from. 'The Tigray.'

'Not Rashaida?'

'No, Tigray,' he insisted.

So from the mountains – like the mountains of Karpathos – not the desert. He dismissed the Karpathos amulet I was wearing as 'modern'. 'This ancient, sister, ancient.'

It glowed weirdly glaucous as I held it in my hand on the bus to Asmara.

Asmara

Leaving behind the gutted buildings, the abandoned tanks and burned-out lorries parched into the sand of Massawa's hinterland, the road to Asmara curls and mounts steeply, first through dry scrubland where camels graze on saxaul, then through a fertile valley, dank with drizzle and mist, where fuzzed green plants move past the bus windows. When the dankness clears for a moment, the plants turn out to be prickly pear, crowding for space among low feathery bushes with rusty-brown flowers.

The bus moves up out of the valley into a mountain range rising two thousand metres, that the Turks, remaining on the coast, never bothered to climb, but that the Italians, like busy insects, bored and webbed with cables, railway and road. Beyond the cacti, and then the terraces of maize, we seem to emerge from a landscape of magnificent mountains rising out of a myriad lakes. Only as the lakes begin to swirl and ripple is it apparent that they are clouds. Clouds creeping up from the coast into every valley and crevasse and hollow. The peaks remain shrouded.

On one, invisible above, stands the monastery of Debre Bizen, founded in 1368 on the summit of the highest peak in Eritrea, by the monk Abuna

Philipos. Here, a hundred years ago – remarked J. Theodore, slightly misquoting Gibbon – the monks lived 'forgetful of the world and by the world forgotten'. And Mrs Bent, having previously refused to withdraw from the precincts of another monastery where no women – or female animals – were allowed, managed to enter here by disguising herself as a man, the braids on her costume leading her to be mistaken for a military officer. Monks still live here, women are still forbidden, Debre Bizen still hides in clouds, though on a clear day the Red Sea lowlands are said to be visible from it, and on starry nights the lights of Massawa.

The years of war with Ethiopia have completely destroyed the farms and orchards that the monks depended on, and now, to try to preserve their way of life and their art treasures – manuscripts five hundred years old, relics, crosses and robes – the monks are appealing to 'all Christians', presumably including women, for money. This they hope to use to turn the monastery into a huge tourist attraction, setting up a souvenir industry and making the road – now steep, ragged and intimidating – more accessible. But at the bottom they will leave the demarcation line, over which no woman is allowed to step.

Nothing betrays the presence of Debre Bizen as the bus passes way below it.

The young mother sitting opposite me cannot have been more than twenty, and her daughter about six. The girl stood, leaning on her mother's knee, for the five hours of the journey and never moved or spoke, except to turn shyly and accept a handful of pumpkin seeds.

The office of the National Union of Eritrean Women in Asmara was approached up an outside flight of stairs and was manned by a group of efficient women in colourful dress. Most rural women and girls are brutalized, they said. From the age of five they get up before dawn and walk miles to collect firewood and water. Then they work on domestic chores all day and look after the younger children. The women are given heavy tasks in the fields and the home – grinding grain manually, for example – and always eat last and least, just whatever is left when the men and boys of the family have finished. They're often married off from the age of twelve and certainly by fifteen: childbearing is then immediate and frequent. Female circumcision is still widespread and so is

wife-battery. Some customary laws even specify on which part of the body
the husband should or should not hit his wife. It seemed irrelevant to
ask whether they embroidered. Yes they do, around Anseba and
Kashbak in the north. I couldn't find such villages on any map.

The Union was working on several projects. On literacy 85-90% of
women were illiterate – on setting up grinding mills, and factories to
produce women's underwear and sanitary towels, on teaching
vocational skills and providing health education. Things had improved
since the war with Ethiopia. That had been the first time women had
been able to leave their homes – many had been fighters. Now they had
a legal right to own land, and the government had made the payment
of dowry and bride price, and marriage by kidnapping, illegal. And
they had set up a system of working for food, so war widows were
building dams and roads. They were also sweeping the streets of Asmara.

Asmara lies in the sunshine above the coastal clouds, an Italian town
set in Africa. Notices 'divieto di affissione', advertisements 'una vita senza
dolore con aspirina', trade signs 'ricambi', rust on its walls. Around its
faded elegance blows the red dust of Africa, like ground cinnamon
sprinkled over a shop cake.
    Catholic bells wake the town at six-thirty and end the day's work at
five. The *muezzin* chimes in quietly. From just after dawn the old
widows sweep the sun-bleached streets with palm fronds and witches'
broomsticks: the palm to swish across the beautiful tiled and patterned
pavements, sending scudding into the gutter purple bougainvillaea
petals, and the broomsticks to gather them up into green wheelbarrows,
each with a number splodged on it in yellow paint. They work up and
down the main avenue, skirting the date palms and the lavender lace
umbrellas of jacaranda trees. They sweep the side streets too, where
only the odd Fiat Cinquecento and horse and cart pass by, and where
kids play football in the road with a stuffed sock, and chalk out hopscotch.
    The smells along the streets are musky, a subtle distillation of the
warmth of sun on human skin, of bread baking, spicy food cooking and
coffee beans roasting. Dust sifts into the nostrils, the inescapable
African dust.
    Public buildings from the first wave of Italian settlers in the late nine-
teenth century look like Tuscan cathedrals with imposing staircases,

porticoes, towers, turrets, and castellated balconies held on fluted supports. One side street offers a glimpse of a Brunelleschi dome. But most of all, Asmara is a town of almost pure Art Deco architecture, unique in the world, built by the Italian settlers who came in the 1930s. Curved street façades are like the prows of ocean-going liners, cafés and shops are named in spare, elegant font, and, hidden behind back stairways of neglected hotels, are peach glass mirrors and rounded dressers of marble and bakelite, edged in chrome, in old Hollywood style.

Most buildings are now weathered and peeling, and a few strafed here and there with bullet holes. But mostly Asmara survived the British damage of the Second World War, and the struggle against Ethiopia. Its isolation has left it in a time-warp of courteous, unhurried people, of a town centre that is quietly residential and devoid of high-rise blocks of banks, insurance companies and offices.

At night the dark streets are safe to walk, alive only with the odd passer-by and with cicadas and exotic music from behind closed doors. Soft coach-lights on the gates of villas, from an era when Italians would ride out in their horse-drawn carriages, blur the intensity of the African stars.

The old Keren hotel lies on a slight hill, a shabby cream tin-roofed building whose symmetrical, pedimented windows are shuttered in pale green. The lace-curtained door marked 'Entrance' is caked in grime. Its dining room is a gem of overblown turn-of-the-century fantasy. The pale yellow walls are encrusted with white plaster decoration: a curly frieze and Grinling Gibbons-type floral swags swathe together Bacchanalian cherubs haloed by bunches of blowsy grapes. 'Anno 1899' is painted in black. In each corner a pedestalled vase is weighed down by gargoyles and crude leafy acanthus, and in the centre of the room rises a spectacular white plaster pillar with a curlicued capital.

Looking benignly down on the few solitary diners were two large masks, probably meant to be Commedia and Tragedia, but in truth one more tongue-in-cheek and the other yawning.

'I have wine' said the waiter. 'Sometime OK, sometime sour, but after open you pay. You try, OK?'

I smiled and nodded. The man at the next table nodded back and moved over to join me. He was very thin, with grizzled hair and a dark face which would have been sharp had it not been furrowed by wrinkles and squashed by a punched-up nose. His brown eyes were slightly glaucous as though cataracts were pending. He was nattily dressed in pressed dogtooth trousers, white Aertex shirt and denim jacket, set off by a flowing scarf. He wasted no time.

His name was Tekleab – 'plant of God'. He had been working in Sweden as an accountant for twenty-eight years – he was fifty-three, he confided. He had a Swedish wife and two kids, 'most of Sweden is half-caste now, they didn't realize when they let all those people in. Even the king's children.' He had come back to see his brother in his home village, 'he draws his water from a well and has eleven children and a few head of cattle. I envy him his peace.'

He was Eritrean now and not Ethiopian any more. 'Things are changing,' he added. 'Our generation based their lives on education. We underlined every word in a book that we didn't know and then learnt it. Now the world belongs to young men. They're different.' He continued with the history of his life and paused only to gather up his goat stew into handfuls of *injera* – the cartwheel of fermented dough that is the staple of the local diet – and put it into his mouth, leaving gravyish stains all over his face and fingers. He gave his thumbs an extra lick, smiled at me and got up and left.

The wine was sour.

A few evenings later Tekleab found me at the Keren again. It transpired that he was staying there – my own place was a little pension up the road, a third of the price. He was drinking double *zibibs* – a strong local anise-flavoured liquor – and evidently had been for some time. He talked of Eritrea, of its promise for the future now that it had enjoyed five years of peace. Its young president, Issaias Afewerki, was eliminating corruption – police and bureaucrats were paid decent wages to avoid temptation – while the president himself received only $12,000 a year. Cars could only be imported for your own use, not for sale – Afewerki's official vehicle was an old Toyota. Aid was only accepted in a working partnership.

But then he would allow no opposition party and there were whispers of human rights abuse. Begging was illegal – and what had happened to the beggars? people asked. Some said they were shot, others that they'd been pushed over the border into Ethiopia. 'No,' said Tekleab 'they're cared for by their families.' He was proud to be Eritrean, but because he hadn't voted in the referendum for independence he had to pay 2% of his annual salary to have his Eritrean identity card ('and that as a

Swedish accountant,' he pointed out. There was no getting round it.) That was what he was here for, to get his identity card.

He spoke again of his brother's life: 'only sunrise, then sunset, and between you go out to sell two eggs. And at night no electricity, only the stars and the great ball of the sky. And water only from the well, and goats, and love and peace and nothing else. Then when you want a servant, you get married.' This brought him, in his own line of argument, to the subject of circumcision. 'It's done with a rusty old blade. For a boy at forty days if the hood is there or not – or later – it doesn't make much difference but the baby screams. For a girl at eight days. They – usually an old woman – cut everything away and then sew it all up leaving only a hole for urine. But then everyone knows the girl is a virgin and the family hang a wet towel – a wet red towel – outside the house, so everyone knows. And when she marries it has to be unsewn, all the skin grown together. Imagine.' He looked straight at me for the first time – 'you look like Katherine Hepburn' – and then picked up his theme again. 'Imagine. So a man is only a reminder to her of all the pain. It is everywhere in Africa. It is to be an African woman.' On this dramatic note he staggered off to his room.

The women walking around Asmara, particularly on a Sunday, looked cheerful and normal enough, and were totally swathed in white. They wore huge white shawls with patterned or red edges, and long white dresses sashed at the waist and embroidered down the front with as many variations of the Christian cross as are found in the silver and wooden crosses for which Ethiopia is so renowned. I searched for their source.

Gere was sitting in a cramped shop, a mass of white fabric on his knees. He was a very small man with a thin, twisted face that bespoke some untended childhood disease. He was actually a priest, he said, at the Orthodox church of St. Mariam – that kitsch twin-towered palace built by the Italians in 1917 on a spur overlooking the city – but as the church was mostly kept closed, his services were only infrequently required and so he spent the greater part of his time embroidering.

He worked slowly in bright acrylic threads – enlivened, as he thought, by bits of sparkly Lurex – a complicated version of the Ethiopian cross in chain and stem stitch. This dress was the traditional clothing worn by the mountain women, he explained, and the designs were drawn by Saloman, who sat beside him at a sewing machine. Saloman showed me how he drew a series of dots and then joined them, so creating hundreds of such variations on the cross.

Did he know the triangle with three pendants, and a diamond above it? Yes, yes. He drew it by the same method and added a cross above it. 'It has to have a cross because it is the church.'

'And what are the pendants?'

'Legs,' he said immediately, and then seemed to hesitate before suggesting joining them up to make a base.

'No,' I said. 'Leave them as legs.'

I then asked him about amulets, kitab, and the fertility goddess, mentioning her triangular skirt, and corn and fruit and greenness, but none of this meant anything to him. 'For us it is the church.'

Gere would embroider my triangular pattern for me. He could do it on white cotton fabric from Asmara, or similar stuff from Axum – a rough, almost hessian-like texture difficult to work a geometric pattern on successfully – or a fine striped cotton from Addis Ababa, which I chose. I would call for it before I left Asmara.

Left for where? I had told Tekleab that I was going over the border to Ethiopia. He advised against it – 'go and see what your consul says.'

The British Consulate was a small bungalow behind a high wall, only the Union Jack visible from the road. The walls were covered with warnings:

> *Eritrea: 5 Europeans (Belgian) and their Eritrean driver shot dead on road near Asmara. 19.2.97*
> *Somalia: Don't go. Nov. 96*
> *Yemen: Armed theft of vehicles and random kidnapping. Jan.96 French tourists taken hostage. Avoid governorates of Al Mahra, Al Jawf and Sa'ada.* (So much for the embroidered triangles on the dresses of Sa'ada, I thought.) *Marib area volatile. Where possible travel in groups. 21.2.97 (German tourists kidnapped, released 7.4.97)*
> *Egypt: Improving, but no travel by road, rail or river through governate of Minya (incl. Tel El Amarna and Beni Hassan). 96* (So much for the tomb paintings of women spinning and weaving linen at Beni Hassan, I thought.)
> *Sudan: Civil war in south, also near Eritrean and Ethiopian*

borders. Don't go near. 14.3.97
Ethiopia: 10.2.97 hand grenade killed at least 2 and injured
15, including 2 British and 2 Europeans in Harar. 2
foreigners also killed in Dire Dawa. Don't go east of
Awash or south through Bale. Bomb explosions at hotels
throughout Ethiopia in 1996. Go only to recognized tourist
areas – Rift Valley lakes, no further south than Arba
Minch, Addis and Highland tourist route. 14.2.97

I set off at 3.30 the next morning to catch the bus to Adigrat in Ethiopia.

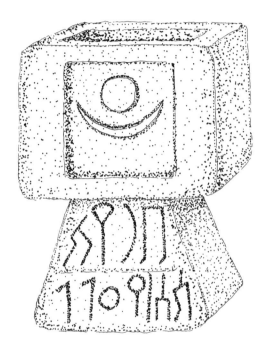

Ethiopia

Tigray

S outh of Asmara, Eritrea blends into Ethiopia in a barren pleating of mountain and plateau, half-concealing in its folds narrow green strips of cultivation busy with people and animals. Here and there a lone sycamore fig tree – immense, ancient, wide-spreading on tangled roots – emerged from the morning mist, so out of scale and time with the human activity around, that it brought its own sense of awe, and of belonging to Africa and the beginnings of man.

The bus had left, as they always do, before the sun rose. A stop was scheduled, but overlooked, at the small town of Metara. This place J. Theodore had commented on, believing it to have been an Axumite city, the first town in the highlands where traders approaching from the Red Sea port of Adulis could buy ivory. Just outside it stood a towering third-century stele, topped by the 'disc over crescent' symbol of Almaqah, the moon god of south Arabia.

The twelve-hour clock begins the day in Ethiopia at dawn rather than at midnight and so the hours are counted lagging six behind the rest of the world, a small point that added to the general confusion at the new, makeshift border. All the passengers were tipped out for the usual bureacratic hassle, some not managing to get back on again as the bus hastened on. The region of Tigray, which we were now entering, was considered volatile as the home of the pink-hued Tigray Peoples' Liberation Front, that had overthrown the red rule of the Derg, and was still in power.

We headed for the first town in Ethiopia, Adigrat, a dusty sort of place where I was the only person getting off and so was left on the nearby highway to walk, assailed by beggars and dirty, screeching kids, to the one hotel in town.

Tekleab was leaning on the doorway, a double zibib in one hand and a cigarette in the other, waiting to surprise me. 'You need looking after,' he said.

Hidden on precipitous slopes of the wild craggy mountains near Adigrat – jagged ranges that pierce the sky above the parched plateau – are the rock-hewn churches of Tigray, wondrous, and hardly known to the outside world. Tekleab quickly established himself as major-domo and hired a guide at a squabbled rate. We could visit them by bus and on foot.

We trekked from church to church – a little procession of guide in a grubby white shift, Tekleab with dapper floating scarf, and me in shabby skirts – met at most by an ancient priest, leaning on a stick, bending his shoulders under the warmth of a ragged shawl, clutching a bunch of keys, and demanding money. He would lead us by the light of a taper from the harsh sunlight into a sepulchral darkness of massive cool stone, into a labyrinth of carved pillars. The walls flickered, like old movies, with biblical scenes and the pale, wide-eyed faces of Ethiopian art, and with winged angels like those on old Russian ecclesiastical embroideries.

The iconostasis of each church usually consisted of three tatterdemalion brocades hanging from a rod, concealing a beautiful, gently flaking screen painted with staring figures dressed in robes patterned with pagan and Christian symbols. In most was a *tabot*, the replica of the Ark of the Covenant, to be found in almost all Ethiopian churches. The Ethiopians claim to be one of the lost tribes of Israel, and the original Ark, the chest in which the stone tablets of the Ten Commandments are said to lie, is reputed to have been brought by them from Jerusalem to Axum and still to be hidden there.

At Wuko Chirkos the priest was off duty, lying yellow-robed and idle on the dry ground outside. The church was a three-quarter monolith cut below ground level, a millefeuille cake of stone, backing onto rock, plants oozing between its layers like cream in a green froth. The façade was topped by a stone cross defiant against an indifferent blond landscape of scrub and tree. Fading yellow signs declared this church to date from the fourth century, but most are believed to have been built from the eleventh century on.

We hitched a lift in a truck, up hill and down dale into a wide, peaceful valley dotted with small huts, and shaded by spreading fig trees. Secluded at the head of the valley was the church of Abraha Atsbeha, fronted by an Italian portico, imposing as the Basilica of Assisi. Inside, the vast dome, supported by a gloomy forest of serried stone pillars, flashed in meander patterns. Beautiful old painted doors led to the sepulchre of the two fourth-century kings, Abraha and Atsbeha, in whose honour the church had been built, but the focal point of decoration was a gaudy arbour with a plastic model of the Virgin Mary, dressed in shiny polyester.

The presence of the church of Mikael Milhaizengi was, like so many, only hinted at by a glimpse of stone windows and wooden doors, clinging halfway up a vertiginous cliff and so deeply incised that the rock face wrapped around both them and the priest who waited with his bunch of keys. In the darkness he lit a taper, dancing the stone into a glimmering, flowing huddle of columns, and teasing the rough T-shaped twigs leaning on them into a vision of the twisted shoulders of a group of penitents. What were these sticks that came alive in flickers of light? I asked. The short twigs were for the monks to sit on, like shooting sticks, and the tall for them to lean on, during the long, long hours of prayer.

We set off then to the next, Petros and Paulos, only visible as a low white doorway high up on a cliff face. The ascent began with a scramble over boulders, but then rapidly became a horrendous vertical climb up a cliff of slippery marble. I looked at this sheer precipice with its ladder of chipped footholds and stopped dead in my tracks.

'I'm sorry,' I said to the priest.

He nodded gently. 'Yes. Last week a young local woman climbed up and slipped. She was gone.'

Returning to Adigrat, the modern Orthodox church there was completely circular, like many in Ethiopia, an architectural form probably taken from the local African tradition of round huts. It was concocted of tin and palm, surrounded by a balcony, on which an old woman sat as concierge.

'She can't come in here,' she shouted at Tekleab. 'We don't like white people. And if she does come here, she must give money. She must always give money,' she continued shouting, then looked at me and spat.

Adigrat was a destitute town of barely-roofed, stone shacks and wide, rutted streets, teeming with beggars, cripples and boys who screamed 'you, you, gimme money' and tugged at my bag and clothes. The atmosphere was profoundly different from Eritrea, where children just said 'hello' and tried to shake your hand.

It had become impossible to shake off Tekleab. He seemed suddenly to have realized that he knew nothing at all about me, not even my name. 'Let's leave it like that,' I said. He was on his way to Nairobi, he told me, where his wallet and all his papers had been stolen on his way up to Eritrea. Could I lend him fifty dollars? I lent him forty, knowing I would never see it again, and feeling it would be better given to the cripples.

On the last night in Adigrat, my attempt at sleep was shattered by another violent downpour, rain splatting off the tin roofs with that sharp African hiss. A man in the hotel courtyard worked through the hours of darkness, killing and skinning goats, their flesh stinking of dung and blood in the hot rain. At four in the morning, chanting from the Orthodox church frazzled the last remnants of sleep. At five, coffee zipped me into life, and then Tekleab appeared and had his usual breakfast of two double zibibs.

I sat on a stone by the roadside waiting for my bus, while Tekleab left on another for Addis and Nairobi. He had no bags or luggage of any kind, only his pockets, and waved a backward goodbye.

I was heading for Axum. In the early morning mist the previous day I had seen a distant range of faint peaks, rounded like the sugar-loaf mountains of Chinese scrolls. I hoped they were the ones enclosing the Axumite kingdom, a kingdom cut off from the world, and forgotten for ten centuries.

The way wound down wide valleys flanked by steep escarpments and over a dry, sandy plateau, divided by stones into small fields being ploughed by pairs of oxen pulling wooden ploughs. Then past fig trees and prickly pear into a wild, harsh and arid land with ancient terracing, that led to the sugar-loaf mountains I had perceived in the mist. Each rose in isolation from the sandy plain that extended for miles and then clustered to a highland plateau where cattle grazed. Here lay Axum.

Axum

It defied belief that this small, dusty town, isolated in a barren African mountain range at more than two thousand metres, should have been the capital of one of the most important civilizations of late antiquity. The Axumite kingdom flourished for six hundred years from just after the birth of Christ, and then lay forgotten for nearly a thousand. It was the only African civilization to leave a legacy of written material – apart from Egypt, and Meroë in Sudan – and was one of the very few early civilizations of the world to issue its own gold coinage, which it did in emulation of Rome.

Though Axum appears to lie in the middle of nowhere, it is in fact set astride trade routes between the Nile and the Middle East, and owed its wealth to that great maritime highway of the ancient world, the Red Sea. And so the city looked east to its port Adulis, but the territory in between has always been forbidding, a fractured mountainous terrain of unpredictable weather patterns. It rises from the hot coastal plain – in turn oppressively humid or scorchingly dry – to the highlands, which are prone to violent storms, and are at times swirled in mist and at others cool and sunny.

The Axumite kingdom traded in luxury goods – exporting obsidian, tortoiseshell, ivory, incense, spices and rhino-horn, and importing wine, olive oil, cloth, glass and metals. Such goods it traded with Rome and the Mediterranean world, even with China, but its closest links were with the Sabaeans of South Arabia.

Axum began as a pagan civilization, its kings worshipping African gods that could be identified with such Greek deities as Zeus and Poseidon, or with South Arabian ones, as Astar and Almaqah. The beliefs of its people appeared to reside in the worship of a Trinity: Beher – who perhaps like Poseidon was god of the sea – together with Meder – whose name derives from the word for 'land' in the Ethiopian language of Ge'ez – and with Astar. These gods may form the Ethiopian Trinity of heaven, earth and sea, or perhaps a Trinity with agricultural significance – could such beliefs possibly embrace the concept of a fertility goddess, and the arts depict her in stylized triangular form?

In the early fourth century, the ruler of Axum, King Ezana, converted to Christianity and the South Arabian disc and crescent symbol on Axumite coinage changed to a cross. But the old beliefs never entirely disappeared, and still the mixture remains. The Ethiopian Orthodox church has many rather un-Christian rituals, some Judaic, others including the incantation of magic spells to ward off devils.

At Ezana's conversion, Axum became a holy Christian city, and when it declined in the early seventh century – mainly because of Persian and then Arab conquests around the Red Sea – it still remained the holy city of Ethiopia. And all that is now visible of this prestigious past is a group of stelae.

Though they mark the sites of tombs of kings, the monumental stelae of Axum look just like the multi-storeyed mud-brick houses of Yemen. Their decoration is architectural: windows, doors and supporting wood beam ends, copied in stone. The tallest, more than thirty-three metres high, has crashed and lies where it fell, its shattered stones zigzagged down the grassy slope like a bombed tube escalator in the London Blitz. The highest one left erect extends twenty-four metres above the ground and three below it. The next highest was looted by Italy and now stands, deteriorating in the traffic fumes, near the Circus Maximus in Rome.

Olga's little shop, where she also lived, was close by the stelae field. It was cupboard size, with a single counter and just room for her bed – for water she had to go to a tap outside. She prepared coffee for me, strewing on the floor flower petals, and branches of a sort of grass that looked like miniature palm trees. She placed a small gas stove by them and lit it. 'It should be charcoal,' she said, 'but all the trees have gone.' In fact all the trees had already been used up thirteen centuries ago, and this was another of the contributory factors to the fall of Axum. She heated a small pan and then roasted the coffee beans in it until they were almost burning, throwing away the pale ones. 'They're bitter,' she explained.

The ritual was always the same: throughout Ethiopia, it later transpired. She ground the roasted beans with pestle and mortar, and placed them on a small basket mat. She then folded this and slid the beans into the water now warming on the stove. Once the water boiled she juggled the coffee to and fro between two pots, and then poured it through a filter of ox-tail hair into a tiny cup. This was the first drink, thick with sugar (had the Turks been here?) Water was added twice more to make the second and third servings, but each tasted almost as strong.

Olga sold embroidered dresses and picture postcards, as did other shops in Axum. 'Cultural clothing', 'curios', 'tourist souvenirs' were signs everywhere, and here also were tourists, the first Europeans I had seen since Asmara. The 'cultural clothing' was the traditional white embroidered dress of the highlands, made by men in small workshops, like Gere's in Asmara, still with variations of the cross down the entire front. Some

women walking the streets wore them, others just had the usual white
cotton shawls over poor, grubby dresses. Most women were carrying wood
on their backs, burdens that were too heavy for donkeys. He felt guilty
about his mother, a young man told me, she was now bent double and
suffered from serious back pains because of the wood she had carried all
her life. And now his wife had to do it too. If women weren't carrying
wood then they had a baby slung on their back in a cowrie-decorated
goatskin. Dirty children, wearing only old vests and amulets of a cross
and a leather rectangle, rushed up to me and screeched 'you, you, pen,
pen, gimme money, gimme money.' Cripples hobbled up on one emaciated leg and an even thinner stick. Eyeless, armless, leprous, feet twisted
backwards, crawling on wooden blocks, all repeated the same shrill
cries. I gave only to timid old women, but felt besieged, and helpless to
solve Ethiopia's economic and health problems out of my own purse. Just
occasionally it was 'va bene' that people shouted, which served only to
confuse.

The roads were virtually empty of traffic but full of people – walking,
cycling, leading donkeys, or riding in horse-drawn carriages, or, more
often, carts. I visited the local museum where there were goddess figures
that were too realistic, but there was a pair of ecclesiastical trousers with
embroidery on the cuffs very like that of Yemen. Another interesting
connection, but boats were no, I remembered.

I spent days investigating tombs and stones, aware of the warren of
archeological treasure buried below Axum. One excavation was of Kaleb's
tomb, seventeen monolithic steps below ground, the walls constructed
of huge slabs of stone interlocked without mortar, like a jigsaw – a
gloomy slumbering cavern lit only by the light of a match, as the electricity had failed. This is how J. Theodore would have seen it, I suddenly
thought. I had almost forgotten about him.

Of J. Theodore Bent, Amulets and Goddesses

J. Theodore, I was discovering, was a dyed-in-the-wool Victorian, the
kind who would certainly have dressed for dinner in the wilds: 'To
what European power will the ancient empire of Ethiopia eventually
belong?' was to him a natural question. His portrait showed him to be

a bewhiskered young man in a stiff, chequered suit. He seemed rather pompous, remarking as he set off for Ethiopia: *'It was reported that the King of England was coming, as no one not royal was likely to be called Theodore. The Abyssinian legend is that King Theodore I, who reigned from 1409 to 1412, was a great worker of miracles, and that another King would arise of this name, who would re-establish the Cross in the Holy Sepulchre, and make Ethiopia the first of nations.'*

J. Theodore's name was actually James.

James Theodore Bent was an archaeologist at the British School of Archaeology in Athens in the 1890s. He married Mrs Bent, whose Christian name he never mentioned, in 1877, and she accompanied him on all his travels. He studied life in the Greek islands and then worked in the Persian Gulf, later becoming involved in the ancient African kingdoms of Axum and Zimbabwe, and their links with the Sabaeans of Southern Arabia.

Because he and Mrs Bent were responsible for collecting the only early nineteenth century embroidered dresses of Karpathos in Western collections – two in the V&A, two in the Benaki, and one in the Met – I had hoped that, if anyone could give any clues as to linen and embroidery in Axum, it would be them. But no. All he says is:

'Abyssinian women wear prettily embroidered drawers, when they ride, with massive silver anklets below. They have a long upper shirt, also tastefully embroidered, and also reminding us of certain Greek island costumes.'

As the embroidery of each Greek island is completely different, this information was frustrating to say the least. And what did he consider tasteful?

The purpose of the Bents' journey between Massawa and Axum in 1893 was that of archaeological research. They rode on mules, scrambled up and down mountains, slept in tents and were always accompanied by armed guards. They endured storms, heavy mists and hoar frosts, looking all the time for Roman, Greek, Turkish and Sabaean influences. They found many.

Some were in inscriptions and in the fact that Old South Arabian writing was known in northern Ethiopia from around the fifth century BC. Other links were the similarity of irrigation systems – the dam at Kohaito in Ethiopia being similar to the Marib dam in Yemen – but the most interesting were those relating to pagan beliefs. The temple at

Yeha, close to Axum and also dating from the fifth century BC, shows signs of the pagan fertility cults of the Sabaeans: found there were a seated goddess figure with Medusa-like locks, formed of stone incised in lines, and other goddess figures with carved heads and formless bodies. And then, deriving most probably from the cult of horns, many patterns of ibex.

As for the circular churches of Ethiopia, comments Bent, with their four doors at the points of the compass, and the surrounding sacred grove – even the dancing of the priests – all this comes from the worship of Baal, the sun god, and relates to the sun-worship of Southern Arabia. Yet another link is the custom of tying rags to trees, or to reeds by a sacred stream 'a custom which prevails all over the East amongst the Persians, Turks, and modern Greeks.' The Bents found sacred old sycamores hung with little offerings – beads, rags, bracelets, rings. They took a great interest in all such pagan and amuletic devices.

'The Defteras of Ethiopia,' wrote Bent, 'do a good business in writing the long parchment charms with quaint pictures thereon, which are tightly bound up in stamped leather cases and tied round the neck to ward off diseases and the evil eye.'

It was just such a charm on parchment, rolled inside python skin, that I bought at a curio shop in Axum. The incantation on it was written in Ge'ez: *'By the name of Ab-Besma Ab-Besma Wold and one God, pray for Baria your slave, against Zar and Womitch, I say salaam. He who sends devils Saint Faneol fight against them, by the name of God some people make mistakes, I say salaam, he who sent devils in the face of God and high power, by speech come bad problems, you are an angel, I say salaam, that you send to me devils, but the awe of God, Faneol the angel, who works very quickly to help, and the Angel Gabriel...'*

'Ab' is 'father', the old man in the curio shop explained, and 'wold' is 'son'. 'Besma' is the Holy Spirit, so that is the Trinity. 'Baria' was the name of the woman the amulet was made for. 'Zar' is a spirit who possesses people and makes them mad, and 'womitch' 'another kind of thing that makes people sick.'

The names of the saints were carefully drawn in red ink – made from red stone crushed with red flowers – and those of the devils in black – made with the charcoal that collects under a cooking pot on a wood fire, burnt with grain and then stirred with glue from a tree. Both substances are mixed in separate containers with a little water and allowed to ferment for one or two years. 'That makes them permanent,' said the old man.

The incantation continued: *'Devils are killing children, and he was locked inside a door, the angels became angry and opened the door, then St. Michael, Gabriel, Raphael and Jehovah* ('the four who carry the Ark,' explained the old man) *stand by to take care of the world. I believe in you. Save me in all these woes of killing children.'*

At this point the old man stopped. These were only the first four lines, he explained, and the scroll was seven feet long. He could arrange for a priest – seeing Ge'ez was now only used as an ecclesiastical language – to translate it all for me. But it would cost a lot of money. I thanked him and said I thought I had got the gist of it.

The purpose of such amulets, he pointed out, was to protect women against the loss of their babies in childbirth or soon after. The infant mortality rate was so high they could only believe that devils were responsible. So they would come to the deftera, the magic man of the church – 'there are only a few of them now,' he commented – if they were pregnant or a child had died. He would tell the woman to buy a sheep and some sort of medicine. They would then kill the sheep and the deftera would wash the woman's body in the sheep's blood, and then give her the medicine to eat. The sheep's skin would be cleaned and the magic words would be written on it.

If this wasn't enough to cure the woman – or her baby – the deftera would put some water in a container, place it in front of the woman, read the whole scroll to her and then wash her with the water. He would do this every day for seven days. Then she would certainly be cured. The deftera would roll the scroll into leather, 'sometimes it used to be lion skin, but better still snake skin. Women are frightened of snakes, they think they make them demented, but she will see the snake has been killed, so she will change her mind. Once he has rolled the scroll into its case, the woman will wear it round her neck for the rest of her life.'

These amulets were commented on by Dr Charles Johnston in 1841 when he noted that the Ethiopians had great faith in 'absurd formulae' inscribed on parchment and rolled into red leather amulets worn around the left arm of a man or the neck of a woman against disease. They were sometimes sold by 'dobtaras' for as much as ten Maria Theresa thalers each. Then they also wore things like red coral and sea shells on their wrist and ankle against all sorts of complaints, including rheumatism and possession by demons.

Such practices still continue, but possession by spirits – the condition known as 'zar' – is today in noticeable decline. The reason offered is that 'the new generation doesn't believe in it, so it can't catch you; when people get sick now they go to doctors.' And the only amulet they seemed to recognise among the plethora hanging round my neck was the cowrie shell.

This was all very well, but where had it got me? I had gone from the embroidered triangular amulets of Afghanistan, containing an extract from the Koran or a prayer from the mullah, to the triangular amulets of Karpathos, not embroidered but sewn with sequins and containing all kinds of pagan devices. So from Turkic and Muslim in Asia, to Greek and Christian in Europe. Now, on these new African journeys, the amulets were a real mixture of religious and pagan.

I myself was a walking manifestation of Islamic, Orthodox and pagan beliefs. I was wearing round my neck not only a triangular amulet embroidered with a horned goddess motif and tasselled by three 'evil eye' beads and shells – from Karakalpakstan – but also a rectangle of leather embossed with a cowrie shell, and on another piece of string two Orthodox crosses, one of wood and the other of brass, and a leopard's claw set in silver. If any one of these amulets meant anything to anyone, surely they would comment on it? Only the cowrie was recognised.

So much for amulets, but what about fulgurite? Though I had looked in hundreds of jewellers' windows and rummaged through cardboard boxes full of stones, I had seen nothing like it. I dismissed it then as a bizarre link between mountainous areas subject to violent storms.

And what had become of linen? Ethiopia was no flax country, and never had been, though one of Justinian's ambassadors described the Axumite king Kaleb – who reigned in the early sixth century – as wearing a linen kilt embroidered in gold. Linen was imported through Adulis, in all probability from Egypt. Even a little muslin was brought from India, and cotton may have come from the Meroë kingdom of Sudan.

Now they grew their own cotton and in rural Ethiopia women stood outside their huts spinning, while men wove on horizontal looms. But it was always cotton. Linen was further north: historically in Sudan and Egypt and, as the Romans planted flax throughout their empire, perhaps

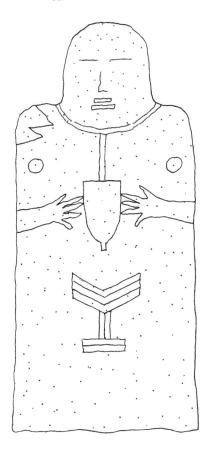

also in Libya. Then, of course, in Europe. But until I headed north again this was cotton country.

And what of the goddess? In the form I was interested in – the triangle with three pendants topped by a diamond – she belonged to linen and the north. But here she was carved in stone, in the form of those strange figures at Yeha. Then, in a region of southern Ethiopia settled probably by people from Tigray, there are mysterious stelae, carved in the form of humans or perhaps deities, that stand as grave markers grouped in clusters. They are decorated with pagan motifs – circles

that could relate to a sun or moon cult – and some hold what appears
to be a cup in their hands. They are exactly like the stelae of the steppes
that are found in the area extending from Kirghizstan as far west as
Crimea. If they are contemporary with the rock-hewn churches nearby
– and therefore erected some time between the eleventh and fourteenth
centuries, as is believed but not proven – then this Rift Valley region south
of Addis Ababa could mark the medieval boundary between pagan and
Christian Ethiopia.

It was precisely following, or determining, such boundaries that had
brought me here. I was hoping to find the south-western limits of
Turkic influence – and were these stelae relevant? And most of all, I
wanted to follow the medieval fault-line between pagan Africa, the
Orthodox church, and their conquerors from the east – Turkic, Ottoman,
Arab, Muslim. The juxtaposition of pagan stelae and rock-hewn churches,
the barrier of the Red Sea mountains that the Muslims had left alone and
only begun to penetrate in the thirteenth century, and the isolation of
Ethiopia's Orthodoxy from the religions of the rest of the world, were
the clearest possible borderlines.

If that was all I had found relating to linen and goddesses, what then
of embroidery? There is goldwork in Ethiopia on ecclesiastical robes and
on garments hired out for marriages and celebrations. There used to be
ceremonial clothing embroidered in silk and hung with silver bells and
balls, as the coat presented to Wilfred Thesiger's father when he was
Consul-General in Abyssinia, but such ornate garments seem to belong
to the past. Now the only embroidery is on the dresses of the highland
women. The white cotton these are all made of is hand-spun and handwoven and comes from Ethiopia, only to be an import in Eritrea. It's a
pretty poor, fine dishclothy kind of fabric of the type I had seen Gere
working on, too uneven to lend itself to counted threadwork, which is
what the triangular goddess really needs. And the motif on these dresses
was always only the Ethiopian cross, crudely worked. Still, they looked
wonderful, all those women in long white dresses, sashes and white
scarves, congregating like snowdrifts around the churches, or walking in
gentle clouds down dusty streets.

There was still one enclave in Ethiopia to look for embroidery and
amulets, the Muslim town of Harar. A grenade had recently been thrown
into a hotel there, killing and injuring several people, including tourists.

It was out of bounds for foreigners. I might as well spend time following the tourist trail of Lalibela, Gondar and the Blue Nile falls, until Harar's gates opened again.

The Tourist Trail I: Lalibela

The airport terminal of Axum was an open-air affair, an improvised hut made of a few tree branches propped up, tied with string and held in place by a tin roof. The runway was a strip of grass alongside it, where the passengers' bags were laid out in a neat row and scrupulously checked. The tiny propeller plane took off over the backs of a few goats and then flew over an eroded plateau gashed into ravines and scarred by mountain crags. It landed at the airport of Lalibela, an even homelier version of that of Axum.

The nearby monolithic churches, hewn on King Lalibela's orders in the twelfth century into the rocks of this remote mountainside, are one of the greatest wonders and mysteries of the Christian world. How they came to be built in such an isolated spot so difficult of access, how they were cut with the simplest of tools out of solid rock, how they were designed to form such a warren of complex levels, planes and turns, and, most of all, why, will probably never be entirely understood.

I found a young guide, Theodros, and we set off together into a labyrinth of old rose stone, deeply incised in the rock below ground level: a labyrinth chiselled by hand alone into tunnels, passages, moats, stairways and walkways, linking in a snakes-and-ladders turmoil the churches themselves. In narrow defiles we brushed our shoulders along cool dusky pink walls untouched by the sun, in wider passageways we blinked at scarps bleached to pale apricot. Here and there hollowed into the walls were hermits' caves and graves, one containing a skull, and, bent close by it, leathery, mummified legs and feet, as if the worshipper in death were still at prayer.

Round each corner we came to a monolithic church, its walls rising sheer out of the massive excavated clefts around it, a church of a size that would grace any parish, any town square, but cut in a single piece out of the mountainside. Huddled everywhere were figures shrouded in white rags, some crouched against the walls, their crooks propped up against them, others standing reading the Bible. A mystical chanting and the occasional toll of a bell eddied around the stillness of the rocks and the men.

The chanting, and the service for which the bell tolled, lasted for three hours, a ritual that has remained unchanged for almost two thousand years. As the mournful blend of monotone Amharic and Ge'ez finally died away, and silence gradually slipped back into the church, Theodros took me inside. In the dim candlelight shimmered a maze of pillars, carved from the same rock as the church, not by being cut and placed within it, but by all the solid rock around those pillars being removed. So, having severed the mountainside to free the monolith that would form the church, the carvers burrowed away inside, creating pillars, pediments, capitals and arches, and then incised in the walls tiny windows of symbolic shapes. These let in shafts of light that fell through motes of dust onto the pillars in the forms of the swastika, the moon and stars, the cross, the flared cross of Lalibela and the curved arch of Axum.

People stood patiently in the gloom, hundreds of them, silently worshipping, still or shuffling, raggedly dressed. The symbols of sharp light touched their penitent faces with moons and stars. Swastikas and stars illuminated the painted biblical faces that stared from the walls, crosses and arches splintered the carving on heavy wooden chests and massive doors.

Lalibela was visually, aurally and spiritually awe-inspiring.

The village beyond wound higgeldy-piggeldy up the mountainside, the circular houses of stone built in two low storeys, those of twigs in one. I wandered around without the protection of Theodros. Beggars tugged at my clothes, leprous, legless, cripples with deformities I had not seen since Bangladesh looked pitifully at me. Filthy children covered in flies pursued me relentlessly. There were women spinning cotton, or grinding maize and wheat on smooth, sloping stones, there were men weaving or making baskets, and chickens pecking around the dirt pathways. The poverty was desperate. And again 'You, you, you' was screamed at me in that terrible high-pitched tone, 'gimme, gimme.'

But the child standing outside the church, his face half-eaten by leprosy, was silent. Hanging round his neck, as protection and cure, was an amulet of cowries and blue beads. And a small leather bag containing the holy soil of Lalibela.

The beauty of Lalibela was stunning, and beauty that is stunning stuns the mind – what else did the word mean before being hijacked to describe every coffee-table book of artful photographs? And in stunning it obliterates the detail. Returning to the rock-and-rose-hewn churches with Theodros the next day, their impact softened by a casual familiarity, I noticed aspects less sublime.

The floors, first, were covered in dusty woolly rugs that appeared to be knitted. The pattern on them was the Ethiopian lion, an emasculated nursery version with its four legs and feet all sideways on, a mane like an Elizabethan ruff, and eyes that squinted short-sightedly. But it did have a vigorous tail, a forked Satanic extremity.

And on these woolly rugs lay an unbelievable assortment of tat that looked as if it had lain there for hundreds of years: old tin cans, kitsch paintings of overblown madonnas, handmade baskets covered with crocheted acrylic doilies – for receiving offerings – piles of grain, dumps of rags, broken candles, corroded ancient Bibles and little heaps of the holy soil of Lalibela for the priests to sell. And leaning on the walls were shabby stained umbrellas, looking as though abandoned in the cluttered back hall of some English country house, covered in labrador hairs and dumped with the green wellies. They must once have been beautifully embroidered with dazzling suns and stars, proudly held aloft in the blaze of every gaudy ceremony.

Then outside, the sunlit apricot and rose stone of several of the churches was caged under rusty scaffolding. This, financed by Norway or Finland the faded notices said, supported tin roofs intended for protection. It was claimed that the Italians had pummelled the churches with bullet holes and left them exposed to the elements. But the pockmarks alluded to seemed too regular to be from bullets, and the holes poked in the walls ostensibly by men with guns, too high for human hands.

As for the priests who were everywhere, though they were splendidly dressed in high gold brocade caps and robes of purple, yellow and gold, and carried immense ornate crosses of gold and silver, ready for any ritual; they actually spent most of their time selling little paper twists of holy ash to the lepers.

A man walked up to me with a clipboard, describing himself as 'Minister of Tourism for Lalibela'. They had almost completed a brand-new tarmac runway so charter flights could come in. In a week or two it would be operational – what did I think that would do for Lalibela?

In the meantime the airport 'departure lounge' was a tree with stones under it, and donkeys were shooed off the grass so the plane could take off.

And two weeks later, when presumably the new airfield had been inaugurated, the priests' gold crosses were stolen from Lalibela.

The Tourist Trail II: Gondar

Ethiopia – its Greek name means 'sunburnt people', whereas Abyssinia, its Arab name, means 'mixed people' – is the oldest independent African kingdom. Its language, Amharic, is one of the earliest written languages in the world. In medieval Europe it was the only African country people knew. On their maps, all of Africa south of the Sahara was labelled 'Ethiopia' or 'here be dragons', and even unknown countries in an easterly direction were named Ethiopia. Until Haile Selassie, descendant of Solomon, conquering Lion of Judah, King of the Rastafarians, was murdered in 1975, Ethiopia clung to its feudal past. It still lives by the Julian calendar, so that just as its twelve-hour, dawn-launched clock leaves it six hours behind everyone else, it dawdles three years behind as well.

Ethiopia is the only African country that was not colonised by a European power, so that even J. Theodore was left wondering who was bound to take it over, as someone was. They never did. The Italians tried their hand at empire-building in the nineteenth century, along with all the other powers involved in the scramble for Africa, but were defeated by a motley band of warriors clad in amuletic fur, and brandishing spears. Perhaps this single defeat of a modern European power by a medieval African kingdom lay behind the Italians' reputation in subsequent wars of having tanks with one forward gear and four reverse.

Ethiopia is also the oldest Christian country in the world, having followed first the Old Testament and then the New. Christianity, with the fervour of the earliest years, touched almost everything in Ethiopia. The ornate crosses, wrought in silver, carved in ebony, stitched in silk, mirrored in their complexity a devotional skill that a simple pairing of upright and horizontal could not satisfy. Even all the years of communism under Mengistu had done nothing to diminish that faith.

As an ancient Christian country, Ethiopia was firmly believed in the Middle Ages to be the home of the legendary Christian king, Prester John. It was in searching for him, and hoping to gain his allegiance in holding off the Muslims, who were threatening their maritime trade, that the Portuguese came here in the fifteenth century, sending soldiers, sailors and priests. By the seventeenth century there were disputes between the Ethiopian Orthodox Church and the Catholic, and the Portuguese, supporting the Catholic, were thrown out.

In the meantime they had built at Gondar an enclave of royal palaces, banqueting halls and stables, now crumbling in an evocative site of crisply dry yellow grass surrounded by a high wall. No one was there, save the restorers chipping away at beautiful deep pink stones piled in the grass, the same stone that had been used in the original ceilings and stairs. The setting was medieval Europe and hardly belonged to Africa, yet it was by Gondar that I saw no more olive-skinned aquiline faces, but only black negroid ones. And the night was warm and African. In the hotel garden cicadas hummed and the low lights silhouetted the trees into torn black lace. A tiny waxbill with yellow breast, and flash of blue as it flew away, swooped down onto a vase of flowers by my side.

The further south the buses took me, the denser and more African the foliage and the more exotic the birds: a huge hooded hornbill raided another bird's nest, dribbling the yolks from the stolen eggs down its breast feathers, amazing birds flew by, from delicate pinky-red firefinches to menacing vultures.

The Tourist Trail III: Blue Nile Falls

James Bruce, passing this way in 1769 in his search for the source of the Nile, had certainly been exaggerating when he said of T'is Abay, the Blue Nile falls: 'It was one of the most magnificent stupendous sights in the creation, much degraded and vilified by the lies of a grovelling fanatic priest.' Or had he? It was not that different today. Problems at the falls, the guide-book said. It mentioned drunken, loutish behaviour, intimidating groups of adolescents yelling abuse and demanding money. Beautiful though the falls might be, it was advisable to give the place a miss: 'you might be better off taking a book to the grounds of the Tana hotel and having a quiet read.'

As the bus pulled into the village by the falls, a young man got on and offered to guide me to them for twenty birr. Unsure how far away they were and what this entailed, I hesitated. 'Fifteen,' he said. I agreed. After all it was only £1.50.

We set off along a well-marked path, when all of a sudden he veered off through rough terrain. 'To see the church,' he explained. I followed, tripped and fell. He picked me up and dusted me down most solicitously and we continued. Suddenly there was a tremendous shouting from the direction of the path and an armed policeman summonsed us over. He grabbed the young man and pointed his gun at him. 'He's taking me to prison. Please help,' the man yelled as he was marched off. I surmised that he had led me off the path simply because he'd spotted the policeman. Even so, I leapt to his defence. But it was no use.

The falls were indeed spectacular and various young men popped up at different locations and looked after me, none asking for money. Then the only way back to the village, without retracing one's steps, was to be rowed over the river just above the head of the falls in a papyrus canoe. 'No chance of being swept down over the falls?' I enquired diffidently. 'No, no. Only perhaps in the rainy season when the river's in full spate. So the crossing is more expensive then. Forty birr instead of twenty.'

The village was one long sandy street lined with square and round huts of twig with straw roofs. Women sat winnowing, others spinning, and all were wearing a loose white dress with a red hem, embroidered at the back and down the front mainly with a motif of diamonds that formed a cross but was less complicated than the crosses of Asmara or Axum. Rows of sashes woven by the men hung outside the huts. It was all fascinating but I was somewhat distracted.

I asked where the prison was. It turned out to be the largest building in the whole village, a complex of shacks around a courtyard. I enquired about my young man and was shown into various offices, innumerable bits of paper being stamped. Finally I got to him. He was in a tiny shack slatted at the front with heavy wooden bars. He peered through them, distraught and shouting. 'Please go to the tourist office and tell them to say they asked me to be your guide.' I promised I would.

The tourist office was one of the little twig huts along the main street. A smartly dressed woman listened to my tale then, casting her one non-blind eye heavenward, said 'he knows it's illegal for anyone but official guides to take tourists. He'll be in prison for a week and he'll be lucky if anyone brings him food, but he knew what he was doing.' She searched for the words she needed, but didn't happen to know 'serves him right.'

Addis Ababa

Addis was, predictably, a hideous urban sprawl. Suppurating arms reached out to me, 'you, you, gimme, gimme' screeched at whistle pitch. The rain pelted down squelching the rags, grime and litter, and the maimed, drugged and poor lying along the roadsides, into a morass of abject misery.

I checked into a crummy hotel where a young couple was emerging at lunchtime from a drab, windowless room with ruffled bed, the man caressing the woman's hair. The room was free for me to take. In the hotel café, a small lean-to shaded from the sun, a woman in her fifties sat alone. We introduced ourselves. 'Gertrud,' she said, 'Austrian.'

Gertrud was exceedingly plain. She had a huge nose and large ears, and long mousy hair scragged across her forehead to one side where it was regimented into a plastic clip and then left hanging in a kind of whip to the waist. It struck me immediately that she was oddly dressed. She wore a baggy track-suit top, polyester leggings, white socks and – seemingly totally out of character – a pair of very fancy, indeed rather silly, sparkly sandals.

She was travelling alone as her second Swedish husband – her first, also Swedish and the father of her children, had died – wouldn't come with her. He preferred to plant his potatoes in the garden at Gothenburg, and in any case he loved Austria and, if he was going to go anywhere, it would be there. So he would visit her family in her place, while she went off further afield, as she loved to do. But this time it had been terrible. She too had been taunted and jeered at, and assailed by beggars, and was trying to go home.

I knew it was rude, but curiosity overcame me and I enquired about her sandals, along the lines of 'do you find those practical for travelling?' 'God no,' she said. She had arrived at Woldia, a town to the north of Addis, after one of those long bus rides that always begin at four in the morning, and dump their passengers ruthlessly in some out-of-town depot in the fading light of evening. She had checked into a hotel and collapsed on the bed, without locking the door. Immediately a group of young Ethiopians had pushed in. She'd hung on to her money, her camera, everything she could that seemed important, but they'd made off with her only pair of shoes.

The Italians did occupy Ethiopia briefly from the run-up to the Second World War until the North Africa campaign, and had left a few traces, notably one or two restaurants in Addis. Gertrud and I treated ourselves to supper – ravioli alla Genovese – at one of them nearby, an old-fashioned place preserved in the time warp of a pre-war Italy long forgotten in Europe, its customers ex-pats who stayed behind when the Italian military left, its waiters ancient grey-haired Ethiopians in white coats as stiffly starched as the table-linen. It was a calm haven of gently creaking wooden floors, of sparkling silver, glass and linen, of prints of old Abyssinia, and of classical dishes of pasta and seafood.

The same evening, two grenades were thrown into a more expensive restaurant further up the road, the Blue Tops, blowing out a French-woman's eye and injuring other Europeans, in particular two British policemen working in Ethiopia who had thrown themselves at the first grenade to protect their wives and others. And a few minutes later another grenade, hurled through a window into a hotel in the centre of the city, killed a woman and injured thirty four people. Having to wear fancy sandals began to seem rather unimportant, indeed their sparkle somewhat defiant.

The next day I haunted the museums of Addis, closing my eyes and ears to the streets around me. On my return to the hotel the manager handed me a note. It was from Tekleab: 'please phone', with a number. How had he found me? I did nothing.

Harar

Harar festers on a rocky hilltop like old vomit on a pavement, its rubbish and sewage lying around on stone too hard to dig. Wild hyenas scavenge at its gates, scrofulous dogs cringe in the shade, flies blanket the detritus. Surrounded by a high battlemented stone wall, breached by one gate only sixty years ago, it was a curfewed town trading in slaves and contraband. From its four gates a cross of roads, lined with ill-lit stalls

and innumerable mosques, quarters the town. In between lies a twisting, rising, falling, stone-encumbered maze of dead ends designed to trap
thieves. It has not changed since Burton's day: 'the streets are narrow lanes,
up hill and down dale, strewed with gigantic rubbish heaps, upon which
repose packs of mangy, one-eyed dogs.'

Its houses turn inward in the Muslim fashion, their lively courtyards
hidden behind blank walls and perceived only through heavy doors
slightly ajar. Harar belongs to the Indian Ocean and the Middle East,
rather than to Africa.

By three of the town gates, bundles of shawled women sit patiently on
the ground, beside them shallow baskets of papaya, banana and mango,
rusty tins of peanuts, deep baskets of fresh rolls, or, laid out on paper,
small handfuls of garlic, red onions, potatoes. Most men stop only to buy
the branches of *qat*, that mildly narcotic leaf stuffed into the cheek and
chewed in much of East Africa and Yemen.

Other women, the beaded Argorba from further north, sit with the
faggots they have brought to sell. They have nothing else.

By the fourth gate, the 'Evil Gate', is the market of the blacksmiths,
weavers and craftsmen; those who, by virtue of their magical powers to
change natural materials into objects, have always been feared and
shunned by a credulous society. And not just in Harar.

If Harar is now an unpleasant market town, in the last century, dealing through Djibouti and Somaliland, it was 'the greatest trading-centre
of East Africa, called by many travellers the Timbuktu of Abyssinia, its
most civilized town, if by civilization we mean houses built of stone,
shops, drinking booths, pawn-shops, and houses of prostitution, slum
quarters honeycombed with sordid streets through which secretive
people slink about their mean material avocations with anxious preoc-
cupied looks.'

'We advise no foreigners to go out alone,' said the hotel owner. I
enquired first about the grenade incident I had read about in the
consulate at Asmara. It transpired that two armed men had suddenly
appeared, shot dead a customs officer and the hotel guard, and then
hurled a grenade into the place. So it appeared to have been a personal
vendetta linked to smuggling, rather than a specific attack on tourists.
'Even so, you should take Abdul.'

Abdul was an Arab – the Hararis are mainly descendants of Arab and

Persian exiles who settled there in the early thirteenth century, and are not African. He waved away the usual hassle of shrieking, grasping kids and staring men. Having discussed – with some surprise on his part – my interest in embroidery and amulets, we began in a house where a marriage was taking place. Or not precisely. We actually began in the bridegroom's father's house where the young man was getting ready, unpacking a flashy tie and holding it up against the crisp new suit and shirt hanging on the wall. 'We can choose our wives ourselves now,' said Abdul.

On then to the bride's house where the women of the family were sitting around in groups, dressed in floral shawls and flouncy dresses. There was no sign of the bride.

We continued to a third house where the actual wedding party was taking place, still without the bride and groom. Here there were only women, the older ones sitting on the ground in the courtyard, the younger dancing. One woman was leading the dancing playing a drum, while the others formed a tight circle around her, singing discordant songs and banging together blocks of wood. These women, Abdul explained, are members of a women's 'association' of which there are quite a number in Harar. They are self-help groups and assist at each other's family weddings and funerals. Each woman comes to the wedding carrying a basket on her head containing twenty injera she has made, but here they are of sorghum and not teff, explained Abdul. Teff is the staple carbo-hydrate of Ethiopia, a type of grass used nowhere else in the world. It is made into dough and then fermented and flattened into grey, tasteless cartwheels used as plates and scoops for greasy stews. Tekleab's favourite.

The baskets the women carried were of coloured raffia, covered by a painted lid. They were the baskets of the local traders, the Harari, whereas the baskets of the Oromo – the local cattle-owning people – are shallow, enlivened by leather and cowries.

And the women's dress? The Oromo wear a bright flower-printed dress, and below it a full white petticoat, which gets grubbier with each flick in the dust. They always swathe their head in a floral shawl. The Harari, however, wear a dress of immense interest.

Egyptian frescoes in the grave of Rekhmara, vizier to Tuthmosis III, who died in 1425 BC, depict women wearing strange dresses about three times as long as the woman's height and immensely wide. These fall from neck to ankle and are then looped up again to be tied under the arms and hang in a double fold almost to the ankle again. Spectacularly vast,

similar dresses were until recently the traditional costume of the Bedouin
women in and around the town of As-Salt in Jordan. Here in Harar they
are slightly smaller, as there are no huge winged sleeves to criss-cross over
the head and, instead of being tied under the armpits as in As-Salt, they
are tied round the waist. Or below the stomach, as in the case of the
particularly fat woman who showed me hers.

And J. Theodore's dresses from Karpathos are the only ones in the Greek
Islands with a similar cut. Shorter than the Harar ones, they double up
with a deep tuck in the skirt. Could all of these have derived from the
same source?

The embroidery on the Harar dresses was predictably a world away from
the Orthodox crosses on the traditional white robes of highland Ethiopia.
Just small diamond patterns and rosettes, on red or black cotton fabric.
A particularly bright version is worn by a young girl to walk around the
town announcing her marriage.

'All hand-made,' said the traders, the blood of generations of lying dealers coursing through their veins, as I thought to buy one. The last man
to make them died ten years ago, I was told, so an exorbitant price was
charged for the one I bought. And it was machined.

It was in the men's quarters that trading in these dresses – and in baskets
and silver – was carried on, and those quarters were extraordinary, a
unique arrangement of platforms I have seen nowhere else in the world.
The houses are entered from an open courtyard and the platforms are
arranged around it. They are of wood, covered with rugs or raffia, and
are used for sitting, sleeping and eating. Each man has his allotted
place. Guests have the first place to the left of the courtyard, straight ahead
is the platform for the young and to its right that for the owner of the
house. Behind them sit the educated and next to them, concealed
behind a pillar, is the spot called the *soutree*, meaning 'hidden place'. This
is for girls reaching puberty, who presumably on first menstruating are
sent to join the women. If there are no prepubescent girls in the family,
the place is filled with quilts. Then behind a curtain to the right of the
courtyard is the area for honeymoon couples. They used to spend a week
in there, without coming out, but now it is only five days.

The houses all have very high ceilings of wood beams covered in
wattle, clay and earth, very much like the houses of southern Baluchis-
tan along the coast of the Arabian Sea. The walls of white plaster are
completely covered with baskets and plates, reminding me of Karpathos.

The old plates and bowls are a beautiful burnished black wood, while the new ones, from Japan, Taiwan or India, are of tin, garishly painted with flowers. Three little niches are cut into the wall in memory of the dead. The centre one used to contain the Koran, but now usually has photos of the sons of the family.

As for the women, they are generally outside this family home, crouched on the earth floor of a nearby hut, their eyes smarting, cooking over a wood fire. Here the walls are blackened and the smoke swirls everywhere, escaping only through a gap between the walls and roof.

> *J'ai vu le soleil bas taché d'horreurs mystiques,*
> *Illuminant de longs figements violets...*
> *J'ai vu des archipels sidéraux, et des îles*
> *Dont les cieux délirants sont ouverts au vogueur...*

Rimbaud wrote what is probably his best-known poem, *Le Bateau Ivre*, when he was only sixteen; by nineteen he had finished writing poetry. Perhaps it was his vision of archipelagos linked to the stars, of the mystic horrors of the setting sun, of sailing around islands under wild open skies that made him leave France for years of wandering, ending up as a dealer around the Red Sea. A French trader in Aden appointed him his agent in Harar and he spent the last ten years of his life here, before returning home to die in France at the age of thirty six, though France had long since presumed him dead.

The house he is reputed to have lived in – though no one really knows – stands at the top of the town, an impressive stone building surrounded by scaffolding. Inside, turned wooden staircases lead up through gloomy rooms to a circular gallery at the top. Windows look out over the countryside around and to the world beyond. Dark paintings round the walls depict scenes that are vaguely Indian rather than African – houses, trees, vistas. The painted ceiling hangs down in torn strips.

Abdul was scathing. 'They've left it too late to restore. It could have been a big tourist attraction.' 'But it's almost certainly not the actual house Rimbaud lived in, and anyway there aren't any tourists in Harar' I pointed out. 'One day they'll come, and they won't know where he really lived,' said Abdul.

Abdul was right. By the time I finished my travels the restoration of Rimbaud's supposed house had been completed – all doubts as to its authenticity brushed under the carpet – and the place had opened with a grand, though dry, ceremony in the presence of foreign dignitaries and diplomats. It was curious to wonder what the effect of future coach parties of poetry appreciation societies, sandalled and socked and clutching volumes bound in sugar-paper, would have on the aggressive marauders of Harar.

Abdul and I left to the usual shrieks of 'you, you, gimme money' and headed for the witch-doctors.

The first had a notice at his door of all the ills he could cure:

> A known traditional healer in Harar
> Shek Mohammed Haji Bushra, branch of
> Shek Turunbedus Shek Mohammed
> The major diseases are treated by
> the above mentioned traditional healer
> 1 Bronchial Asthma   7 Gastritis
> 2 Diabetes Mellitus   8 Gynaecological d.
> 3 Paralisis   9 Mental illness
> 4 Liver disease   10 STD (V disease)
> 5 Heamorrhoides   11 Epilepsy
> 6 Cancer
> The treatment is given by the help of 'God'.
> Although the Medicine is given without payment
> the patient (and all other peoples including
> organizations) help us if you can. Thank you.

But his cures were achieved without the use of amulets. We set off for the healer by the Evil Gate who was reputed to work with such devices.

Mohammed Abdullah's house was up a stony path from the gate, set in a walled courtyard with a papaya tree. It was a single dark room with an earth floor and wood ceiling. A platform ran round three sides and the walls were of white plaster with a shelf of wattle and several niches displaying small phials, and wrapped bundles of plants. There were dusty plastic bags and flies everywhere.

Mohammed was an old man, his beard dyed with henna, wearing a wrapped skirt. He lounged back, chewing qat and staring at his Koran. In front of him a kettle steamed on a small earthenware brazier. He was attending to three patients.

One a young boy, also chewing qat explained that his problem was
that he was always hungry. He would eat and then immediately want more
('Tape worm?' I suggested to Abdul). Another was a woman lying on the
floor who was sure she had a live animal or insect in her stomach – she
could feel it move ('Pregnant?' I wondered). The third was an old
woman complaining of terrible pains in her back and her stomach ('Too
many years bent double carrying heavy loads' was clear). To the women
he gave a glass of plants infused in hot water and to the boy some more
qat, looking all the time at his copy of the Koran.

He had learnt his trade from his father, he explained, and could cure
anything. He made amulets by writing spells or extracts from the Koran
which the people then rolled up inside plastic or leather and hung
round their necks or tied round their upper arms. 'Plastic is better if you
have to wash the body,' he said. The problems he gets most often are heart,
miscarriage, abortion, and the evil eye. He has many cases of the evil eye
and showed me spells he used. They were a scribble of vaguely Arabic-
looking writing filling a square or rectangle, with sometimes an inner or
outer border of red. He promised to make me one against the evil eye
being directed towards me by a particular Italian woman. It would be
ready the next afternoon. He asks no payment for his work, he added,
but people bring him presents when they're cured. He offered me an
infusion in a glass encrusted with flies.

The next morning, emboldened by the success of the previous day, I
set off from my hotel, without Abdul, to walk into Harar, modestly
dressed as usual in long skirts and swathes of scarves of gloomy hue. First,
it suddenly pelted with rain, turning the piles of filth into such quag-
mires that even the mangy dogs slunk away. Then, as I walked along, I
was attacked by men and boys, even women and girls. They tried to grab
my bag, they jeered, they screeched as usual, adding this time 'farangi,
farangi' to the 'yous' and 'gimmes'. One man kept running up and
pulling my scarf and hair, to the great hilarity of the crowd.

I turned towards the Evil Gate and Mohammed Abdullah's house, but
was met by a pack of teenage girls who hurled stones at me. By twisting and turning to avoid them, I lost the way to the old man's house, so
I never did collect my amulet. It seemed his powers of protection did not
extend very far beyond his garden wall. I walked back, dishevelled and
soaked. Then caught the bus to Addis and phoned Tekleab.

South of Addis

Tekleab strode into the pension, ordered a double zibib, and sat down beside me. 'It's taken me all this time to find you,' he almost shouted. 'I've been round every cheap hotel in the guide. How could I have left you sitting on that stone by the roadside with your little bag, waiting for a bus that would probably never come, looking so pathetic.' I glowered. 'Why didn't I stay with you? What on earth was I thinking of? Well, I'm here to look after you now.'

Though I hate being looked after, I'd had enough of beggars and hassle. We set off the next day for the British Embassy. I paid our fares on the minibuses. Outside on special display stands were four large colourful posters, one showing Harrods' Fruit and Vegetable Hall, another Harrods' Meat Hall, another a joint of beef with brussels sprouts and roast potatoes labelled 'British Beef' (with no hint of any mad cow controversy – perhaps some hope of a market here?) and the fourth 'Crown of Lamb', a British delicacy, with cabbage, roast potatoes and gravy. The hungry sat on the dirt around, and would have been grateful for an old injera.

The Embassy was closed. It was Friday afternoon.

I had gone there, I told Tekleab, because I needed their help to send threads to the nuns of Eritrea who were teaching wounded and orphaned girls and women, victims of the war with Ethiopia, to embroider so as to be able to support themselves. 'You're nuts,' he said, stopping to buy two local cigarettes from a street vendor and putting them in an empty Rothman pack. 'But I love you. I've fallen in love with you. The way we met, everything, I can't forget you. Please stay in Addis. I'm with my family here, they'll take care of you, they'll pay for you. When they knew I'd found you they were really happy. "Good," they said. "Now" – you'll excuse the expression, but it's the only one we have in Amharic – "now you're going to pump a white woman."' He stood looking very pleased with himself. 'No way,' I said, heading straight back to the hotel. Tekleab followed me.

His family wanted to ask me to lunch, he continued, but of course guests must be offered chicken and as it was fasting time there was no way they could kill a chicken, so they couldn't formally invite me. But they would look after me with 'fasting food', and friends would lend us a vehicle, and he'd have the forty dollars for me on Monday. The hotel manager hovered protectively by and, appreciating the situation, chased him off the premises.

At five in the morning the manager sent one of his staff to escort me to the bus station. 'It's dangerous there,' he said. Sure enough a man tried to grab my bag but only succeeded in dragging me to the ground. The hotel man put me safely on the bus heading towards the Rift Valley lakes and the south.

It always seemed curious that so many people got onto the buses and then got off again before the bus left. This time I saw why. A man sat down next to a woman and asked if she could give him five one-birr notes for a five. As she did so he grabbed her purse and ran. She was still weeping hours later.

The countryside was flat and fertile, marred by maimed and carelessly felled trees. Oxen were ploughing, cattle and goats wandered across the road. The houses were almost all circular – made of wattle and with conical straw roofs – clustered in small groups, usually surrounded by a wattle or brush fence. The abject poverty and degradation looked infinitely worse in the driving rain.

We moved into a region of lush foliage, of mango and papaya trees. Two priests in cheap, tinselly brocade came on the bus with a cardboard collecting box. A few people gave ten cents, most hung on to the money they'd got ready to buy sugar cane along the roadside. A tyre burst, the rain finally stopped, the hot sun turned the bus into a sauna.

The curtains on Ethiopian buses are thin and inadequate for their supposed purpose of keeping out the sun. Instead, they serve for people who have been sick out of the window to wipe their mouths on, or for those who have partaken of goat stew at wayside halts to clean off the excess grease, and even more frequently they are a convenient cloth to blow away the snot and dust gumming up the passengers' noses. On such an insalubrious pillow I fell asleep. Some hibernating bug, sensing new pastures, must have crept out and entered my ear.

The lakeside hotel was charming, the monkeys scurrilous, the birdlife exotic as ever, but I had no real reason, beyond escape, to be here. I was way outside any Turkic, Ottoman, Muslim, Middle Eastern or Red Sea influence. There was no evidence of embroidery or amulets. Even J. Theodore hadn't come here.

I lay for two days in intense pain, dozing, wakeful, somnolent, until

I finally asked whether there might be an English-speaking doctor in the vicinity. It seemed a ludicrously manic idea. 'Yes madam,' the hotel owner said. 'At the polyclinic.' I imagined the polyclinic – as it was in southern Ethiopia – to be a medical centre besieged by the maimed and halt clamouring at its door. It turned out to be two quiet huts in a clearing between palm trees, with no one waiting.

I was registered with professional care and expertise (blood pressure, temperature, heart, suffering from any illness, malaria, for example?) and then taken to the doctor. He peered into my ear and, without the benefit of any modern equipment, pronounced a serious ear infection and prescribed antibiotics, instructing me how to get to the rural drug vendor by horse and gig. But, just before I go, he would like to ask what disease I had that the backs of my hands had brown flecks on them? He seemed pleased to learn that even white skins not only wrinkled but blotched with age. He had never treated a white person before.

I sat that evening by the side of the lake and watched the rainwashed, lowering sun until it was almost colourless. Its last rays caught the edge of the pleated ripples as they unfurled shorewards in sharp horizontal lines, grey and then silver, almost as a closing Venetian blind. And as the dusk settled down like a nesting bird, the sky was suddenly jazzed by a display of distant lightning. Fulgurite vaguely crossed my mind but I still had no reason to be there.

The next morning I went by another horse and gig to the bus station and then, packed around with big bundles of qat wrapped in banana leaves, by minibus to a small hut by another lake. But it was no use. I still had no reason to be there. The doctor's antibiotics only made me sick and I lay racked with pain.

And still there was the relentless rain. That African rain that slices the air into steel sheets, then calms itself to split into slivered glass, ricocheting off tin roofs and finally coming to rest steaming softly on dank, dark green foliage.

Sudan

The Way There

Almost a year elapsed before my return, my intention this time being to head north from Eritrea into Sudan, still tracing that fault line between the Ottoman, Muslim and Arabic world, and that of Christian and pagan Africa.

But Sudan was in turmoil. It is a sharply divided country – the hot, arid north the home of mainly Arabized Muslims, the torrid south that of Africans, most holding animist beliefs, but with a significant minority of Christians. The attempt by the north to impose Islamic values, and then Shari'a law, on the whole country has led to a civil war that has been dragging on since 1983, and has by now fractured the south into separate warring factions of the main Dinka tribe, and the smaller ethnic groups. Two million dollars a day are spent on the war, while education, safe drinking water, roads and electricity are neglected. The south is routinely devastated by famine – the world's newspapers are full of gruesome pictures of the starving – while it is feared that the imposition of fundamentalist Islamic law rides roughshod over human rights, and torture is said to be commonplace.

Transport into the south of Sudan was non-existent, and in any case I had no business to be in a place where only the presence of aid workers – and perhaps a few journalists – could be justified. As for the west, there was banditry and war there too, and again no transport. A few old buses ran in the north and east.

I planned, then, to cross from Eritrea into the north east of Sudan and follow the Nile, making a detour to the Red Sea to see the Sudanese Rashaida, and leaving through Egypt. It was not going to be easy. The Eritrean border was mined and subject to sporadic shelling, the

Egyptian one completely closed. I had heard that even the old Wadi Halfa to Aswan ferry, which used to be the only way through, hadn't been running for about four years.

I began by surfing the internet on my neighbours' computer. Things didn't look good. First the Egyptian end:

> 'Anybody recently gone overland to (or from) Sudan from Aswan via Lake Nasser and Wadi Halfa? Is it possible? Is the ferry regular? Would appreciate info to help a dream come true! Regards, Chris.'

> 'Sorry to ruin the dream, but not this year, or any time soon. The border is closed, Sudan is not issuing tourist visas, and they're in a virtual state of war with all neighbours. Plus, the ferry is sunk at the wharf. I tried, also, but got only as far as Aswan. Sudanese embassy told me to get lost. Boat was sunk. Flew to Ethiopia instead. Ken.'

> 'Guess you could fly into Khartoum, but you'd probably be risking some banditry heading west to Chad, and no public transit into Egypt... I did learn that there's a refugee truck going from somewhere near Abu Simbel into Sudan every day, and that they would take one foreigner per trip (probably not a long wait!) but didn't investigate it further. Good luck. Handy.'

Logically, if a truck went into Sudan every day it must go back. That's how I would get out into Egypt.

As for getting into Sudan:

> 'Circa early 1996. You could not travel from Eritrea to Sudan. In the reverse direction officially it was closed, but unofficially you could cross anyway. Now, I believe with the fighting in the area this border is firmly closed in both directions. Bob.'

Worth a try at least.

I returned, then, to Asmara, to the early warmth of mornings, the sharp midday heat on the sunny side of the main avenue, the dim cool on the other, shaded by villas the Italians had built in a sun hotter than Sicily's. On Sundays the women and little girls still promenaded in their white embroidered dresses, but for the teenagers the *passeggiata* was now in T-shirts and jeans, or sassy tight skirts and out-of-date Italian shoes.

At the British Consulate the warning notices had changed slightly in the intervening year:

> 'Egypt: In a major incident near Luxor on 17 Nov 1997 gunmen killed more than 60 tourists, including at least six British visitors. Extremists have warned tourists not to visit Egypt. In April 1996 gunmen killed 18 Greek tourists in Cairo. On 18 September two men, acting alone, killed ten people, mainly German tourists, also in Cairo.'
>
> 'Sudan: The security situation in southern Sudan and the Nuba mountains remains unstable due to the continuing civil war. Only those engaged in essential relief work should visit south Sudan. There is continued military activity near the Ethiopian and Eritrean borders, and banditry and tribal clashes in western Darfur. Visitors should avoid these areas and not attempt to cross any Sudanese land border. 7.11.97'

The notices continued with dire warnings about muggings and armed attacks in Kenya, murders in South Africa, violent street crime in Nigeria, land mines in Rwanda, military road blocks in Zaire, drugged food in Tanzania, armed aggression in Zanzibar, rebel attacks in Djibouti, road ambushes and car hijacking in Uganda, sporadic bombing and banditry in Ethiopia. For Somalia the notice still simply said 'Don't go' and the FCO map covered the country with a red explosion.

Could Africa really be so bad?

The consul himself was decisively negative about crossing from Eritrea into Sudan. 'As far as we're concerned it's a closed border.' The whole area was mined and just the previous week the border villages of Awad, Oulsah and Hudrah had been shelled. Like the villages in the north of Eritrea where women were said to embroider, I couldn't find them on any map.

The bus, taking several days, descends a couple of thousand metres from Asmara to the western lowlands, twisting first through arid mountains, rucked, tucked and deeply pleated, the colour of butterscotch, gashed in shades of green mould and fondant pink, just like tourmaline. Tall flowering cacti, candelabra euphorbia, clustered together in groups or stood in isolation, multi-fingered on a thin base so that they seemed unstable. But none was fallen and it was the lacy thorn bushes that blew around like tumbleweed, rootless in the stony ground.

Keren was the first halt, a sandy market town woken by the muezzin and crowded with men in long white robes and white turbans, one of whom asked how much gold or silver he would need to marry me. The commerce of Keren was, however, mainly in fruit and vegetables and firewood. Hundreds of camels were driven each morning from the surrounding countryside into a dry river bed on the edge of town, laden with wood. There they sat patiently in the dust, a seemingly timeless, unchanging biblical scene. But Keren had been a battlefield of the Second World War.

The Italian cemetery was beautifully kept – paths of gravel massed with bougainvillaea, and gravestones mostly marked 'ignoto'. The ages recorded on the stones were nineteen, twenty, twenty one. So young, so many, so painfully unnamed, for a forgotten battlefield where no one now called.

One commander buried among his men was Colonel Lorenzini. A delightful man, Colonel Sir Hugh Boustead had said. Lorenzini had entertained him and a group of British officers ten years previously in Sudan, cooking the dinner himself, serving it with copious supplies of chianti and presenting it elegantly on starched tablecloths with silver cutlery, the best china and glass. Toasts were drunk in spumante, and Lorenzini told his guests that he couldn't imagine anybody being stupid enough to want to acquire territory in this part of the world. He was killed fighting at Keren to preserve it for Italy, though many of his men, it seems, died of starvation and thirst. But there was water now for the flowers.

The cemetery of the British enemy was on the outskirts of town on a spur looking west towards the mountains. Equally well cared-for, but with most of its dead named, it had no flowers. 'There's a problem of water here,' said the keeper. 'The British chose this place because of the view.'

The westerly mountains, that the dead could not look at, were different from those to the east: softer, tawny in colour, humped and hillocky

like the haunches of so many sleeping lions. The bus passed villages of
round thatched huts, with burnt-out tanks and lorries on the edge of
them, and small 'martyrs' cemeteries' from yet another war – that with
Ethiopia.

The first town was Agordat, a quiet place of wide streets where camels
sauntered. The mosque was its heart and in the shop opposite worked
a woman called Dahab. She spoke excellent English, having spent two
years with the Tucker family, she explained. They were in this area for
ten years and had established schools in Keren, Berentu and Tessenei and
a hospital in Haykota. Then the Ethiopians had come and destroyed them
all and given the Tuckers twenty four hours to leave.

I ventured to ask Dahab about embroidery and amulets. No embroidery here but amulets, yes. They're worn around the neck or upper
arm, mostly by women and children – a few men as well – but they keep
them hidden as they feel ashamed of them. If they have some problem
– enemies, a sick child or whatever – they go to the sheikh and he
writes out a prayer, a kitab, which they then put in a metal or leather
container. Never fabric as it isn't strong enough. The amulet can be rectangular or triangular and the pendants are just for decoration, she added.
It was the same old story, all the way from Afghanistan.

Beyond Agordat and towards Berentu the countryside was rolling
semi-desert, the only vegetation flat-topped acacia bushes like green lace
parasols, and the odd primeval-looking baobab tree. Trucks and trailers
overloaded with cotton headed in the other direction, leaning precari-
ously sideways or already toppled in the ditch. The road passed by
rusting military hardware and the small villages of thatched stone huts
and concrete shacks that were the homes of the Muslim Nara. These
villages, and others like them throughout Eritrea, were destined to be
replaced, the man at the Development Agency in Asmara had said, by
terraces of proper houses. His windows displayed 'before' and 'after'
photographs, while on the walls of the office, in pride of place – though
they hadn't built any yet – were examples of Barrett-type houses, detached
with garage and tarmac drive, and named 'The Wentworth', 'The
Newmarket'.

Berentu lay at the top of a mountain pass and was guarded by armed
soldiers who checked the identity of everyone on the bus. There was
already a whiff of the border. 'One day soon the road will be tarred,' the

Development Agency man had said, 'and Berentu will be a big city.'

The main square of Berentu is a parched space centred by a low-walled roundabout. Clustered around it and alongside the sandy road that leads down from it to the market, are the solid tin-roofed buildings of the town: small, open-fronted shops, shacks and houses. Crowding up against their backs are compounds of round huts of wood and palm, stockaded by the tall, spiky branches that camels transport around the countryside. Electricity in the town is non-existent or sporadic, water is brought in hessian sacks on the backs of donkeys.

On the hill above the dusty square stands an old baobab tree and a sordid hotel whose one loo at the back is full of shit and cockroaches, but whose terrace at the front commands an agreeable view of the small town.

Gudrun sat on the terrace, her long blonde hair blowing across her face while she spoke, though she made no attempt to smooth it back. She wore a gorgeous turquoise necklace and a sleeveless top, and was here recording and photographing the customs of the local Kunano people, with a grant from the Eritrean Ministry of Information.

No, the Kunano do no embroidery; yes, they wear amulets against the evil eye and illness. These were rectangular, in metal or leather – she hadn't seen any triangles. Inside were roots and plants collected by moonlight, by women or men 'who knew' and were considered healers. Then there were the special ones the bridegroom's mother would give the bride to ensure the success of the marriage. Made of rows of metal discs, with three cowrie shells hung below them, and then more discs and leather, these were actually triangular in shape, when you thought about it. 'And, to keep away the evil eye,' she added, 'I remember seeing an old woman stamp on an egg at the edge of a compound.'

'Though it is claimed the Kunano don't practise female circumcision, in fact they do,' said Gudrun. 'They do it to dancing and lots of noise so that the screams of the child can't be heard. It's the grandmother who does it. She's always crying, but she knows the girl won't go to her ancestors if she hasn't been circumcised.'

'What about their religion?' Some were Muslim, some Christian and others were not really animist, but believed in one god Ama (a word very similar to that for 'mother' but with a slightly different pronunciation) and in one prophet. They had no earth/mother/fertility goddess that she knew of, though they were a matriarchal society. 'Oh, and they bury their dead east to west and pray to the east.' That sounded solar rather than Muslim, particularly as Mecca was to the north.

The Kunano women in Berentu mostly sat in the dust around the market, ablaze with coloured beads as if they'd been showered in Smarties. Their woolly hair was caked with rancid butter, two matted locks hanging over their ears, the rest then plaited to the scalp and released in a frizzy tangle. When they weren't sitting with their piles of firewood to sell, they were staggering along bearing them across their shoulders on heavy wooden yokes. Even little girls of about six. A few of their menfolk strode around doing nothing, tall, muscular, their hair in matted ringlets, and wearing only a loincloth draped like a nappy.

On moonless nights before dawn Berentu is pitch dark. Dim paraffin lamps in the main square aureole shadowy figures sitting around at low tables. Women fan braziers, and boil tea. The buses gradually fill and leave in the darkness. The one for Tessenei was the last to arrive, a small, local-looking bus, rusty, windowless. I was to sit on it for nine hours and the only diversions were to be the sight of one baboon and four guinea-fowl ('good to eat' the girl sitting next to me indicated by gestures.)

Then, nearing Tessenei, armed soldiers ran through the shrub, smoke billowed on the horizon, trucks bearing shrouded machine guns passed by, and soldiers checked passengers' papers as the ramshackle bus plodded on like some old donkey.

And it was only a matter of weeks after I left Eritrea for Sudan that war broke out again with Ethiopia. All foreigners were flown out of Asmara, leaving it as quiet as a small town in Umbria when Ethiopian jets weren't screaming overhead, heading with their bombs for the airport.

Though the dispute was ostensibly about some remote stony piece of ground on an ill-defined border, in reality it seemed the resentment the Ethiopians harboured at the loss of their Red Sea ports had boiled over. After all, Asab, the port through which they shipped most of their goods and now in the hands of Eritrea, was fairly easily accessible to them, whereas for the Eritreans it was a ridiculous three-day drive through a long strip of the forbidding Danakil desert from Asmara, or was served by one plane a week, and a couple of slow boats. But then again, it was claimed that Eritrea had struck the first blow.

After a few weeks the war slipped out of international headlines. But by the time my travels were over, the uncanny peace over Asmara had vanished and the slumbering town had been overrun by aid workers, military observers, do-gooders and hangers-on, all driving around hell for leather in four by fours. And the children had put their hopscotch chalk away.

Over the Border

In Tessenei, Amanuel, a road engineer whose teeth shone white in the surrounding dark, pressed on me during the evening triple neat gins of local manufacture, redeemed only by a squeeze of fresh lime. He treated me to a dinner of goat stew which I ate, with some misgiving, by starlight alone, surreptitiously slipping most of it to invisible cats. He himself had spaghetti alla verdura as he was fasting for Lent. 'You'll get across,' he told me.

Outside the restaurant we met his friend, Omar. 'No way,' said Omar. 'Forget it. You won't get anywhere. Tomorrow is clean-up day.'

Once a year Eritrea shuts down for the sake of the environment. Towns are sealed off, shops and offices closed and everyone is legally obliged to clean up their property. Tessenei, with its wide sandy streets, verandahs and huge open spaces, usually has a Wild West feel about it. This morning everywhere was empty of people, and all the shops shuttered and padlocked, as if the sheriff's posse were expected. Lorries went round picking up piles of swept-up twigs and the odd dead cat from the doorways, tractors collected domestic rubbish, armed police hustled two householders into a truck – presumably they weren't scrubbing hard enough. In a few streets men swept the sand with palm fronds, simply swirling it here and back again. Plastic bags blew untended everywhere and more fluttered down from the collection lorries and tractors. By twelve it was all over. Men gradually crept back on to the verandahs and sat in disconsolate little groups in their long white robes and huge turbans, huddled like meringues on a cake-stand. Only slowly were the padlocks undone and the blue doors opened. A few men lit up in relief and threw their fag-ends on the ground.

And in my hotel room at the end of the day the old bottle tops were still lying around on the floor and only the dead cockroach had gone.

Though the town had gradually come back to life by the afternoon, it was too late to leave. 'You need the sun behind you when you go to the border, not in front,' said Omar. Three gentlemen were to escort me there in the morning to make sure I was safe – Amanuel and two tall, courteous Sudanese in stained jellabyya. They would go with me on the bus to the border village and then find a donkey-cart to take me across no-man's-land. It was the best way to go, as the donkey-drivers knew where the mines were and, if they made a mistake, it would be the donkey who would lose a leg. They provisioned me with halwa, cinnamon and dried ginger for the journey.

In the event it was Amanuel alone who took me to Village 13, the last before no-man's-land. Just a few grubby shacks jostled along its baked streets where white-robed men with nothing to do sat on low string stools, drinking endless glasses of hot sweet tea. A donkey cart was negotiated, the cart being simply two old pick-up wheels held by a rickety axle and surmounted by a flat piece of tin. The deal was that I would give Amanuel money and he would wait in the village until the donkey-cart returned with a note from me to say that I was safely across, and then he would pay the driver.

We trotted off through an empty landscape dotted with a few bushes, the driver, Abraham, sitting on the front part of the tin and me on the back. The heat was intense and, pinioned on our metal sheet under the merciless sun, we might just as well have been two lamb chops on a grill pan. We passed the odd browsing camel and a furry ground-level animal with a long tail that shot out from cover and ran to another bush.

Otherwise the silence was total, perhaps enclosed even more preciously between the shelling there had been the week before and undoubtedly would be again the next week. A few obvious holes showed where mines had been removed. Abraham was very fond of his donkey. Though he shouted 'Waha!' from time to time, he never hit it, and enjoyed running his fingers through its bristly fur when he was bored. I hoped it wouldn't lose any legs, but in fact I felt both the donkey and I were absolutely safe in Abraham's hands. We had been sent off to cheers and laughs from his fellow-villagers, and he was certain to have to return, his head held high, his mission achieved and his money waiting.

Twice we came across armed guards sitting in the sand, hidden behind bushes. Abraham seemed to know where they were as he headed for them. They waved us on. We had been going for something over an hour, when

Abraham hobbled his donkey with green rope and tied it to a tree. He then unshackled the cart and indicated that I was to walk the rest of the way. We seemed to be nowhere at all and I wasn't very happy about giving him the note confirming my safe delivery. In the end he walked on with me for ten minutes or so and then waved towards a yellow building in the far distance. 'Sudan Immigration,' he said. He made it clear that it would be dangerous for him to go any closer. I wrote his note, slung my bag over my shoulder and walked on.

Though it was only early morning, the heat was unbearable. When I finally reached the yellow building – a Sudanese flag flying over it – I found it was a border post long since abandoned. On the horizon were the sugar-loaf mountains I knew to be near Kassala. I carried on over open ground towards them and came to a spread-out village of straw huts. There was no sign of life. Then I spotted a soldier squatting in the sand, his gun spiked beside him. I walked straight up to him.

The border guards' headquarters was a small straw shelter. A fire of twigs burned on the ground and a couple of armed men lounged around on string beds. They made me tea, then handed me over to a police officer, who searched my bag, took my camera away to open it up, and confiscated my maps, but, annoyingly, displayed no interest in whether I had any alcohol.

I had been severely warned not to take any with me. The law against alcohol is very strict. Not only would it be seized but I could also be thrown in jail, perhaps for life. It was just like taking heroin into Thailand. So I had come without vodka and anticipated an attack of the heebie-jeebies around six every evening. For the first couple of nights I devised some displacement activity to occupy that time, like eating a mango or sorting out my travel bag, which took all of five minutes, but I didn't miss my evening drink at all, and was to emerge at the other end of Sudan, weeks later, in perfect calm.

However, I was not to know that, as the guards searched and seized and questioned, but made no mention of alcohol.

Finally I was taken to Kassala in a series of pick-up trucks and then, until ten o'clock at night, harried in one police station after another. I was feverish from the sun, my tongue stuck to the parched roof of my mouth, I had had nothing at all to eat all day, having given my provisions to Abraham. By the last police station the electricity in the whole town had failed and I was stood outside in the pale moonlight to be questioned. 'What are you doing in my country?' a bumptious, armed youth of fifteen asked me.

Kassala

It was time to take stock. My maps had gone. They had thought me a spy, I was later told, because I had underlined certain places (actually where I might find embroidery) and, worse, I had ringed a large part of southern Ethiopia, writing across it 'MINING'. Many years before, Haile Selassie had offered my husband the job of 'His Royal Highness's Mining Engineer', based in the south near the Kenyan border, and I had intended while in Ethiopia to see what the area was like, before realising that it was too volatile to visit. Explaining that to the border guards was impossible.

My camera had been returned, with light in the film. I had a small supply of survival food as, before leaving England, thoughts of famine and refugee camps had prompted me to bring some sunflower seeds and dried apricots past their sell-by date, so as not to be a drain on the locals.

Then I had my sheet sleeping bag, and a Pakistani outfit of *shalwar-kameez* and shawl, all of which had tipped my small travel bag up to six and a half kilos instead of the five I usually carried. But I had thought of the typical hotel room – a dormitory of iron bedsteads with bug-infected mattresses and no bedding – and the warning that women not dressed in correct Muslim fashion would be publicly flogged, so I felt it worth bringing them. I was prepared for everything, just sorry about the vodka.

Kassala was the favourite honeymoon town of Sudan. It was considered a green and fertile oasis in the surrounding desert, though a heavy pall of dust blanked the sky. It was a town of cracked streets and crumbling concrete buildings with reinforcing rods for a second storey, never to be built, sticking up like aerials. The hotel I was taken to in the dark turned out to have three storeys, and just one honeymoon couple as the other guests.

The next morning a plain-clothes policeman was waiting for me at reception and the trail from one police station to another resumed. If I had come to see the costume of the Rashaida, then I had to have a special permit to go to their villages. They couldn't issue it here, I would have to go to Khartoum and come back again. They finally stamped my passport with an entry permit for Sudan, marking it with ominous large black crosses. 'You should have gone to Khartoum first,' they added.

It was in Kassala that I began to feel ill. Breathing the stifling woolly air of Africa, especially when I was captive on my tin slab, had sealed up my lungs. I was prescribed the local pink grapefruit by the hotel staff and set off to the market to buy some. It was a scene of torrid decay – overblown fruit, wilting lucerne, putrid rubbish – for, though Kassala produced wonderful fruit and vegetables, there was no transport to get it out of town.

At one end of the market a group of young men lounged around a pickup. They were instantly recognisable: wavy black Italian-like hair, aquiline, olive-skinned faces among the mainly negroid all around. And scallywag eyes that came from generations of inbred rascally traders. If not downright thieves. I stopped. 'Rashaida,' I said to them. They crowded round and immediately produced silver jewellery to sell me. A couple of women came up, wearing triangular headscarves embroidered in gold thread with solar motifs, and the traditional silver veil and appliquéd dress. They tried to clip silver bangles on to my wrist. I hardly had time to protest when I was grabbed. It was the plain-clothes policeman. 'You make a mistake,' he shouted. 'You were told no Rashaida without permission from Khartoum.' He marched me back to the hotel. 'You stay in your room and tomorrow morning you get the bus to Khartoum.'

'I've already got a ticket for Suakin,' I said.

The Red Sea

The flat featureless desert and leaden sky melded into a blank of alabaster, swirled only rarely by the clouds of dust that stirred in the distance around small groups of moving donkeys, people and camels. The Red Sea mountains began as huge piles of loose stones on the sand – bucketfuls tipped out by some giant – and then coalesced into a sharp, bare range as the dry air suddenly held the barely perceptible scent of the sea.

It was Suakin I had come to see. A small island, linked to the main-land by a causeway, it had been an important Red Sea port since at least the tenth century BC, and had been, like Massawa further down the coast, an Ottoman stronghold, its first Turkish governor installed in 1518. The town was mainly constructed of fragile coral and had been falling into ruins since the 1930s, when the merchants left. Now hardly a building stood, bar a couple of minarets – Suakin was simply a white tip of rubble and broken coral, in which only a few squatters lived. An aggres-sive pye-dog barked, the voices of children came from a sacking shack pitched against a heap of stone. But these sounds quickly faded and the ruins were again mummified in silence.

On the mainland opposite the causeway a few more buildings stood: a crumbling house with a Turkish latticed window protruding over the street at first floor level, where it was easy to imagine the whispering voices of the Ottoman women concealed behind it; the remains of a palace of 365 rooms that the Mahdi had built for himself; a row of huts that had once been banks and shops but were now all barred by faded shutters; and a shabby tea-house made of palm matting stretched over posts, where a few men sat desultorily drinking tea. A shawled woman passed bearing firewood.

It was the establishment of Port Sudan by the British that had killed Suakin. Now Port Sudan itself had an air of decay about it, the colonial sea-front villas flaking under a coating of sand, the offices and business premises boarded-up, the hotels closed down.

The police were waiting for me on my return to Kassala.

More Rashaida were back in the market – the men in lilac robes, the women in flouncy skirts decorated with appliqué, and gold and silver ric-rac. Thrown over their heads they wore a black ankle-length shawl, their silver chin and head veil stitched into it. They were hung with coins and amulets, and wore silver bracelets, anklets and rings, which they again persistently tried to sell to me, tugging at my sleeve and bag. The wealth for all this adornment they derived from smuggling. Not just over the Eritrean border, where as nomads they crossed almost freely, but also over the Red Sea. The long silver veils they cover their faces with on special occasions were embroidered in exactly the same technique and style as the dresses of the Tihama – the coastal plain of Yemen – and the trousers of southern Iran. The Rashaida are Arabia in Africa.

But gradually their hand embroidery is being replaced by purchased and garish braiding, and their appliqué by machine-stitching done by men in the market. As far as I was concerned, this would probably be the end of embroidery for a while. Travelling northward I was likely to find nothing more, except a few caps in Khartoum and Nubia, until the oases of the Western Desert of Egypt – Siwa and Bahariya – where patterns were of solar symbolism, rather than the Christian cross or Islamic twists.

I set off for Khartoum, jolting in a bus across an utterly empty desert.

Khartoum

I n my childhood, all the possessions of the British Empire were coloured a rather faint red in school atlases. Only Sudan was an exception – it was striped diagonally red and yellow. Any child could see this showed dusty, red-coated soldiers marching in lines across the sands of the desert. The country was resonant with conflict, with the names of Gordon, Kitchener, the Mahdi.

The story of the political turmoil that followed Gordon's resignation in 1880, and the rise of the religious leader, the Mahdi – whose soldiers lay siege to Khartoum and then stormed Gordon's palace and killed him, as the relief expedition of Wolseley and Kitchener moved slowly up the Nile just days away – was in every school history book.

The palace still stands, on the southern bank of the Blue Nile. Knowing almost from infancy that the Mahdi's followers beheaded Gordon there on the 26th January 1885, and that Kitchener's help arrived, so nearly on time, on the 28th, gave the place a sombre poignancy. The approach to it, and the proximity of the Nile, was announced by a damp sniff in the dessicated air of the city. Along the river's edge, colonial buildings were guarded by an avenue of banyan trees planted by the British. Imposing hotels of the British era, and brand new ones of Gulf-style architecture, were all barricaded behind corrugated iron, the nearby Christian church was securely locked. As for Gordon's palace, it was forbidden to go near it, or even to walk along the road in front of it. It had now been taken over by the President as his own.

If Khartoum during Gordon's years had been a battle site, it was now an abandoned building site, where the desert blew and skirmished, blanketing bricks in sand before they could even be laid. Its heart, where there used to be a park laid out in the form of a Union Jack, was gutted, a deep hole in the ground surrounded by idle cranes and unfinished buildings. The city gave the strange impression of having recently been rich and bustling, of having only a few years before had real shops, busy cranes, smart hotels, and that suddenly the shops had emptied, the cranes had stopped in mid-air and the desert had moved in.

The Ethnographic Museum was a small building like a private house, each room laid out with the crafts of a different region of Sudan. It was delightful, but there were no visitors. The reserve store in the back yard was inches deep in sand, and the little embroidered caps (bought in the souk of Omdurman in 1938 by Abdulahi Ebb and presented to the museum by the British administrator G. W. Grabham, the labels said), though fluffed with dust, were exquisite, and bespoke a more prosperous, leisured era. Now the men wore only white machine-embroidered ones.

It was in Omdurman that the Mahdi and his followers had camped while they lay siege to Khartoum, and it is there that his tomb still stands, its silvery dome rising above the mud houses and the narrow lanes where goats wander. And it is in Omdurman on Friday nights that the dervishes still whirl.

They gathered at the cemetery and tomb of Sheikh Hamid el-Nil, a sandy place sparingly shaded by dry rustling trees, where robed men sat around and a few shawled women made tea. By the pretty little domed mosques a few rather elderly men in bright patchwork clothes and jester hats began to move, followed by younger dreadlocked ones dressed in green. They moved forward, their whirling more a knee-bending, rhythmic lunging. They were joined by the crowds of men in white waiting at the edge of the cemetery, who followed the dervishes' movements, until no one was still. In the frenzied throbbing one or two men began really to whirl around, some slowly, some so quickly they fell to the ground.

Among the spectators was a handful of Europeans, including a couple both carrying large camcorders and wearing flagrant gold Rolex watches, the man dressed in designer clothes of suspect, oriental manufacture, she in an ill-fitting trouser suit, shiny sandals, and – instead of the headscarf every woman is required to wear – a gilt plastic hairband. To the mutters of the crowd, they kept taking photographs of one another standing by each dervish as he succumbed to this mystic religious experience, the woman posing, the man digging into a large wad of notes stuffed in his open shirt pocket and thrusting money at the dervish. 'They're from the Russian Embassy,' someone said.

Khartoum lies at the confluence of the Blue and White Niles, the old city to the south of the Blue Nile, the industrial town of Bahri to the north, and Omdurman to the west of where the rivers meet. I had imagined the scudding Blue and the turgid White flowing side by side like duo eye-shadow, but they merged into a wide expanse of grey water crossed by a couple of bridges hazed by traffic fumes. In Gordon's day boats up the Nile were the only transport – now because of the civil war, they no longer run. In his day too, in a country of almost one million square miles, there were no roads – now, more than a hundred years later there is merely one from Khartoum to Port Sudan and another from Khartoum a few hundred kilometres north to Atbara, where it peters out. And there were no railways – the British were later to build one from Khartoum to Wadi Halfa, which still has only one train a week. But now for transport there were also a few lorries, buses and pick-ups known as 'boxes'.

It was my intention to follow the Nile through the territories of the ancient kingdoms of Meroë, Napata and Kerma, north to Wadi Halfa. And it was in Khartoum that I began to hear rumours that, after a lapse of more than four years, the Wadi Halfa ferry to Aswan had just started running again.

A government permit was issued to me as Sheik Rosemary Paine to visit Shendi, Dongola, Karima and Wadi Halfa. While historical facts on Sudan had been dinned into me, I was vaguer on the detailed geography and missed my confiscated map. Profuse and courteous apologies were offered for its removal and I was allowed to call at the Survey Department to ask permission of the Minister to buy a new one. He sat eating breakfast under a ceiling fan in his upstairs office, and I was further allowed to wait while he finished his toast. The maps I was permitted to buy, one for the districts of Dongola and Berber, and the other for Wadi Halfa, were remarkably detailed. They were the work of the British, though that was not acknowledged, and showed Dinka cattle camps, and Christian remains. Bluffs, 'low clay mounds', 'large cracks in cotton soil holding water', and places with no water were clearly marked. They were infinitely superior to the one I had had taken away.

I called at the British Embassy, too, to ask for advice on travelling north and, in the meantime, for the name of a doctor. My small knife, my table fork and simple camera were removed from me before I was allowed two feet inside the grille.

'Was it true that the ferry to Egypt was running again?'

'No.'

'What help and advice could they give me?'

'Don't go.'

They could have told me I needed a permit from the Ministry of Antiquities in Khartoum to visit the archaeological sites of the ancient kingdoms of the Nile. They could have warned me about Eid al-Adhah. And they turned out to be the only people to deny that the ferry was running.

But they did give me the name of a doctor.

The place to stay in Khartoum was, and always had been, the Acropole, an old-fashioned, now rather shabby, hotel run by a Greek family. The only people there when I arrived in Khartoum were a few aid workers, reading the out-of-date copies of *LeFigaro*, the *Herald Tribune*, and *Frankfurter Allgemeine* stuffed into locally-made baskets on every table. A tall man wandered around barefoot in an old T-shirt emblazoned 'Waikiki Surfing Club', while the Greek owner of the hotel worked in suit and tie. A white-coated waiter brought me cold lemon juice.

The Acropole cost $75 a day, which included three meals, the owner had told me. He then immediately recommended a little place up the road, for $75 was way above my budget and I certainly couldn't face three meals a day. I was ill. My usual policy: 'leave it and it'll be better in the morning' hadn't worked and the dense African air in my lungs had now turned to thick soup. I had progressed from pink grapefruit and the Temple of Heaven Tiger Balm Tablets from Singapore given to me by the staff at the Kassala hotel, to serious antibiotics the Embassy doctor had prescribed. They had cost $44 (how many Sudanese could afford that?). I had pneumonia.

George was the closest to a gorilla of any human being I have ever seen: forehead sloping back from bushy eyebrows, pummelled nose, thick pink lips rolled into black. He spoke flawless English, was a devout Christian and a trained accountant. He was also a Dinka and as such could only obtain the most menial work in the north, in this case manning the small hotel near the Acropole where I was the only guest. George looked after me. He ran the hotel deftly with water that came and went, phones that seldom worked, and electricity that spluttered on in the morning and cut out again after an hour until late evening, pitching the windowless reception area into a candlelit cavern. The local men who came every day to watch the television sat patiently in the gloom in front of its blank screen. The one small lift was never used, the men far too afraid of finishing up trapped between floors. The kitchen produced English-style breakfasts and bean stew. I lived on water from the Nile filtered through iodine, until one morning scrambled egg seemed a good idea.

The first place to call before leaving for the north was the German Embassy, where I had that age-old device of the traveller – a letter of introduction. This was to the ambassador, who immediately invited me to dinner at his residence. What on earth could I wear? I set off for the Omdurman souk.

A hundred years ago slaves were still the market's principal commodity, shackled wretches sitting in the dust at the feet of their Arab owner. Now solicitous, robed dealers sold hairgrips and plastic keyrings from China, goldsmiths hammered away at sheets of metal, and small shops around the edge of the market displayed dried-up crocodiles, zebra heads and useless trinkets made of ivory and reptile skin.

I looked around for something stylish, but there was no hope. I had with me an Indian cinnamon-coloured skirt, the Pakistani kameez I had brought to save being flogged – both old and somewhat travel-stained, but still acceptable – so I bought some coral beads to go with them, and then strung them on to the plastic cord I always carry to tie up doors at night in dicey hotels, to make bracelets and a necklace. I bought a bottle of 'Deep Violet' nail-polish by Carol Celeste of Wigan, that was actually cinnamon in colour. I washed my trekking sandals and hoped to be able to hide my feet under the table.

The residence was a cool haven of elegant white marble and sober architecture. Half a dozen guests were there. Oh-so-welcome gin and tonics were served, then vichyssoise, followed by a fish dish, accompanied by the best German white wine, and then a sorbet of mint and grapefruit. It was another world. The ambassador, a sensitive and erudite man, led the conversation. No remark passed without receiving his considered attention, a slight quivering flushing his face as he reacted to it. He switched from Arabic to English to German, from Sudanese history to Yemeni architecture and from Meroitic archaeology to iconoclasm. After a while he seemed to consider the subjects of conversation adequately covered and looked straight at me with intense concentration. 'Now tell me,' he said, leaning forward slightly, 'just what made you walk across a minefield?'

Kingdoms of the Nile

North of Khartoum the Nile switchbacks in a thin green filament through desert ever more desolate. Its fertile sliver snakes through an empty land of trackless sands, shifted and hummed by the wind. It is a land of courteous tall black men in long white robes and white turbans, who cuff each other on the shoulder in greeting and then shake hands, exchanging a volley of good wishes for peace, health and the blessings of Allah on themselves and on all those dear to them.

Along the narrow banks of the river lie small villages and towns, dependent on the date groves and irrigated patches that cling close to its shores. And in the arid wastes that fringe these settlements stand the pyramids and tombs of the ancient kingdoms of the Nile, enclosed in wire fences, encroached by sand.

It was tempting to think that those towns and villages would be linked by a road following the Nile, but no such road existed. Each settlement turned its shoulder on its neighbour and at best had only a ferry to the opposite bank. Though there was the tarred road from Khartoum to Shendi and then on almost to Atbara, after that there were only rough desert tracks.

Travelling north, I was told, I would have to go in lorries, or local buses that were nothing more than tin shells. Just a lorry chassis roofed in tin, a few wooden benches for seats, no windows and no shock absorbers. Hours and hours and hours of being bumped to hell and covered in sand. And then there was virtually nowhere to stay. Before I left Khartoum I would need more letters of introduction, Isam, whom I hardly knew, had said. His uncle Mahjoud was a very important man, and his relatives in Karima and Maqal would care for me. He took me down miles of black alleyways in Bahri to Mahjoud's home. A pristinely white-robed elderly man with intelligent eyes, who spoke perfect English, Mahjoud sat dictating letters that would help me. 'You will need these,' said Isam, 'or you will have nowhere to sleep.'

'In Shendi,' said Peter – a jolly Danish engineer in yellow shorts, who was in Sudan installing and maintaining power stations – 'you can stay in my house.' Following the dinner with the German ambassador he had appeared at my hotel and offered to take me to Shendi in his pick-up.

Shendi had always been a miserable place, seemingly in the middle of nowhere. But it lay, in fact, at the great crossroads where the caravan routes from Ethiopia to west and north Africa meet those of the Nile. The Nile here is at its closest to the Red Sea, so this small settlement of a few yards of riverine green surrounded by sand and stone – Bruce found only twenty five huts there when he called in 1770 – could trade in spices from the East, swords and beads from the North, gold from the West, ivory and slaves from the South. Though the place was nothing, its market was once fabulous, one of the liveliest in Africa.

Now Shendi was a poor spread-out settlement of low mud walls, concrete shacks, a few stalls of vegetables, and open sandy spaces littered with plastic bags and refuse, attended to by goats. Everywhere were shattered pick-ups, impossible to repair, and men rode around on donkeys. A few camels sat in the sand. Two men rowed a ferry across the Nile to the empty bank opposite, where the passengers caught a donkey shuttle to and from the nearby village.

Peter's house turned out to be made of four old shipping containers. It stood in the grounds of the power station, so there was a heavy throbbing all through the night and the electricity never failed. It was luxuriously equipped with fluorescent lights and Axminster carpets squirming with beige and brown. The walls were decorated with Danish posters of smiling broad-faced blonde girls in gingham, holding baskets of flowers; views of the port of Copenhagen and sea scenes of a land where water is as sand is here. There was even a video, and I spent a wholly unexpected evening watching *Fried Green Tomatoes at the Whistle Stop Café* dubbed into Danish.

Travelling from south to north, I was going in the opposite direction to the ancient Nubian kingdoms of the Land of Kush, those royal cities built along the fertile strip of the Nile that formed the trade route for the slaves, ivory, gold, ebony and incense on which the Nubians built their wealth. The oldest city, Kerma, was the nearest to Egypt, but the Nubians had gradually moved south from there, first to Napata, and then to Meroë, close to Shendi, where they established their capital around the third century BC. It lasted until about the year AD 400.

The royal pyramids of Sudan are smaller than those of Egypt, slim and graceful. They stand, huddled witnesses of a distant past, on the flank of low stony hills, swirled by sanddrifts, isolated, deserted. No one is there to offer rides on mangy camels or sell plastic scarabs. The silence is absolute. But at Meroë forty one of the pyramids have their tops sliced off, like breakfast eggs. The culprit was one Giuseppe Ferlini, a doctor from Bologna, who went to Sudan in 1821 on the military expedition of Mohammed Ali, Turkish Viceroy of Egypt, and then returned on his own account in 1834, looking for treasure. Lopping the top first off the pyramid of Queen Amanichakheto, he found a cache of fifty-odd superb pieces of gold jewellery in a bronze bowl, including a magnificent bracelet of gold and blue cloisonné. Afraid for his life, he wrapped the bowl in a cloth and hastened back to Europe, where he tried to sell the treasure. As no one had ever seen anything like it before, he was dismissed as a fraud, and it was with some misgivings that Louis I of Bavaria eventually bought half the pieces. Ferlini was unable to sell the rest.

In 1844 the German archaeologist, Richard Karl Lepsius, went to Meroë and reported to his patron King Frederick William IV of Prussia that the jewels were genuine. The king bought those Ferlini still had, as a result of which half the jewels are today in the museum of Munich and the other half in Berlin, while in Meroë itself the mutilated pyramids, stripped of their treasure but awe-inspiring on their sandy crest, still evoke the power of man's faith over his greed.

The nearby Meroitic temples of Muzzawarat and Naga lie some distance into the desert. Peter's Sudanese assistant, Babakir, found a man with a pick-up converted into a minibus who said he knew the route well and could take me there. 'You need a four by four,' said Babakir, 'but there aren't any.'

The man did not know the way at all and, heading for Muzzawarat, we reached Naga. Here a small temple to the Lion King was carved with the portraits of Egyptian-looking gods, and close by it stood a kiosk that, with its Corinthian pillars, could as well have been in Greece or Rome. Like the oases of the Silk Route, these Nubian kingdoms along the Nile were the transit points between the Mediterranean world and distant, unknown lands, exchanging riches and influences.

From Naga the driver headed off into the desert and, after four hours of constantly digging the minibus out of the sand and pushing hard, we reached Muzzawarat, tired and parched. A German archaeological team were working there. It was verboten. I needed a permit from Khartoum to visit the site, they said, but as no one ever came, they would consider making an exception. But just this once. A young student on the dig told me he knew England well, he'd been to Durham. The work here was very interesting, he said – pouring himself a cold Pepsi and drinking it before our eyes – he was very happy in the desert. Babakir scowled: 'No desert man would leave us without a drink,' he said. 'It's an unwritten law. This man shouldn't be here.'

Babakir took me on to Atbara, a sleepy railway junction, a town once captured by Kitchener that became an important British administrative and railway centre. Close to the Nile, grouped together in high-walled gardens planted with trees, were palatial pastel-coloured villas with long cool verandahs slatted in green. Sudan had once been the most desirable posting in the British Empire after India. Now most of the villas were decaying and there was seldom a train. Railway scrap lay rusting in the sand.

Babakir returned to Khartoum and I spent the next few weeks moving slowly down the Nile, travelling in trucks, lorries, anything that moved. I slept mostly in Peter's shipping containers beside power stations, lulled by what sounded like the rhythmic beat of breakers crashing on a beach, but was merely the pulse of electric turbines. Where the Nile took a big loop to the north, I left it and cut across the desert to Karima in a battered old Bedford lorry. I scrambled up into the back and found a perch on piles of oil drums and sacks of flour, squashed in with crowds of men and boys whose black faces vanished as darkness fell, but whose robes and turbans glowed white in the moonlight. The passengers were so tightly crammed, with heads and hands all round my feet, that I feared for the money hidden in my socks, but it was my glasses I lost in the scrum, so that the stars blurred into melting snowflakes.

For seventeen hours the lorry followed a tangle of almost obliterated

tyre tracks across the rough sands, pitched and tossed like a small rowing
boat in the Outer Hebrides. By late morning we lurched on to a wobbly
ferry and, finally, on the west bank of the Nile at Karima, the passengers fell in a bundle off the back of the lorry, filthy, exhausted and
more thoroughly shaken than Harry's best gin sling.

Around the twelfth century BC a weakened Egypt withdrew from
Nubia and the kingdom of Napata flourished, with its capital at the foot
of the sacred hill, Jebel Barkal, at Karima. This kingdom by the year
750 BC had conquered Egypt and remained in power there for a hundred
years, until the Nubians in turn were ousted by the Assyrians.

The Napatan temple at Karima, dedicated to the 'Sacred Spouse of
Amun' lies in ruins at the foot of the hill – two pillars standing, the rest
in pieces half buried in the sand. The sacredness of Jebel Barkal derives
from its strange form. With its almost detached cliff-face, it resembles
the Egyptian royal uraeus, the upreared cobra worn on the pharaoh's forehead to signify his kingship and divinity. Crowned with a solar disc, the
uraeus of Ancient Egypt was also a goddess amulet, the eye of the sun,
spitting fire at the king's enemies. It was the symbol of the king's right
to rule over both Egypt and the South, given by Amun, king of gods.
Because of the formation of the cliff, whoever held power in Jebel
Barkal could rule both Egypt and Nubia.

The setting sun fired Jebel Barkal, its fearsome power almost tangible,
and silhouetted a cluster of thin, pointed pyramids on a nearby crest –
with their tops still intact they looked like a pile of discarded magicians'
hats.

The journey on down the Nile from Karima would be tough – a
chain of long days and nights shaken in buses and lorries over rough road-
less terrain, with nowhere to stay, or at best, stops at lokandas, small
cockroach-infested rooming houses with no facilities and ominous
rustlings under the bed at five in the morning. That I knew. But here
in Karima I was still in a shipping container – this one, from its full
ashtrays and grimy sheets, clearly not used by any Danes for some time
– and there was absolutely no onward traffic to be found. Nothing.

And so I spent days inside the high wired enclosure of the power station.
It was a long way out of town – or at least a long way from the little
central market – and I would walk each day across wastes of sand to a

few small shacks, not lined in streets but set at random a wide space away from each other. One was a small shop, easily found from the languid plants trained up a netted fence around it. Here I could buy tomatoes and eggs. Then another had two small windows at eye level where a floury baker would appear, his black skin dusted with white, his fingers still flecked with dough, and sell me a round flat loaf.

Each evening women dressed in the bright shawl covering them from head to ankle that all women wore – I never saw one veiled – came to the gate of the power station. They carried large plastic containers on their heads and had walked for miles. A huge distance, the gate watchman said, to fetch water, which the management allowed them to take from the one tap. We stared and smiled at each other. And every evening when they came I was still there, and there was nothing leaving Karima.

I called on Mahjan's important friend, who immediately invited me to dinner – beans, eggs and tomato – but was unable to help with transport. Then, several days later, I heard about a 'box' that was reputedly crossing the desert, west to Dongola. I was up and ready at six. By late morning I had heard it was definitely going to leave, but was waiting for the train from Khartoum to arrive at two o'clock. Or three. At five the train could be heard whistling across the sands, and at seven the box stopped outside the power station. It was a small pick-up truck with seats around the back, already filled with luggage and a very large family. My small bag was added and a goat, with its supply of lucerne, was made comfortable on top of that. It was Eid al-Adhah in a few days and everyone killed a goat for the occasion. It would be six hours to Dongola.

The driver seemed to find his way across the desert by constantly switching the headlights off so that he could discern some shape or horizon that would guide him. Every time he stuck in the sand, we all dug him out. After three hours, one puncture and six times stuck in the sand, we stopped, at a place lost in the emptiness where there was a little water tower, five trees and a hut. A man and his wife and children were selling tea. A little girl of about six brought mine. She was dressed in a ragged shift encrusted with dirt, an amulet round her neck. You knew immediately that she had nothing underneath and had no other clothes. Her hair and eyelashes were matted with sand, but her pale brown face was beautifully fine and her eyes and teeth shone white.

Everyone lay down on the sandy floor of the shack to sleep till morning. I preferred the open air of the desert by the pick-up truck. The goat bleated all night. There was a lorry parked nearby with the driver's goat for Eid tied high up on top of the load. Ours wandered dolefully round and round and underneath the truck, knowing there was a lady goat somewhere around but not able to find where.

The next day the edge of the desert was sudden – small square fields of wheat, then houses, cows and the thin green line of date palms on the horizon that everywhere announced the Nile.

Dongola was a ferry ride to the far bank, a small town that had a centre: a souk and a main street. It also had a couple of hotels. They were closed. Ready for Eid al-Adhah. Only a small depressing room with no window in a seedy lodging house was available. And there was no onward transport. I would have to go back to Khartoum – two days on a lorry – then wait for the train that went once a week to Wadi Halfa and took two days to get there. At least rumours that the ferry into Egypt was running again were confirmed. Everyone was sweetly helpful – there would be a bus coming from Khartoum at six or seven that evening and going on to Wadi Halfa, or even just as far as Abri. No, said someone else, not that evening but the next morning, wait on this side of the river. Wait on the other side of the river; go to Kerma, you'll get a bus from there; go to Abri then it's only six hours (double that I thought) to Wadi Halfa. Amidst all this conflicting information, one message was loud and clear: though I might find something that evening or the next morning, after that there would be no transport of any kind for at least a week. Eid al-Adhah. I took the dismal windowless room.

The main street of Dongola was bustling. Men walked along dragging a single sacrificial goat by its front legs, the tea vendors boiled kettle after kettle on their charcoal braziers, the small jewellery stalls were packed with women. I joined them.

As there had been no evidence of linen at all – and here not even of cotton – and the only goddesses those of the sun king Amun, I searched instead for fulgurite. In one stall I spotted a small ring of the same cat's-eye green as the Massawa stone. My questioning, and arm-waving depictions of thunder and lightning, enlivened by groans and zizzes, gave the jeweller such concern for my sanity that he reduced the price immediately from three dinars to two, and threw in a George VI Africa Star.

As for amulets, they were always the leather box or piece of fabric containing the Koran, but no one admitted to wearing one, though I saw several children with string visible around their necks. I knew they would flee in terror if I tried to see what was hanging on it.

By late afternoon I was at the river's edge. Single-sailed markar boats, made of hard acacia wood, were moored on the shore. They were the only boats able to negotiate the cataracts and sail into Egypt. I wondered if I would ever follow them. The ferry plied to and fro, a tumble of people, trucks, donkeys, goats. I waited on the river bank until the last one crossed on the cusp of dusk and night, and the stallholders by the jetty turned off their kerosene lamps. No bus had come.

To Wadi Halfa

Next morning I was back, to find a holiday scrum of donkey carts, goats, men in clean white robes and shiny shoes, women in their brightest shawls, and vendors squatting behind piles of fresh vegetables, crowded along the river bank. Donkeys were decorated with red tassels and their carts carried shouting families squashed among unwieldy bundles tied up with string. And there was always a bewildered goat lying on top. The goats tethered singly at every available hold seemed to sense there was something amiss and bleated mournfully at each other. 'Get the box to Kerma,' everyone shouted.

Kerma was the earliest of the great Nubian kingdoms on the Nile. It flourished from about 1750 to 1500 BC and – among other achievements – produced breathtakingly elegant pottery. Now it was just a another dusty small town, where I was bundled by the men who had been sitting next to me in the box from Dongola on to another one that set off across the desert at high speed with just them and me on it. My experience of the Sudanese led me to accept this situation with no fear but with the absolute assurance that it was devised solely for my own good. Sure enough, we caught up with a bus lurching through the sand, luggage and men piled on the roof, men hanging on the sides, faces at all the side holes. It was not going to Wadi Halfa but to the town before, Abri. From there I would be sure to get another bus or lorry on to Wadi Halfa, even if I had to wait a day or two. If not, there must be a pick-up or something.

The bus was again simply a lorry roofed over in tin and provided with bench seats, but no other refinements, like windows or shock absorbers. I was squashed in at the back and thrown against the roof so many times that I put my hat on, on top of my Muslim scarves. The passengers around me were wrapped in a fine coating of sand, clouds of which flew off each time the bus bounced.

The bus skirted the Nile, continually veering off into the desert where endless wastes of sands shrouded the remains of those ancient kingdoms between the fourth and second cataracts – shattered stones of temples, palaces, necropoli – but always returning to the dark green line of date palms on our left. The Nubian villages were of neat mud courtyard houses, their doors decorated, their walls edged in coloured paint, and the sandy spaces between them swept clean. It was an isolated, forgotten world, the Nile no longer a great seaway from equatorial Africa to the Mediterranean, but a local source of water for little date groves, for diesel pumps to irrigate patches of wheat, for life along a tiny narrow stretch of shore the people never willingly left.

Some who had left were coming home for Eid. At every village passengers climbed down clutching cassette players, blankets, onions and bags of squashed tomatoes, to be greeted by handshakes of blessings, and the tears of mothers. On into the night the bus went from village to village, playing chimes like an ice-cream van, to stop by clusters of waiting people, only the white robes of the old men visible in the pale moonlight. Only two more hours to Abri, everyone assured me, there they had electricity and light, and from there you will find buses and lorries. And the ferry from Wadi Halfa to Aswan they were sure was running again.

There was no approach to Abri. Just the darkness and the desert track, and then the bus suddenly stopped. Only half a dozen people were left on it, all ghostly figures smothered in sand. I climbed down and found myself in a stage set: a tiny sandy square, confined on the left by two little stalls, each dimly lit by a fluorescent strip – one a general grocer, the other selling aluminium kettles – as a backdrop a blank stone wall, and to the right a small verandah with a stand holding half a dozen large pottery amphorae. In the distance I could dimly discern a row of shuttered stalls. And that was all. Could this be Abri? This was a village, not the town I was expecting. Where was the souk, the lorry lot, the bus stand? The pickup trucks, the tea stalls? Why ever would any lorry or bus call at such a tiny, forgotten place? And what chance of a lift on a pick-up when there were clearly no vehicles at all? How would I ever get away from here?

There was one lokanda in town, the last passengers said, and kindly took me there. It was locked, bolted, shuttered. Closed for Eid al-Adhah.

Gaby's great-grandmother was no doubt a Swabian goosegirl. Gaby had inherited the strong big frame, thick limbs, capable hands and round, heavy-featured face of the European peasant. Bundled round now with a Muslim scarf, her face seemed even rounder and more moonlike, and a quality of sweetness shone from it. Barbara was older: cropped grey hair and bony face. The night breeze blew her long dress against her body, defining its thinness. Of course I could stay, as long as necessary, I was most welcome.

In fact, I would have to stay, they insisted. Nothing would open, nothing would move, there would be no buses, lorries or anything at all for a week. But in ten days' time, they had heard, the ferry from Wadi Halfa would leave for Egypt.

I reflected that when I set out originally I had expected to have to try to find a refugee truck in the wildest of desert terrains, and ask for a lift across the border and, if that hadn't worked, I would have had to wait for the weekly train across the desert from Wadi Halfa back to Khartoum and then fly from there to Nairobi, then to Addis Ababa, then Cairo. That would have been the only way to get into Egypt. I was happy to be stuck in Abri.

Gaby and Barbara were German nurses working at Abri hospital. Barbara had been there on and off for almost twenty years, Gaby for five. They coped with every imaginable disease, having almost nothing in the way of facilities. Adults succumbed to illnesses that elsewhere would be cured, children died of malaria, TB and malnutrition, bottle-fed babies were always brought to them too late. Away from the pressures of the hospital, the nurses indulged in girlish giggling and elbow-shoving, and, having lived alone for so long, didn't think to pass the salt at table.

Their house was in a street of stone, tin-roofed houses by the hospital, set in the desert away from town, a cool high-ceilinged place full of buckets and bowls of cloudy water. Some days, without warning, water came for a while through a pipe in the garden, suddenly disgorging uselessly into a muddy flowerbed if the nurses were away on duty. If they were there, they ran to and fro filling their water-butt and every plastic container they could lay their hands on, ready for the days the pipe remained dry. Electricity might come on half an hour after dusk and, if it did, always went off at ten, so there was no need for light switches. The government had once installed electricity at Abri but had made a charge of one pound a month. The people couldn't or wouldn't pay and now there were just lines of poles for street lights but no lamps. Only the hospital and the small town centre had evening light. 'The West has electricity,' was the reaction of those who wouldn't pay, 'they can give it to us.' Most simply couldn't pay. They were the ones who lived on beans and the bread they made themselves, and could only look at the bananas in the market. Nor could they afford any medical care.

Until March 1993 the hospital had always been cram-jam full of people. Everything was free, food was left lying around, rats scampered everywhere and were thought to be a normal feature of hospital life. Then, overnight, charges were introduced for everything from anaesthetic to breakfast. Even visitors had to pay to call. So now the place was almost empty and people came only in extremis. In the children's ward were just three little girls, all suffering from various effects of malnutrition. The ragged bedding of a fourth awaited her return as she had been taken to prison along with her mother, incarcerated for brewing liquor.

The nurses had a small garden enlivened by a few bright flowers, a frisky cat and a sickly lemon tree, but mostly it was of sand, yellow grass and dry flowerbeds, and full of glass boxes in which they did their cooking by sunlight.

Eid-al Adha came and went. People called on each other in their best clothes, offering and accepting sweets or, more often, breakfast. This was a basket-covered tray of bread, beans, eggs, tomatoes and, most especially, meat, as Eid was the time for meat. The houses of Abri were divided into two courtyards – the women's always bigger – surrounded by rooms. In front was an open verandah with beds, on which people lolled, listless in the intense heat. And always hanging on the verandah would be the skinned back half of the goat whose forelegs we were eating.

As days passed, news on buses, lorries and boats was conflicting. There would be nothing for a week. There might be a pick-up on Saturday. There should be a boat on Wednesday, so there might be lorries on Monday to meet up with it. There could even once have been a train, had the Nubians not ripped up the track between Kerma and Wadi Halfa, preferring their isolation.

In the market, Solomon, a tall kindly man, his face like polished ebony, his robes and turban crisply laundered, his black shoes shining, promised to find out for me what possibilities there were. He was the owner of the snuff stall and came up every so often from the south – where the tobacco was grown but where no one was interested in sniffing – to provision and man his stall for a week or two. The next morning I waited at the snuff stall. Solomon came striding up, smiling in a phalanx of glistening white teeth. 'Good news, good news!' he shouted. But the news was nothing to do with lorries. 'Ireland has a peace treaty. I heard it on the BBC World Service!'

But nothing was moving out of Abri and I would have to stay on with the kindly nurses.

There had always been many occasions on which, on my return to England, the choice of food available in my local supermarket had seemed obscene. But the shortages people suffered in the countries I had been travelling in – Slovakia, for example, where the range of vodka extended from buffalo hide to gentian, but where an apple was never seen – I had shared in only for a short while. But to live for years in the deprivation of Sudan, to endure the monotonous diet, the lack of every basic need from the society of friends to safe drinking water, had been a deliberate choice of the nurses. In the name of Christ, but not just for Christ, they said. For the medical care they could give.

Before we partook of any meal, grace was always said. Mostly by Barbara, but Gaby also took her turn, and when I murmured 'For what we are about to receive, may the Lord make us truly thankful', I was asked to serve in the rota. Which I did gladly, for the words had acquired an urgency: after my departure, the summer heat would suffocate both people and land, there would be only dried okra and bread – the tomatoes finished, the aubergines and dry festive biscuits a forgotten memory. And then the nurses would be sent back to Germany. It was already forty eight degrees, and summer could add on another ten.

In the silent emptiness of the desert around Abri, the sky was always clear, at night free of the pollution of light from the earth, by day bleached by the sun. For seven days its blazing heavy heat crushed down and for seven nights its cool moon and starlight lifted the burden. And on the eighth day a lorry went to Wadi Halfa.

On to Egypt

At least, a convoy of three lorries went, for it was unsafe for one alone. Not from the point of view of the fundamentalist terrorism that had erupted in southern Egypt – ostensibly filtered over from Sudan – but more because of the total isolation, the wild terrain, the inevitable blow-outs, the certain breakdowns.

The nurses had kept a visitors' book, sparsely entered, but it did contain the record of a couple of people who had come down from the north in the preceding five years, including a cheerful note from a Swedish girl cycling to the Cape. 'Did she make it?' I asked.

'No, of course not. She was picked up just outside Wadi Halfa and brought to us on a lorry. When she recovered she caught the bus to Khartoum and married a French archaeologist there. Then there was the Dutch cyclist. He was discovered lying semi-conscious at the side of the road, by a passing lorry, and brought straight to our hospital.' It was a harsh landscape. 'No one ever makes it on a bike.'

Leaving Abri, the lorry driver stopped at every shack, and women came out with greetings and with letters and parcels for him to take: the mail service between Wadi Halfa and Abri had ended when the mail van broke down and was never repaired. The nurses had received no mail for a year or more. Post for them from Europe, or anywhere, was flown to Khartoum, then simply put on the train to Wadi Halfa and abandoned there.

After only a few miles the lorry wheels skewed into the most forbidding of skidding, boundless wastes. Tumbled boulders, dappled with glinting blown sand, piled into low, cliffed hills on each side of the little convoy, holding it on a vague track. As the sun set behind those to our left, they formed a barricade, hemming us on one side while opening up never-ending yaws to our right. As night fell, if it were possible to define a track, it was only by the lights of the lorry ahead, each of whose relative position changed with every breakdown. For the thirteen hours of the journey absolutely nothing passed in the opposite direction.

The lights of Wadi Halfa, when they came, were extraordinary.

Reflected in the choking waters of Lake Nasser, strung along its shore, they looked as if they belonged to some Swiss resort comfortable in its photogenic lakeside setting. The truth, as we circuited around the lights, bucking, pitching and tossing through slipping dunes, was very different. As we crossed great stretches of empty sand, the lorry headlights would pick out here and there a cluster of a few miserable shacks, then we would be grinding through desert again. At each group of shacks the lorry offloaded its passengers until I was the only one left. The hotel that should have been there was boarded up, the driver took me to another and dropped me off. It was simply a collection of rooms around open courtyards, with metal bedsteads littered around. There was at first no sign of life.

It was easy to imagine them in Paris, meeting perhaps at a party on the Left Bank. 'Come with me to Africa,' he must have said. 'We will make love under the stars, we will live as the Africans do. We will take nothing with us, but share their lives, cooking our food on a wood fire, outside in the warmth of the sun. Come with me, chérie.' Now they were sitting on broken plastic chairs in the hotel in Wadi Halfa, eating tomatoes. There had been nothing else for the week they had been holed up waiting for Eid al-Adhah to end. 'Tu es insupportable,' the man was shrieking at the girl, 'stupide.' He turned and introduced himself: 'Jean-François.' He was an aggressive, grey-haired man in jeans. I told him I had just come by lorry from Abri.

'How much did it cost?' he asked immediately. And when I told him: 'Too much for two hundred kilometres.'

I narrowed my eyes. 'You haven't seen the two hundred kilometres.'

Apart from a German couple we heard had come down from Aswan a week or two before, and rumours of an Australian who had done the same, they were the only foreigners to have entered Sudan since the ferry had started running again.

Eid had caught them with no money, but the hotel owner was happy to wait until the bank opened again to charge them for their room, and in the meantime lent them money for tomatoes. They ate them raw at lunchtime and cooked them on a few sticks of wood on the floor of the hotel yard at night.

The next morning Jean-François went down to the market for their tomatoes, and came bounding back. 'There's a lorry to Abri at 12.40,' he said. There seemed an unnecessary precision to the hour.

'Make sure you take plenty of water,' I said. I had had to sit for the whole journey on top of the engine, just like basking for all that time in a sauna, and had needed all the water I'd taken, and been very glad of the thermos of tea – and sticky rice pudding – that the little café near the hotel had sent over for me when they saw me arrive. The kindness of the Sudanese still bowled me over.

'We didn't bring water bottles with us. We drink the same as the Africans. My copine is afraid of the desert,' he snidely confided. She was much younger than him, a simple girl with round face, round glasses and hair in plaits. When Jean-François wasn't around she came and quietly asked me questions about the journey, in worried tones.

When I left for Egypt a couple of days later they were still there, waiting for a lorry.

The first morning after my night arrival in Wadi Halfa, I had set out to find out about the ferry. In the early light the 'town' revealed itself to be nothing but a scattering of a few shacks spread out over a huge area of desert, with not a single road or tree. No building was higher than three metres and most were roofless. There was a pervasive smell of rotting fish. I walked down to the jetty. The abandoned settlement near it now had a population of squatters, Nuban refugees who had escaped from the war in their homeland of the Nuba Mountains to the south. They seemed to live mainly by brewing illicit liquor. 'They make our *araghi* for us,' the Muslims said. It was an African enclave of mud huts, stately women bearing water, and dire poverty.

Wadi Halfa had been an important trading post and military outpost. The grandest building in town was the Nile Hotel, a pretty place with verandahs and balconies, and a beautiful garden leading down to the river. In the hotel's tourist shop ivory, silver and ostrich feathers were sold, and in its bar the British used to gather, including Winston Churchill, who found Wadi Halfa 'brown and squalid, an African slum'. Thomas Cook steamers plied the Nile, and one, the S.S. Sudan, served as an annexe to the hotel. A pleasant avenue of date palms lead through the town. There were plenty of mosques and a motley populace of Jewish moneychangers, Syrian drapers, Egyptian ironmongers and Greek grocers – in the old colonial days a Greek grocer was always said to accompany a British officer to provide him with his whisky ration. 'Here we find the British and Egyptian flags floating side by side.'

All that was now seventy metres below water.

In 1963, when the Aswan high dam was built, fifty thousand Nubians lost their homes in the floodwaters, leaving their villages, their date palms and river banks for an arid and distant desert landscape. As the dam was constructed, the waters of the Nile gradually rose, slowly, inexorably. Hassan Dafalla, who supervised the evacuation, slept with his bedsheet dangling down to the floor in the hope that the water would wake him before engulfing his house. It flooded first his garden, so that shrubs, sere for lack of water, suddenly freshened up and their curled leaves and drooping branches straightened. In the town around he could hear the dismal roar of falling buildings, followed by clouds and splashes of water.

When the town of Wadi Halfa and all the villages around were evacuated and left empty, Dafalla returned alone for a last look at the gentle riverine landscape that had been wrested from the desert over centuries. He walked into the deserted mud houses, their walls, windows and doors still edged with pretty white painting like cake frills. He found the hyenas, used to picking up scraps around the streets, had slunk scavenging into the empty houses. Even they, as the scent of rising water reached their nostrils, moved up and away into the surrounding desert. The rats were the last to leave, picking up their babies in their mouths and scrambling up the banks and the buildings, until the top of the last minaret vanished below the waters, and the crocodiles moved in along the new shorelines.

There was a buzz of excitement when the ferry came, though it brought only sixty two people when it used to carry eight hundred. The same evening the connecting train from Khartoum arrived, so that the hotel the French couple and I had shared was suddenly full of crushing, invading people. They moved their beds into the open yards and were sleeping and cooking everywhere, blocking the only shower that worked, by using it for their washing-up and laundry. The pottery amphorae that stood in the central yard, holding the hotel's supply of Nile water, protected from the sun by a canopy, were suddenly empty. There was no drinking water. Local women sat in the sand outside the hotel making tea, the market stalls opened, selling tomatoes, onions and stinking fly-blown fish. The temperature was still in the high forties.

The military and trading importance of Wadi Halfa lay solely in its position on the Nile where the river crossed an international border. Otherwise before the British built the railway across the desert to Khartoum, its isolation was extreme. It is still hardly less so: desert to the north, south, east and west, only the Nile as a channel to the outside world, and that impeded to the south by the eight miles of volcanic boulders that form the second cataract and allow the river to pass only in narrow thrashing channels. And to the north, a twenty four-hour journey to Aswan across a flooded lake more than three hundred kilometres long.

The ferry was, predictably, decrepit and smelt of stale fish. It chugged through Lake Nasser past a coastline of inlets, promontories, bays, peninsulas and creeks, and around groups of islands. But mountain tops do not make islands, and waters that simply find their level on a mountain slope that they have not eroded, can never form a natural landscape. The coast and islands were weirdly detached from the water that simply choked them. The reconstructed cliff face of Abu Simbel loomed in the dusk and, near it, lights. Lights in such desolation. They were from a small town in the distance and from two deserted hotels – one owner had spent a million dollars on improvements over the last few years, but after the tourist shootings at Luxor hardly anyone came.

Then at last Aswan. Aswan! the southernmost point of the Roman Empire. The first step into the orbit of the Mediterranean. Fairy lights along the corniche, floodlit tombs across the Nile, the wonderful Pharaonic excesses of the Old Cataract Hotel, where Agatha Christie and celebrities from what now seemed another world, once had stayed. The soft pleasures of Aswan were like a velvet wrap around my shoulders.

I walked its streets, wandered into the vegetable market as if in an egg-tomato-bean-induced trance, and bought wildly. Then to the general market, where I found an embroidered Nubian cap – there was plenty of cotton here, but for all that remained of the linen of Upper Egypt, it might as well have been just thistledown.

I gawped at Western tourists in shorts and it was a while before it occurred to me that there were very few of them. The pall of Luxor, I was to find, hung over Egypt like the smoke of the machineguns. The piled bodies of grandmother, mother and daughter, the bloodied clothes of Swiss lovers, impinged on the mind more strongly than the grandeur of Hatshepsut's temple. Life in Egypt now was 'since the incident at Luxor' or even just 'since Luxor'. It was never referred to as a massacre.

Egypt

Linen and Guns

The linen of Ancient Egypt, the finest in the world, was used in scraps to wrap small treasures in boxes, as if it were tissue paper; old sheets of it were ripped into strips to bind countless mummies of people and cats; swabs of it mopped up excess brain fluids, as in the mummy of the young priestess Tjentmutengebtiu. The best, the very best, was made into royal and priestly clothing, funerary vestments, and bedsheets that served as currency. And almost all of it was plain white.

Embroidery was not a particular skill of Pharaonic Egypt, neither during the Old nor the Middle Kingdom, and examples are very rare. One is a tunic of Tutankhamun, embroidered at the neck with his name and the design of a cartouche of magic rope, all certainly Egyptian. But round the hem is a row of small embroidered panels of real and mythical animals and plants, whose motifs and stitches betray Syrian workmanship. Tapestry weaving, weft-looping, woven stripes were the decorative techniques preferred in Egypt to embroidery.

Of Egyptian motifs only the symbolized papyrus and lotus, nearly always in tandem as they represented Lower and Upper Egypt, might conceivably be considered triangular, their jagged petally, leafy edges resembling almost a horticultural tasselling of pendants. Otherwise on triangular patterns I had drawn a blank.

Then the amulets of Ancient Egypt were small objects, usually of faience, steatite, glass or metal. They were both worn, and set into the wrappings of mummies – Tutankhamun had 143 of them – sometimes even being considered to have transferred their magic to the linen itself. Scarabs, eyes and toads, sacred baboons and falcon-headed deities, vultures, cobras, cats and dogs, they were a talismanic zoo irrelevant to my task.

The traditional journey down the Nile from Aswan to Cairo, by felucca, cruise ship or train, would thus serve no purpose, except perhaps for the stepping stones of Asyut and Beni Hasan.

Asyut was reputedly the source of those net shawls fashionable in Europe in the 1920s, heavy with silver, that clung to the thin shoulders and flat chests of flappers. To make them, flattened strips of silver were cut to a point, pushed through the net, twisted and then cut again, forming patterns of diamonds, cypresses, triangles. Would they still be made there?

At Beni Hasan, about sixty kilometres to the north of Asyut, near Al-Minya, almost four hundred tombs decorated with paintings of everyday life in the Middle Kingdom are cut into the rocks. The tomb of Khnemhotep, from the second millennium BC, and those of father-and-son Baqt and Khety, depict the bustle of temple and domestic linen workshops. Men ret, women spin; men weave on vertical looms, women on horizontal ones, the older version by at least three thousand years.

There was no question of going to either Asyut or Beni Hasan. Both were out-of-bounds to foreigners. Anyone who tried to go there was simply bustled back on to the train or boat by armed police. The consulate in Asmara had been right.

There remained the Nubians, displaced by the construction of the Aswan dam, about fifty thousand of them. Though most were resettled in the inappropriate, dry terrain of Kashm el Girba, east of Khartoum, and now known optimistically as 'New Halfa', some were rumoured to have moved to the oases of the Western Desert, notably Kharga. Of their traditional costume, the men's caps, such as I had seen in Khartoum, were particularly pretty, swirled around with colour and topped with a sharp peak of multicoloured circles. Would the men have worn them until the flooding of the High Dam? Would they have taken them to the Western Desert?

So my destination would be the oases. As road links to them from the Nile below Aswan were now closed, they could only be reached from Cairo. Those of Kharga, Dakhla and Bahariya, settled originally mainly by Bedouin, were today being swamped by schemes to rehouse the exploding population of the Nile Valley. The original women's dresses of those oases were embroidered in styles reminiscent of Palestine and Jordan. The exception was the oasis of Siwa, much further west near the border of Libya, and settled by Berber people, not Bedouin. There the women's dresses were covered with embroidery of solar motifs – double axes and whorls in yellow, orange and red. And they also made triangular amulets of beads.

I caught the train from Aswan to Cairo.

The Muslim militant group Jamaa Islamiyya had been taking pot-shots at tourists and killing them since 1992, in an attempt to destroy Egypt's economy by wiping out the tourist industry. Then in 1996 the worst attacks had begun. As the consulate in Asmara had warned, eighteen Greek tourists had been shot dead outside their hotel in Cairo and fourteen wounded. The next year ten tourists were killed and many injured, mostly German, when their bus, parked outside the Egyptian Museum, was machine-gunned and bombed. Tourists panicked and left for home – Kuoni and Saga offered to transfer theirs to the safety of Luxor. And now there had been 'the incident' at Luxor, when more than sixty had been shot and stabbed to death – including a girl of five – during a forty five-minute orgy of calm and purposeful savagery. As a result, when I reached Cairo, literally every few yards along the streets stood a white-uniformed, heavily-armed, bored policeman, waiting for the tourists to return.

The Agricultural and Cotton Museum complex in Cairo lay in tranquil gardens, a life-threatening walk through traffic almost as murderous as any terrorists of Asyut and Beni Hasan could be. The gloomy buildings of the Agricultural Section looked untouched for a hundred years. Neat rows of dead birds lay on their backs in glass cabinets, labelled illegibly. Mundane butterflies and beetles were stuck on the wall with pins, a scattering of broken-off legs and wings lying on the discoloured paper below, while the more colourful were artistically arranged as fans. A Nile crocodile, whose 'young ones soon learn to shift for themselves', basked in the dust. Unshaven attendants in grubby jellabyya badgered for *baksheesh*.

Textile production merited two small rooms, one featuring silk – showing mostly reconstructions of a silkworm's gut – the other wool. This displayed small models of sheep and goats, a few knitted hats, and drawers full of wool tangled with dead insects and larvae, dried out over the years into transparency. In a folkloric diorama caked in dust could just be spotted a typical dress of Siwa and another from the oasis of Bahariya, crudely worked in vertical lines of red and orange, and hung with silver coins. The rest of the dress appeared to be tie-dyed – a strange technique for Egypt – but on closer inspection the shaded dots turned out to be incrustations of mould.

As for flax, though Egypt's main crops were listed in French and not in Arabic – barley, lentils, sugar-cane, onions, maize, rice, broad beans and cotton – I could see no mention of it. That was the Agricultural Museum. The Cotton Museum was shuttered and closed.

The Coptic textiles of the third to seventh centuries – those medallions and strips of fine linen and wool decorated with small goggly-eyed figures, with dancers and the god Pan, with rabbits, lions, flowers and Christian crosses – are acknowledged to be among the most extraordinarily skilful ever made. But they are mostly tapestry-weaving. The few embroidery stitches there are, are added catching threads in natural linen that emphasize details like the spots on a leopard, or Hercules' nipples. Most look like small flying birds.

The Coptic Museum in Cairo had a wonderful display, but all the figures were quite definitely real humans or real gods, sporting proper legs and feet and toes, rather than triangular skirts with pendants. A few weird figures excited me, needlessly as they turned out not to be goddesses. The only object of any conceivable relevance was a small plaque in the case 'Objects used in Everyday Life, in Bone or Wood'. It could have been anthropomorphic, some sort of fertility amulet, maybe. But in all honesty it just looked like a jelly baby run over by a steamroller.

I sat down in the Church of the Virgin next door. The interior was of sombre wood inlaid with ivory, the vaulted roofs of its nave and side aisles sliced with massive curved beams so that they looked like the keels of upturned galleons. Because of a recent earth tremor, scaffolding held them in place, clamps encircled the pillars. Over all lay a pall of quietened earthquake swirl and eternal dust. A few people sat on intricately fretted benches, like Victorian hall settles, the men on one side, the women on the other. On the empty benches the outline of the bottoms of previous worshippers was clear in the dust. A priest chanted the Orthodox rites.

From a cacophonous medley of vehicles below the floodlit Citadel, I left that night on a bus, with what looked like a Pickfords' load strapped to its roof, heading for the oases.

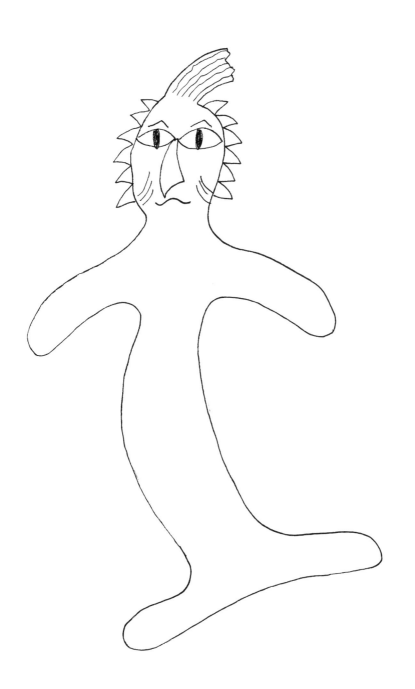

And by now I had learnt that the Americans had launched a missile attack on the pharmaceuticals factory near Isam's uncle's house in Bahri, northern Khartoum.

Oases of the Western Desert

I awoke in Kharga to the sounds of the muezzin and the wind in the palms. Kharga was a boom town, the main resettlement site of people from the Nile valley. The pressure on that narrow valley of ten-children families, ever-diminishing fertile land and shortage of water, was inexorably pushing more and more people into the oases where water at least was plentiful, though life was hard. The shoeshine man, a thin fellow with pinched face, dark brown eyes and large ears, dressed in a grey jellabyya and rubber shoes, stood at the bus stop, waiting for trade. He had a small old wooden box, a few dirty rags, a brush and a tin of black polish with its lid missing. You could live on just that.

Kharga was no picture-book oasis of palm trees, isolated in the desert sands. It was one long main street and a grid of dusty side-roads, where concrete blocks had been hastily cobbled around uncleared, crumbling mud-brick shacks. The market was a small lane-side affair offering piles of aubergines, garlic, onions, and enticing figs bursting with pink seeds and flies. As some of the people resettled in Kharga were supposed to be Nubians flooded out by Lake Nasser, I looked carefully at all the old men shopping and trading there. Some were in Western dress, but those who did wear turbans had the usual Egyptian white knitted or crocheted caps underneath. If any were indeed Nubians, then their lovely old embroidered caps now, too, lay deep under water, along with their homes, date palms and minarets.

Kharga was now called 'the New Valley', Mahmud Youssef, director of the grandly-named Al-Wadi Al-Gadid Antiquities Museum told me. There were no Nubians in Kharga, he added. They had all gone to Kom Ombo, a town forty-five kilometres north of Aswan, two million of them, he assured me. I wasn't going back, not just for a few caps, and on information that sounded suspect. I contented myself with looking round the museum.

There was a showcase of amulets, unlabelled. The usual scarabs, toads and so on, and then from the next oasis of Dakhla various beads and cowries, and necklaces of cloves and coral. There was also a late Graeco-Roman version of the god Horus, whose shape almost formed a cross. 'Coptic,' suggested Youssef. There were caps in velvet, wool and linen, excavated at Dakhla. They were Ottoman of the seventeenth and eighteenth centuries, and worked in patchwork and quilting, but not embroidered. I paid the equivalent of three nights' board and lodging for my entry ticket – special price for foreigners. 'Since Luxor,' Youssef explained. As no tourists come now, the few who do have to pay five times as much as they used to, for entrance into all the museums and monuments of Egypt. He seemed to find this perfectly logical. The ones who still bother to come and risk being shot, pay up.

The brand new five-star hotel on the rim of the oasis was completely empty. Just beyond it, an evening walk past palm trees, irrigation channels and new road signs, was the beautiful stone temple of Hibis, dating from the sixth century BC, but mainly built by Darius in the fifth. It was set in an isolated clearing surrounded by a metal fence, and was supported by rusted scaffolding. An open courtyard was walled by pillars topped by capitals of lotus flowers, one row open and the next closed, golden in the evening sun. The main part of the temple was firmly locked, and guarded by a toothless curator in dirty jellabyya, attended by three armed white-uniformed policemen, there to protect any tourists that might come. The curator unlocked the door while the police stood back. On the walls were exquisite carvings and paintings of Egyptian gods and goddesses, and rows of hieroglyphs. And on one wall the graffiti: *'Cailliaud fut le premier européen qui prit connaissance de ce temple 1818.'* It was Cailliaud, a French mineralogist, who had first visited the Meroitic pyramids near Shendi and had drawn them in 1821 before Ferlini lopped their tops off.

The oases lay along the caravan routes that linked Equatorial Africa with the Mediterranean: the Forty-Days' Road that brought camels and salt from Sudan, the route that linked Ethiopia and Libya. While the caravans were the source of the inhabitants' wealth, they also entailed the risk of attack, so the old towns of each oasis were defensive: mysterious enclosed refuges of concealed entrances and serpentine paths. They were each built on a slight hill – which also raised them above the water table – and were a labyrinth of tortuous paths of intrigue, roofed over by wooden beams and baked mud, at a cowering height that allowed no stranger's camel to pass.

Beyond Kharga towards the oasis of Dakhla, was Balat. Softly curved walls of adobe rounded the twisting curves of the dark, narrow lanes. Fresh sand was laid on the pathways each day. Low mud roofs, held by heavy beams at little above head height, still kept light and sun at bay, now that attacking camels were no longer a threat. Wooden shutters high in the walls were opened by women who sang out greetings. One sat on the pathway embroidering a dress. 'Come back next year. I'll make one for you.'

In the nearby village of Bashandi, the advertised 'girls' training centre of making and embroidering old clothes' turned out to be a showcase for two women doing terrible embroidery in puce floss, though the old dresses they were supposed to be copying were worked in soft shades of dark red silk and then hung with silver coins, while vertical bands in pale orange cotton herringbone stitch decorated them from shoulder to hem. In Bashandi some of the mud brick houses had a red hand stamped on the wall – if a hand is steeped in the blood of a newly-slaughtered goat or sheep and slapped onto a wall, the image will keep away the evil eye, or the *jinn* or any other demon one might imagine, the women told me.

The heart of the main town of the Dakhla oasis, Mut, was another such labyrinth, but unroofed, its mud-brick houses falling into ruin, the one piled into rubble against the standing wall of the other, a squalid tip of stones heaped up the hillside and, unbelievably, still lived in. As I climbed towards the top, a terrible wailing led me to wander inside a derelict hut to find the cause. A small kitten lay dying in a dump of putrid rubbish. When I passed back down again a few minutes later, it was dead.

As I emerged from the ruins on to the road, a well-dressed man was waiting for me.

'You have a camera?' he asked.

'Yes.'

'Did you take any photos of Mut?'

'No.'

'Thank you,' he said.

The third such defensive town was Al-Qasr. Like Balat it was tortuous and roofed, but uninhabited and built not in adobe but in mud brick. Tiny and compact, it was set on a protective foothill, an exquisite jumble of mud and wood, of light and shade. Its sanded paths twisted between close, shadowed walls, pitched into darkness where the roof lay low along the lane, and suffused by sharp sunlight where the space of an old madrasa lay open to the sky. Carved lintels of acacia defined the low doorways, massive beams held corridors of passage, gaps high in the walls served as windows. Only in the evenings was there any life, when the people from the nearby village walked through it to their homes: the muffled footsteps of shawled women, the creak of donkey carts, the hushed chatter of schoolchildren stirring the quiet air. But during the day a creepy silence, a threatening emptiness, a deserted calm hung over it.

I had begun to come into contact with 'camel people'. The first was Marie-Claire. We were staying together at a 'Rest House' above a cafeteria on the highway near Al-Qasr. It was a simple place of hard beds without sheets, high bolsters of iron consistency and a host providing stewed vegetables and hot bread, and a genuine welcome for absolutely peanuts. Or if not peanuts, a slim slice of grubby notes.

Marie-Claire was a bank clerk from Nantes who, having no family and few friends, was always willing to work over Christmas and whenever no one else wanted to, in exchange for extra holidays to travel. Her face was thin, her body boyish, her hair cut into tufts that no French hairdressing salon, even in Nantes, was likely to have been responsible for. Her shoes were sensible. She had passed through the White Desert, and had been left with a great desire to venture there alone on what she referred to as 'a camelle'. She had negotiated with someone called Ahmed and got him down from 350 Egyptian pounds to 200 for two days, a real bargain, she told me. When I last saw her she was still waiting to be collected and carried off by Ahmed.

The road on to the next oasis of Farafra ran through real desert where the telegraph lines finally ended and there was nothing but featureless sand. Just here and there, where there was one tree and thus water, there would be a huddle of concrete buildings around it: the desperation of resettlement. Farafra itself had been, only five years before, a small oasis of one thousand five hundred people. Now there were five thousand at least. Twenty even, some said. The town, again built on a hill, but along wide sandy streets, clung to the edge of the 'garden' of date palms. Only the original people of the oasis were allowed to own plots in the garden and they kept their dates for themselves – even in the village it was impossible to buy them. The heavy wooden peg locks on the doors of the houses served only to enhance the secrecy of the place.

But half a kilometre up the road, the Swiss had taken over. They ran, together with some local people, a smart new hotel. A sequence of ecologically low arches decorated with zigzags concealed a Swiss development of Bedouin-style rooms and real showers. In these luxurious surroundings two more 'camel people' were staying.

One was Elphie. A German Swiss well into her fifties, she was dressed in an altogether more provocative manner than Marie-Claire. Her cotton jacket, printed in a vaguely African, ethnic design of animals and palm trees, blew aside continuously to display a thin see-through top, below which she wore no bra but flaunted very flat nipples surrounded by rather sagging flesh. She was off again on a camel trek, she said. The last time she had been taken into the desert by a Bedouin who had strict instructions to return with her, but she had insisted on being left alone in the desert with her camel. She had made her own fire, then cooked her meal, and rolled into her sleeping bag. The next morning, early, the Bedouin had come back for her.

The other was Eric, a young Dutchman, whose rather shaggy hair was pushed under a baseball cap. He refused to be sponsored by makers of expedition clothing – like the make of shirt I happened to be wearing, he pointed out. He wore instead an old T-shirt that he had bought locally, with loose trousers and heavy boots. Two lethal knives lay hidden in his belt, and he had two camels, Noura and Rania. Every year he spent seven months in the desert with them and then, back in Holland, he sat at his computer writing books 'about myself', he said.

He seemed to be fleeing some thwarted love affair, or perhaps just disliked mankind.

Eric spent an entire morning in the hotel yard loading up his beasts. They carried all the equipment and food, one hundred and fifty kilos each. He always walked. And he did carry a long stick – for protection. Rania had wanted a male on one occasion and had gone for him. Dangerous, they could be dangerous, though he caressed their necks, whispered into their nostrils and said sweet nothings to them.

The camels hated being loaded up. He captured them by placing bags of dried beans over their noses, which they chomped noisily while he tried to balance their loads and get them to sit – 'grrgrr', or stand – 'up,up'. He had to repeat this six times a day, he said, when he was out in the desert. Hours later he set off, not at a nice easy ambling pace, but up a sharp incline where each camel hesitated and he pulled one and then the other. He was making for the little dunes seventy kilometres away, he had said, and then the open desert at a hundred and eighty.

The hotel organised overnight camping trips into the White Desert – I would go there, I thought, to spend the night in starlight and silence, but a group of Swiss were gathered to go with me. They all smoked incessantly and bickered in the ingratiating whine of Schwyzer-Tutsch. One was Elphie. She was a free soul, she confided in me, opening her jacket. Another was a lady wearing uncrushable travel clothes that clung round every bulge of her body and her money belts. She wore diamanté sunglasses initialled Emanuelle Khan, and carried a handbag 'Déesse First Collection' whose diamanté outshone even the sunglasses. She was deeply concerned that the cows in the oasis had no grass or drinking water. Then there was a couple dressed for a desert dream: he entirely in white safari clothes with knee-high cream boots, she in floating red and gold chiffon that hung from her mantilla-like chignon to her ankles. They all somehow failed to conceal their characters of plebian, stolid burghers of Appenzell.

The last one of our little band was a sensitive artist, who had never exhibited or sold a painting, but who was not to be disturbed in his absorption of the atmosphere of the primeval world. He lacked any animation save a slow blink of the eyelids, and contributed only one remark to the night's conversation 'The cucumber has a good taste here', and that in a tone dirgelike even by Swiss standards.

As the Bedouin driver kneaded dough and prepared bread for our meal under the stars, the most hellish squabbles broke out among our band of adventurers, some crying, some shouting, some sulking. Only the beautifully-costumed couple, who along with me turned out to be the sole paying customers, behaved impeccably and walked away into the emptiness around.

The squabbles subsided, the local owners stopped swearing, and the monotonous singalong of Swiss German reasserted itself. I thought of Eric, alone with his camels in the true silence of the desert, lighting his fire, cooking his meal, and wondered to what end of the earth love can drive you. I walked away into the far distance with my sleeping bag.

The White Desert was a bleached, skeletal landscape of huge white limestone rocks hollowed out by wind and sand, and scattered wildly around on the sands, some like blown meringues, others eroded into the atomic mushroom of Hiroshima. By sheer good luck and no planning, a silver full moon was rising on one side and a blood-gold sun setting on the other. As the sun blazed below the horizon the gilded rocks seemed to stand in the silence, like witnesses of the western death the ancient Egyptians believed in. It was an eerily beautiful scene that had existed for millennia and would continue to exist for millennia to come. Unless, I reflected, the world were shattered by a nuclear blast, in which case, we are told, it is only the Swiss and cockroaches that are expected to survive.

Bahariya was an oasis of palm groves, hot springs, orchards of apricots, and fields of grain, that exuded a simple rural calm. Four thousand years ago it was famous for its wine, and seemed not to share the history of attack by strangers' camels that the other oases had. The street of its main town, Bawiti, was wide and paved but overblown by sand at the edges so that it wound as a trickle through the dun landscape of the few adobe houses and desert that flanked it. Donkeys and bicycles were the main traffic. The bus from Farafra was met by a young man, Talad, who took me immediately to the Alpenblick, the one hotel in town, he said.

A straggly, neglected garden, a teahouse of reed matting, and half a dozen rooms painted blue comprised the entire premises, and of the Alps there was no sign. A rusty barrel in the garden provided washing facilities for the guests, of whom I was the only one. Bare adobe floors, bare adobe walls, bare light bulbs, for which there was rarely electricity, completed the amenities.

Nearby was a rickety wooden construction that seemed to protect an entrance to steps below the ground. 'A cemetery,' Talad replied when I asked what it was. 'No one is allowed down there.' I accepted this, to my later regret, and concentrated on Badri.

Badri had a small shop on the main street of Bawiti and was doing all he could to help the poor. He bought the wool of the local camels, and of those from Sudan or Giza, as all of these were white, and the brown wool of the Libyan ones. He then commissioned men and women to spin and knit it into sweaters, gloves, socks and scarves. Traditionally garments in white, or white and yellow, were for women, and brown, or brown and white, for men. Then he bought red and yellow floss silks from Cairo and black fabric in the local market and got the women of the village of El Argus, who had a reputation for fine embroidery, to make dresses for him. He sold some of the things in his little local shop, but most went to Cairo. Egyptian women there liked to wear traditional costume on special occasions, he said.

The embroidery women of El Argus, on the northern fringe of the oasis, lived in a street of concrete shacks, alongside which ran the mud channel carrying spring water into the 'garden'. They sat in groups of two or three doing really crude, rough work in stitches that were at least traditional. They also kept to the old style of working red tasselling over the breasts – anything to do with the evil eye? protecting the milk of the newborn child? They didn't think so.

But Badri knew about amulets – *heejab*. Only two men were known to make them, one a farmer in a village forty-seven kilometres away – one of those small settlements in the middle of the desert where a few palms grow and the presence of water can support a family or two – and the other a man in Bahariya. Secrecy was paramount, he said, so if I ever told anyone I should not name the oasis and I should now call him Abdul and not Badri.

Neither of the men who could make a heejab were mullahs or had any religious training, but they were 'men who knew'. They could write out an appropriate excerpt from the Koran and the 'wrapping' would be made by the person who ordered the amulet. Normally that would be a newly married man anxious to protect his bride from the covetous evil eye, or a mother whose child appeared sickly. Even sometimes someone in love who wanted their beloved to enjoy happiness and good health. My case was different. What did I want the amulet for? Wasn't the one I was wearing round my neck good enough? He looked at me carefully. 'You've got golden hair. It's gold, and it doesn't help you. We don't like it. Can't you change that for a start?'

Well, maybe I needed an amulet to protect me on my travels, Badri, now Abdul, suggested, in a more kindly vein. He would have to think about asking one of the men on my behalf, but I would have to swear not to tell anyone. The man would need my name and the name of my mother – it didn't matter that she had been dead for some years. My date of birth might be relevant, he wasn't sure, but he took it down anyway as he liked the rhythm of the numbers. I was told not to breathe a word to anyone and to come back that evening.

I complied with these instructions, and returned that evening with a scarf over my hair. Abdul handed me a rather slippery black object with a safety pin dangling from it by a sliver of twisted yellow thread. The dear heejab man – and no, I was permitted to know nothing about him beyond the fact that he was old – had not only written out a blessing for my protection, but had also decided to make the 'wrapping' himself. This consisted of a slightly nasty shiny black fabric folded into the correct triangle and sealed with amateurish white stitching, which, of course, precluded my seeing what charms and incantations he had summoned on my behalf (and maybe my mother's). It was to be attached to my clothing by the safety pin and left there all the time. I would be safe in all my travels.

'He just sent one message,' said Abdul. He continued in a 'Beware the Ides of March' tone of voice:

'Don't take the desert road to Siwa.'

Siwa

There are no roads to Siwa that are not desert roads. The Siwa oasis lies close to the Libyan border, isolated in an arid void, the Sea of Sand to the west, a sea of sand to the east. The way to it was usually by the old caravan route that cuts south from the coast, from the ancient port of Paraetonium. This nine-day camel trek was the one taken by Alexander the Great when he went to Siwa in 331 BC to consult the oracle in the temple of Amun. It was the route followed by Herodotus in the fifth century BC, by Strabo in 23 BC, and it was the one I decided to take, simply because it was the way the bus went. It was a long and tedious loop, via Cairo and Alexandria, but perhaps the heejab man could foresee some disaster occurring during the next day or so to a hired 4x4 on the direct track west from Bahariya.

Whereas the journey from Farafra to anywhere significant was daunting, and few people seemed to want to go anywhere anyway, Cairo was almost Bahariya's local market, and men with large bundles wrapped in blue plastic and tied with string clambered on the early morning bus. It left from near the Alpenblick and toured around the oasis. It passed the local museum where I had bought two amulets, one a silver disc engraved with a long-armed goddess with spotted shawl, the other a poor affair of dirty red fabric stitched round a piece of paper. It passed the mud sculptures of grotesque women and animals, the work of the village artist Mahmoud Eid. It passed the hot spring of Ar-Ramla, where I had had a jacuzzi-like bath in the pitch dark and had given the last of my vodka to Talad, who needed it for medicine, he said, and who had massaged me without groping. It circuited the olive groves, the small outlying settlements with their fruit and vegetable stalls, their narrow lanes, their braying donkeys, before heading out across the empty desert.

In little over a year, this simple world was to disappear for ever. For the 'cemetery' turned out to be a labyrinth of sandstone caverns that concealed probably ten thousand mummies, in particular that of Zed-Khonsu-ef-'Ankh, governor of Bahariya nearly two thousand six hundred years ago, who was buried with all the glory of a pharaoh. His wealth and importance were immense. He was second prophet to the god Amun, his sarcophagus containing six gold amulets, symbolizing different gods including the falcon god, and a bird and cobra, was made of alabaster brought to the oasis from hundreds of miles away. A cache of golden mummies was also found, so that the whole oasis of Bahariya was dubbed 'Valley of the Mummies'. Zed-Khonsu-ef-'Ankh's sarcophagus was opened in front of American TV cameras, and the information relayed on the internet. A new hotel was built to replace the Alpenblick, and Bahariya was shaken out of its millennia-long slumber.

Innocent of this imminent future, I slumbered on the bus until it reached the horror of Cairo overspill.

'Green Valley' was the beginning: line upon line of plastic greenhouses, and puny plants struggling against the swamping sand. Then the housing developments – 'Dreamland', 'Golf Hotel', 'Garden City' – stark, bare buildings stuck in the middle of the desert and surrounded by acres of scaffolding, that floundered in my mind into collapsed heaps of matchsticks as the massive, steady, familiar outlines of the pyramids appeared on the horizon above them.

Then in Cairo walking through the chaos of roadside bus depots under thundering flyovers to pick up a bus on to Alexandria, and then, finally, the next day, one along the road west.

The road follows the coast where the desert touches the sea and where Bedouin used to herd their goats. Now the land between road and shore has been parcelled off into strips divided by high walls and approached from the road through imposing barricaded gateways. 'Tourist Village', the notices said, 'Miami Sands', 'Santa Monica', 'Cannes Invest'. Each enclosure was solid with blocks of matching concrete flats, mile upon mile of them – seemingly enough for every living Egyptian – rising gaunt from the sand, devoid of any shred of green. Almost all the developments were unfinished, most of the rest unlived-in. They were like so many cemeteries, row upon row of identical slabs, graveyards of the greed of investors and the dreams of the alley-dwellers of Cairo, row upon row until they joined the true graveyards of El Alamein.

More than eighty thousand men were killed or wounded in the campaign that led to this decisive battle of the Second World War. The bus passed first the seven thousand tombstones of the British and Commonwealth cemetery, set in dead straight rows in a walled enclo-sure several miles east of the town, and then to the west, overlooking the sea, the fortress-like monument of the Germans and the imposing marble memorial to the Italians, all resolutely separate. 'Manca la fortuna, non il valore' was inscribed on a roadside stone. I thought of the cemeteries in Keren, the same war, but Eritrea now seemed so far away. I glanced at my watch. Totally by chance, it was eleven o'clock GMT on the eleventh day of the eleventh month. I knew if I got off the bus it would be almost impossible to get on to another, on to Siwa. I felt like a mother out shopping in town, not bothering to call and see her sick child in the hospital there.

At Marsa Matruh, the modern name of the old port of Paraetonium, the bus turned south on to the caravan route. The few wisps of low green shrub, survivors on the fringe of the Mediterranean rain-belt, soon vanished, and for the rest of the journey the road, now tarred and skirted by a line of telegraph poles, sliced through bleak and barren sands, until it dropped down the escarpment into the depression of Siwa. By this time it was night and only the rocks caught in the headlights along the edge of the road gave any sign that the landscape had changed. The bus pulled into the centre of Siwa, into a town square of donkey carts and low mud buildings shuttered in green, flanked along one side by the dramatic jagged outline of a high, crumbling, fortified city of mud, lit by one fluorescent bulb.

The messages on the Christmas cards had been slightly different each year:

*For 1994 we extend positive vibrations and powerful energy
from the oracle of Amun-Siwa. For a virtual vision of a
peaceful planet let us begin together to meditate, live and
transmit to each other universal harmony.*

*From the magical Oasis of Amun-Siwa we transmit mysti-
cal vibrations and a peaceful vision for a friendly
environment on planet earth for Nineteen hundred and
ninety-six.*

They were sent from the Nile Hilton in Cairo by a Swiss woman whom
I had never met. An Arab newspaper described her as a 'self-proclaimed
social anthropologist', she herself preferred 'social-ethnologist research-
ing the unknown mysteries of Egypt, The Oasis of Amun Siwa'. I
responded every year to her kind greetings and sent finally a note to say
that I was coming to Siwa. The cards abruptly stopped.

Now that I was here, I set about finding out who she was. Opinions
on her work were divided: she had done a lot of good, some felt, promoting Siwa, setting up a centre for women's health and social development,
creating a Siwa Cultural Festival, putting on exhibitions in Geneva and
the Middle East. Shocking, others thought – by promoting the well-being
of women she had shattered traditions that had existed for millennia. Then
suddenly the Egyptian government had given her twenty four hours to
leave Siwa. It was rumoured that her crime was to have photographed the
women, which everyone knows is forbidden: Siwa tries to hold tight to
its Berber traditions though television, education, tourism, breeze-blocks,
and the tarred road with its daily bus, shake it by the throat.

I began with the women.

Hoda's house lay a short bicycle-ride away from the Palm Trees hotel
where I was staying, close to the Mountain of the Dead. A small boy took
me there and rang a bell attached by loose wires to a high blank wall. A
child peered round the gate, eased it open and led me in – no woman
can show her face to the outside world, nor would any man outside the
family be allowed in. We crossed a courtyard into the low mud-brick
house and then entered by a dark corridor. The floors throughout were
of earth, and two rooms opened off the corridor on each side.

Hoda shared a room with her sisters, one of whom lay on a bed with a new-born baby completely hidden under a dirty quilt. She would return to her husband once the baby was out of harm's way, safe from the evil eye. Hoda was twenty three and divorced – divorce was very common, she said, but women usually remarried. She spoke a little English but normally had no occasion to use it. She spent her time in this room embroidering. She did mostly piece-work for a German woman in Cairo, who provided the fabric and thread, but sometimes she made shawls to sell in Siwa or for the girls of the family to wear themselves. I would come back to watch her another time.

The Mountain of the Dead, Jebel al-Mawta, is a rocky hill rising above the palms of the oasis, honeycombed with tombs dating from Roman and Ptolemaic times. I leant my bicycle on a palm tree, climbed up the hill and was sitting down to enjoy the sunset when three men appeared, two Italians and an Englishman working on an agricultural development project. Siwa has serious drainage problems, they explained, as we looked out over the palms and the mud town, to a vast lake and the distant hill of Fantasy Island. It is the lowest of the depressions in the Western desert that form the oases, and water has nowhere to drain away, a situation exacerbated by new wells being dug, and by an increase in population. The engineers pointed to the lake – 'there's a scheme to channel the excess water through that saline lake, feed it off into those dunes' – they waved over to the south to the Jebel Dakrur – 'and grow trees. The channel and causeways have already been built' – they waved again to the salt lake – 'but they're useless on their own and now there's a rival project to divert the water to the Qattara depression. As for Fantasy Island, some Egyptian – not a Siwan, of course, they have no money to invest – has bought it and is building a luxury hotel there. We tried to visit the island but weren't allowed in. It's probably the same investor who's built the other four-star hotel, the Paradise Safari.'

'Soon will be no good 'ere,' said one of the Italians.

The Paradise Safari was a discreet, low cluster of tawny huts amid the palms, priced in dollars, and fenced all round. My own hotel, the Palm Trees, was a modest affair of forty-watt bulbs, sunken mattresses and capricious plumbing, managed by Salar and various men who sat around the reception area all day, draped over plastic chairs. To the back of the hotel lay its garden of massive date palms, whose fronds hung into my balcony and tangled with my washing. The small water channels of the garden

were choked with litter, broken furniture was dumped around and the
dates left over from the last harvest lay mouldering on a sheet of plastic. To the front of the hotel was a dirt road leading out of town, and
on the other side of it a cracked and crumbling adobe house with small
square holes for windows where occasionally a woman's face, her shawl
modestly held across it, would appear, while at its low open doorway a
child would sometimes sit.

Next door to the hotel was Mohammed's bicycle shop. It was with
Mohammed that I negotiated the hire of a bicycle. 'Is OK?' he asked,
of a blue model, its frame slightly out-of-true, its bell-top missing. 'It's
absolutely fine,' I replied. 'Absolutely fine!' he almost shouted. 'Absolutely
fine!' he did shout. 'Real English! The best! Not Australian!' Then he
calmed down. 'For the bicycle you help me with my English?' And so I
spent the next two days cloistered in my room with various useless
recorders that Mohammed had managed to borrow – bulbous, rah-rah
type things that impress the lads but don't work – recording lessons on
'Nick, a schoolboy at Eton'. Life at Eton held no relevance whatsoever
to Mohammed's life in the bicycle shop, but he was very grateful, and
rewarded me with three kilos of dates.

Siwa has about three hundred thousand date palms – and seventy
thousand olive trees – which still provide a living for most of the population. And the dates of Siwa are famous, the best in the whole of Egypt.
Salar recounted that 'at the time of Luxor' he went to Cairo and was questioned by the police. He told them he was from Siwa, though he originally
came from Al-Minya, close to Asyut, and all his papers said so. The police
were ready to arrest him for terrorism, he said, when he brought out some
Siwan dates. 'The best, you will know them immediately.' The police tasted
them. 'Yes, from Siwa,' they said 'just come with us for five minutes.' They
clapped him in jail for five months and as they'd imprisoned so many men
'because of Luxor' there was only room to stand, day and night, crushed
together. 'It was horror,' said Salar, 'and since Luxor we have few tourists
in Siwa.'

Most there now were young backpackers, half-a-dozen or so. They wrote
comments in the old exercise book in one of the cafés: 'chilled-out
place here and, hey, the food's great.' And then there was Klaus, and Mr
Mustafa. Klaus was Swedish, a soft, slightly fleshy man in a check
lumberjack shirt, with pale, unfocussing eyes behind thick glasses. He
spoke with a gentle Swedish accent and came to Siwa every year. The

minute he met me and discovered I was here for the embroidery, he fetched out a linen tablecloth he was embroidering with flowers. The linen came from Sweden, 'here in Egypt it's no good,' he said. You could find it in the market in Cairo, but it came from outside Egypt, he didn't know where from. He liked to buy the best linen for his tablecloths and could always sell them at the Swedish Embassy fêtes.

Klaus had been a 'sandwich man' in Sweden for fourteen years, supplying office workers with sandwiches, he explained. Then he met a woman who talked to him about Egypt. He asked her for addresses: 'she didn't give,' he murmured sadly, but he set off nevertheless and since then had led a life of wandering. Dog-and-cat-sitting in Washington – his greatest ambition was to look after the dogs and cats of America's wealthiest homes – and travelling around Egypt and Tunisia. He didn't do anything, except embroider, but just wandered aimlessly, hoping to find someone to play backgammon and dominoes with him. Here he'd been lucky enough to bump into Mr Mustafa and they were to be seen every day sitting in the cafés of Siwa playing together.

Without Mr Mustafa, Klaus would go to Cleopatra's Bath, the Spring of the Sun that Herodotus boasted of on his return to Greece after visiting Siwa. 'Like bathing in champagne,' said Klaus. It was a hot spring pouring into a scum-surfaced brick pool, on the edge of which local men lounged around in the hope of seeing tourists undress. Klaus had suddenly had a new idea of what to do with his life. He would buy this place, he said, clean it up, live in the palm grove by it, and earn a living hiring it out to tourists for swimming. He would either do that or mind the Clintons' cat in the White House. Meanwhile he spent his days with Mr Mustafa.

Mr Mustafa, as Klaus always called him, was a slightly stooped little man with a friendly smile, who knew all about olives. He was from Cairo, and was a friend of Ahmed, the owner of a stall in the town square where plastic bottles of different types of olives broiled in the sun. Ahmed lived there in a dark, rickety dirt-floored shack just behind the stall, and had fixed a washing line between the two, where his shirts and underwear were always hung up to dry. He lolled around on an unmade bed, surrounded by drums of olives, brewing tea on a primus stove, waiting for customers to bring him empty plastic water bottles. These he would fill with olives and salty water. Mr Mustafa spent half an hour choosing the best for me, big dark ones that dyed the water pink. They turned out to be inedible.

Siwa was a seductive place: the chickens and turkeys that scrabbled around the side lanes; the goats that browsed in the litter; the donkey carts that were everywhere and that thronged the main square on market day, driven by an assortment of men and boys, laden with huge baskets of alfalfa and carrots; the vegetable stalls themselves, resplendent with dazzling displays of colour fit for a Parisian greengrocer – a bank of fragile handmade wooden crates bursting with aubergines, tomatoes, onions, and cauliflowers munched by idly-parked donkeys. And the people: the shrouded women, the albinos from generations of inbreeding, the negroes from the slave trade, and the Egyptians from the Nile overspill, selling garish acrylic jumpers. And every evening at five-thirty the sound of the muezzin, and then the glorious sunsets sharpening the spiky silhouette of the ruined fortified city that was the theatrical backdrop to all the activity of the town. I would stay.

Muffled homosexual giggling came from the floor of the shop behind the counter, where two men were rolling around together. I had gone in to look at the embroidered dresses they sold, but finally walked out in exasperation. For there were many such shops around Siwa, small shops outside which hung rows of embroidered dresses and shawls. They were in the main square, down the side lanes, next to the cafés, the olive stands, and the vegetable stalls.

In the second I went into, a couple were crouched on the floor with their teenage son and two daughters. Hanging above them, strewn around them, were terrible embroideries, roughly worked, dusty and mildewed. Their stock of the traditional baskets of Siwa, which range in size from the biggest for marriage, then bread, peanuts, sewing, down to the smallest for salt, was just as bad, split, caked with dirt and devoid of the usual decorations of silk, buttons and strips of red leather.

Tatty postcards of Catholic-looking saints were stuck with flossy glue to the counter of their shop, drooping over each end. 'We're Christian,' they said, looking at me pleadingly. I bought a pathetic neckband.

The shop across the road, belonging to Abdullah who was often away at prayer, had baskets buried under a tousled wig of orange and green silk pompoms, as they should be, and superb white trousers cuffed in vivid stitchery.

The embroidered costume of Siwa is well known. In particular the white and black dresses, worn with the white trousers, that are cut wide and square and embroidered over the entire front with a sunburst of solar

motifs – whorls and double axes – in sunshiny colours ostensibly inspired
by the ancient sun cult in the form of the god Amun-Ra. These were for
marriage, the white worn on the third day when the family of the bride
brought presents and furniture to her, and the black on the seventh
when both families ate together at the bridegroom's house, and married
life began. For the wedding itself the bride would wear seven dresses –
as in Tunisia – the first white and transparent, the second red and transparent, the third black, the fourth yellow, the fifth blue, the sixth red silk,
the seventh green silk. And on top of all these the wedding dress of
striped silk embroidered round the neck. Were these still worn, were they
still made?

Mr Bahri ran the town museum in the mornings, had an afternoon job
with the council, and sold local crafts in his shop in the evenings. The
museum had been set up by a Canadian diplomat anxious to see the traditions of Siwa preserved. I called to see Mr Bahri. He wasn't so sure about
the solar aspects of the embroidery. As far as he was concerned, the five
colours only ever used related to the dates of Siwa: green at first, then
yellow, then orange and, when fresh and ready to eat, red, and finally,
when dried, black. As for the buttons, those on the dresses – mother-
of-pearl on the old, plastic on the new – were a matter of personal
choice, but for the shawls the rules were precise. Those with buttons were
for best, while those without were for everyday.

The shawls – *trokhoat* – were made of black fabric striped alternately
with transparent and opaque lines: thirty one and thirty seven lines for
everyday, forty seven and fifty seven lines without buttons also for
everyday, while with buttons they were for special occasions. Women
would have five to ten shawls, and two to three dresses made for them
by their mothers. Whether they were still worn or still made, he had no
idea, being a man, as he was never able to see or speak to a woman.

I returned to Hoda's house. Her sister was still there lying on the bed
with her new baby, her children of one and two running around. The
other three daughters of the family were in the kitchen, sitting on the
earth floor in the dark around a small gas burner, a few pots glinting on
shelves along the walls. One girl was kneading dough in a huge bowl,
rolling it into balls that she passed to Hoda, who flattened them into the
discs that are the usual bread of Siwa. Another girl sat in a mire of blood
and feathers plucking tiny birds without a scrap of meat on them.

2. *Haile Selassie's bombed summer palace in Massawa, Eritrea*

<1. *Rashaida woman and daughter, Massawa environs, Eritrea*

4. *Art Deco Fiat garage in Asmara, Eritrea>*

3. *Orthodox church of St. Mariam, Asmara, Eritrea*

6. *Rock-hewn church of Mikael Mihaizengi, Tigray, Ethiopia*

<5. *View of the valley from the church of Abraha Atsbeha, Tigray, Ethiopia*

8. *Woman in highland costume, Axum, Ethiopia* >

7. *Stele in Axum, Ethiopia*

9. Back street in Lalibela, Ethiopia

10. Rock-hewn church at Lalibela, Ethiopia

11. Remains of dead pilgrim in wall niche at Lalibela, Ethiopia

13. Blue Nile Falls at Tissasat, Ethiopia >

12. Portuguese fort at Gondar, Ethiopia

14. *The Evil Gate at Harar, Ethiopia*

4. *Muslim woman in a street of Harar, Ethiopia* >

15. *Restoration of Rimbaud's house at Harar, Ethiopia*

18. *The Market at Berentu, Eritrea*

<17. *Fruit and vegetable sellers at the camel market, Keren, Eritrea*

19. *Rashaida woman in the market of Kassala, Sudan*

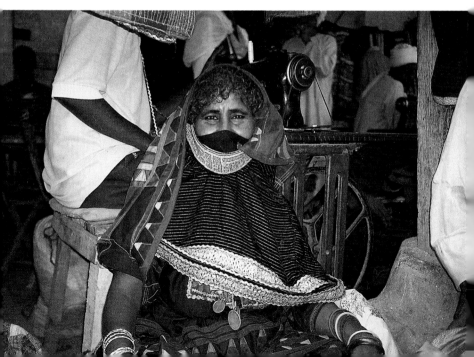

20. *Ruins of the old port of Suakin, Sudan*

22. *Whirling dervish at Khartoum, Sudan >*

21. *Woman spinning cotton for her husband to weave, Shendi, Sudan*

23. The Pyramids at Meroë, Sudan

24. *Girls returning from market, Al Qasr, Dakhla oasis, Egypt*

26. *Woman embroidering, Bahariya oasis, Egypt* >

25. *Woman with embroidery materials, Bashandi, Dakhla oasis, Egypt*

28. *Lane by Palm Trees Hotel, Siwa oasis, Egypt*

< 27. *The White Desert of Farafra oasis, Egypt*

30. *Vlach woman at Metsovo, northern Greece* >

29. *The ruined citadel, Siwa oasis, Egypt*

32. *Ali Pasha's residence at Ioannina, northern Greece*

< 31. *The coastline at Skafia, western Crete*

34. *Car ferry across Vivari channel, Butrint, Albania >*

33. *Town transport in Korça, Albania*

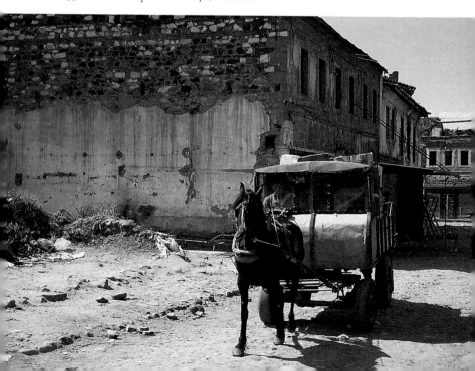

35. Village scene in Dardha, Albania

36. Ruins of the baptistry of Butrint, Albania

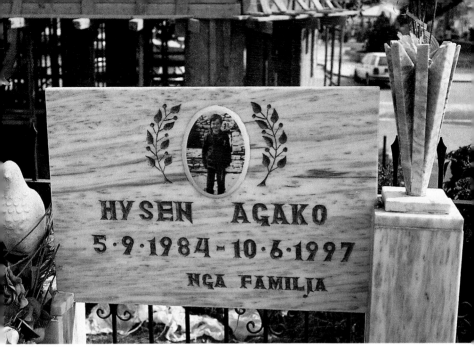

37. Grave of a boy killed in the centre of the town during the uprisings of 1997, Saranda, Albania

38. Old Turkish market street at Kruje, Albania

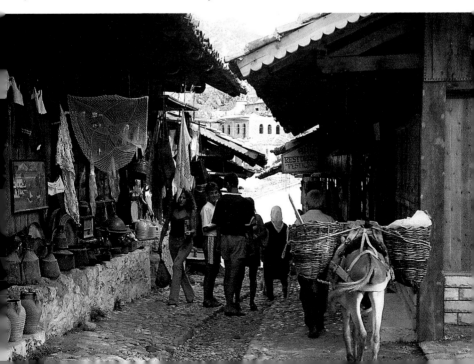

40. *The bouleterion at Apollonia, Albania*

< 39. *The church of St. Michael, c. 1300, clinging to the hillside of the citadel, Berat, Albania*

41. *Woman spinning in the fields near Apollonia, Albania*

42. *German tanks guarding the bridge in the centre of Prizren, Kosovo*

44. *The Drin River at Kuman, Albania >*

45. *Haas mountain woman in framed apron, Prizren, Kosovo >>*

43. *Street scene in Shkoder, Albania*

Hoda clapped the flour off her hands and took me to her embroidery. She was making one of the cloths – the *milaya* – that always shroud married women from head to toe when they go outside the house. These are made of two loom widths, joined by a seam that is covered by embroidery, a style of shawl that the women of Djerba in Tunisia also wear. The threads she worked with were a tangle of the five traditional colours and with them she followed the line of the centre seam, outlining the patterns in red and then working mainly simple couched stitches of six strands, using no frame. The patterns all had names: a triangle with five pendants was a comb and was not amuletic, a diamond with a tail was a fish. If she worked at the shawl constantly it would take a month, but making bread and looking after her child as well, meant at least two months.

The black and grey, or paler blue and white, striped fabric of these shawls was specially made for Siwa in the town of Kerdassa, which until the 1920s was the starting point of all the caravans to Siwa from Cairo. It was also where all the threads came from, so who chose the date colours?

And, I reflected, as I sat on my balcony in the midst of palm fronds, perhaps the sunburst pattern too was only dates. The palms in the fading light of dusk exploded in the same burst, almost like a peacock's tail, and if the colours are inspired by the cycle of the date palm, why not also the disposition of the embroidery? And then Mr Bahri had said that some of the patterns look like the old Siwan alphabet, though no one remembers the meanings. The Libyco-Berber script of the peoples of the Sahara and the Sahel was probably first used by about the sixth century BC and is believed to have vanished at the end of the Roman colonisation of North Africa in the fifth century AD, though the Tuareg people still use a derivation of it. It is a non-cursive script of isolated symbols that would lend themselves well to being embroidered, but sadly I could find no obvious connection. The only sign to resemble the embroidery patterns of Siwa was the double axe which denoted the sound 's'. As for the simple dots that in the Tuareg alphabet formed a square for the sound 'q', a triangle for 'k' and a horizontal line for 'x', and otherwise were grouped in twos and threes, when such dots were used as embroidery patterns, they were always set in lines linking one clear solar symbol with another.

Siwa's most famous site, the stone temple of the oracle of Amun-Ra – Amun the ram-headed god of Egypt, known to the Greeks as Zeus,

linked to Ra the sun god – lies on a hill a short way from town. Clinging to the hillside is the rubble of a town of mud crumbling into
stalagmites, entered by a heavy wooden door. Alexander – himself often
depicted with ram's horns – came to consult this most famous of oracles
on becoming Pharaoh. After two thousand seven hundred years, the room
in the temple, where he sought to know his future, still stands, now open
to the skies. Running beside it is a hidden passageway where no doubt
the priest whose voice was that of the god, stood concealed.

Alexander's visit still raises a glint in the eye of Egyptian businessmen.
They rushed to buy land – at less than the price of a newspaper for a
square metre – when a Greek archeologist claimed to have discovered
Alexander's tomb in a temple on the edge of Siwa. The claim was subsequently discredited and the archaeologist's licence to excavate in Egypt
revoked. Siwa breathed a sigh of relief.

Just outside the wooden door leading to the temple of Amun, an
armed policeman stood guard in case any tourists came, while a little old
man sat in the sand with trinkets, ready to sell to them. I rummaged
through. Glistening among the plastic beads was a yellowish-green glass
triangle set in silver and hung with three silver bells. Fulgurite? Were the
oracle's resounding pronouncements timed to coincide with dramatic
displays of thunder, and of lightning striking the hill on which the
temple stood?

'Heejab,' said the old man.

'Jinn haunt the population of this village,' wrote Al-Maqrizi in the
fifteenth century. 'Anyone who is alone is carried off by them. The
whistling of jinn can be heard distinctly all over Siwa.'

Jinn – those destructive creatures believed in the Islamic world to be
created from the fire of hot wind – still hover around Siwa, and the evil
eye still threatens babies, women's milk, animals and crops.

'Islam now forbids the wearing of amulets but it has made no difference,' Mr Bahri said. The museum has several, usually rectangles of
leather hung with silver bells, and with some sort of magic spell inside.
There used to be magicians in the oasis whose task was to make these
amulets and to recite certain incantations when someone was threatened
by evil or was sick. Babies always wore an amulet round their neck, he said,
and he remembered the women of his family wore a small glass bead –
blue, green or red, but he did not think yellow – set in silver, pinned inside
their dress to improve their milk supply. And the embroidered dresses often

had a pendant of plaited silk hanging over each breast, decorated with small bead triangles that had five pendants, one kinked to form a thumb. The hand of Fatima, that might bring the approval of Islam after all.

The triangular beaded amulet from Siwa that I had found in Cairo was not Berber, but Bedouin. I set out to find where the Bedouin camped. They had, it seemed with some reluctance, half settled in the desert close to some Roman tombs across the lake to the east of the oasis. Their village was a mixture of traditional tents, long and low and made of goathair, and one-room shacks in which the government had rehoused them. In these they had no furniture, only two wall shelves trimmed with fancy paper and holding crockery and old tins. The floor was earth, covered here and there with straw mats, and cooking pots were piled up on wooden boxes. The walls were of bare concrete and by the one small window a decoration of three branches had been made of fabric and looked like the tree of life.

The women who stood around me, their curiosity slightly aggressive, were dressed in bright floral print dresses, tied round the waist with a wide red sash hung with keys and bits of coloured rag. Unlike the women of Siwa, they were not veiled but showed their tattooed faces openly. They were weavers.

They wove mainly from camel hair – white with coloured inserts – mats and bags, and long sashes that their menfolk wore. The bags were tasselled and one or two had triangular amulets of fabric hanging from them. Against the evil eye, they said. I asked to see their looms and they threw down on the ground in front of me seven wooden sticks and the tip of a deer horn. It was the same horizontal loom recorded in the tomb paintings at Beni Hasan and used since neolithic times. The Sahara was once fertile, and it seemed there were still a few deer left, though they were getting harder to find. The horn tip they used as a reed.

The women were as open as the veiled ones of Siwa were secretive. Apart from Hoda's, I was never invited into any other household and so was reduced to stalking the women walking around town to photograph the patterns across the back of their shawls. Married women never left their homes unless wrapped in a shawl, the *milaya*. In the past girls were married at twelve to fourteen years old, now it is more usually sixteen. And, until recently, once they were married they were only allowed out to attend a wedding or to congratulate a new mother. Now they ventured out more frequently but still furtively. Mindful of the fate of the sender of my Christmas greetings, I hid in the doorway of the Palm Trees hotel and round the side of the bicycle shop, I sat in cafés, a camera concealed on my lap, I lurked round corners, but I never seemed to be ready when a woman passed, or I was ready – focus and aperture set on my unwieldy manual camera – but too much in the public eye. I followed these fleeting figures, forever trying to capture them on film, as a lepidopterist pinning down a spectacular specimen. They hovered in dusty lanes before vanishing through gateways, they rode in donkey carriages past the bicycle shop just when a crowd of boys walked by, they crossed the street outside the café when the men gathered at the shrine opposite, they walked into the old town just as the men came to buy their morning falafel, they stooped to slip quickly into the low doorways of the mud building opposite the hotel. These snapshots could never capture that fugitive image of a sequestered woman venturing out of her gloomy mud-baked confinement into the sunshine of an outside world, where men and boys, and foreigners on bicycles, shared the few yards of sandy track that led her further into the palm groves, the piles of harvested dates and olives, the hot springs, the totality of her oasis that had been her life for ever and would be for ever.

And one day, as I sat in the square waiting for the women to go by, wondering about the meanings of the patterns on their shawls, wondering what Kerdassa, where the silks and fabric come from, was like, two huge tourist coaches drew up, like invaders from Star Wars. One had the somewhat inappropriate 'Everest Tours' painted along the side, the other 'Extension Travel'. Seventy five elderly French clambered out, blinking in the bright sun and immediately pointing their camcorders at everything and everybody, including straight at any women they could see. They were staying at the Paradise Safari, someone said. Most were women, whose flabby arms and legs protruded from tank tops and shorts they would surely never dream of wearing at home in Lille. The Siwan men in the square stopped and stared, some laughing, some looking horrified. The few women fled. The justification for a massacre flashed through my understanding.

It was time to move on.

The Lower Nile

Though Kerdassa was once the throbbing terminus of a thousand camel caravans, it was now just a long string of shops selling dresses. 'Before Luxor', coaches used to ferry tourists out from Cairo, to buy clothes more cheaply. Kerdassa was still an important textile centre. Traders paced outside their shops – 'come, come, just looking' – and offered tea. Hanging in windows, inside shops and outside doors the entire length of the street were embroidered dresses. A few were genuine old black Bedouin shifts worked in vertical bands of cross-stitch over the bodice and much of the skirt, others were the work of Badri's protegées at Bahariya, their vivid red and yellow floss making the Bedouin shifts look dull, but most were loose dresses of pastel colours embroidered over the bodice with a panel of cross-stitch bordered by curling lines of couched braid. There was something not quite right about them.

I found the factory a short distance away. Scraps of Bedouin hand-worked cross-stitch, cut from old dresses, lay around the floor and on the large table, and by them were huge rolls of cloth embroidered in the same patterns and colours and stitch. By machine. It was easy, said the boss, who looked so like The Fat Controller I never caught his name. 'I do it by computer.' The computer wasn't there, he explained. It was in a bigger factory in Cairo, this was really just a local workshop. Men sitting at sewing machines couched the braid around the bodice sections, which had been cut from the machined cross-stitch fabric, and the dresses were made up by a small boy of twelve who had worked in the factory for four years. 'And school?' I asked.

'Oh, he goes to school in the mornings.'

'But it's morning now.'

There was an embarrassed shuffling of feet and the boy bent over his machine again.

The workshop where the shawls of Siwa, the milayah, were woven was a short distance away, a careful walk through a nauseating squelch of mud and litter. The weaver, one man alone, sat in a windowless room, working at a vertical loom, exactly as on the paintings of Beni Hasan. All their weavings now were of cotton, though they had used linen until a few years ago, the owner Mohammed Issi, said. A couple of spools of linen thread labelled 'Orient Linen & Cotton Co. Flax' had been in the cupboard for years – did I want to buy them? Then, I noticed among the dresses hanging in their shop – most of which were machine-embroidered, computer-created, tourist-aimed jellabyya – one in linen. The last they'd ever made. About fifteen years ago, but no one had wanted it. It was stiff, though it would soften on washing, Issi assured me, and was far too long for any woman to wear. I could have it for very little.

It was decorated in Egyptian style in a brightly-coloured appliqué of an entwining rope, perhaps a version of the magic protective rope of Fatimid belief. But no threads had been pulled or counted to form a goddess, or even a plain triangle.

As for flax, that no longer grew in Kerdassa, though Issi thought that in nearby Narya it still did, probably only now used to make rope. The tradition of weaving linen fabrics in Egypt, thousands of years old, had died, he thought, fifteen years ago.

Grace Crowfoot went to Narya in 1930: 'rich fields lie round it,' she wrote, 'but the desert edge is not far away. I shall not easily forget my first sight of the green waves of flax, bright in front of a line of tall palms and, behind the palms, yellow sand and the pyramids of Giza sharp against the sky.'

I suspected the fields would no longer be there, but went to see anyway. Where they had once been, half-finished apartment blocks rose, washing strung over the balconies, bleak stretches of sand between each block. But along the waterways, I was assured, people were spinning flax, and hemp.

The dried-out river was scummed by rotting food, filthy rags and batteries leaking acid. Plastic bags glittered prettily in the sun, coke cans glowed red in the slabs of shade. On the opposite bank from where I stood ran a long, low building, and in the shadow of its wall some men were spinning. At one end a group of them turned the heavy metal wheel of an old machine, while a boy walked away from them, holding a bundle of flax and twisting it against the rotation of the wheel. He walked the whole length of the building, along the narrow strip of earth between the wall and the river, tied the flax on a post, then turned and walked back again.

There was no access to the strip of land from the end of the bridge, so I took the road behind the building and skirted its walls. As I turned the corner my whole body heaved. The building was the camel slaughter-house. It was where the camels who made the long trek across the desert from Siwa, the Forty Days' Road from Sudan, the crossing of any of the trails of the most arid territory on earth, were slaughtered, and always had been. A white camel stood tethered outside.

The hot stench gripped the breath as if the still living blubbery fat and pulsing blood of a million camels were pounded straight, straight without any softening, any dilution of air, sickeningly into nostrils, sinuses, throat, brain. Thick, acrid blood was everywhere. It was coagulating in the sludge underfoot, it was smeared on the hands, aprons and clothes of the slaughterers, it was splashed on the walls, the gates, the carts outside, it seeped into the water channel hard by. I staggered away, without ever seeing the spinners.

Not far away, close to another waterway – small, narrow, slow-flowing, dammed with detritus, squalidly putrifying – an elderly couple plied the ancient trade of rope-making. The woman, plump and clad in black, sat at the wheel. From there two rows of warp had been stretched onto pegs close to the water's edge. Though it was now hardly visible through the morass, water is essential for this process. Her husband, a strong caved-in old man in a ripped and ragged shirt, walked to and fro along the warps, his body wrapped in tangled linen threads, a fuzz of flax gripped under his arm, spinning the flax into rope. It was a craft that had existed in Egypt, benefiting from clear waterways and historic skills, for thousands of years. Now, it seemed, the buffers were there. The flax was no longer grown in Narya but brought there from somewhere between Alexandria and Cairo.

I returned to Cairo, a ball of flax in my hand, and the smell of blood in my nose, wondering whether it wasn't hemp rather than flax that was used to make ropes.

The Museum of Islamic Art in Cairo is a musty, imposing place, the textiles tucked away upstairs: Abbasid weavings of the third to fourth centuries, an entire range of Fatimid tapestry work from the tenth century through to the twelfth, Mamluk of the fourteenth and fifteenth. But the motifs were animals, and mottos: 'perfect blessing to the weaver'. I went back downstairs and wandered aimlessly round the displays of carved window shutters and Persian-style pots. Then suddenly I saw them, two small linen pieces, one worked in black – or it could have been dark indigo – in the pattern of my goddess. There she was, even alternated with the tree of life. The embroidery was in double running, a stitch used on the earliest English samplers, and the motifs were edged with tiny hooks, as in the embroidery of Bulgaria. The second piece had no

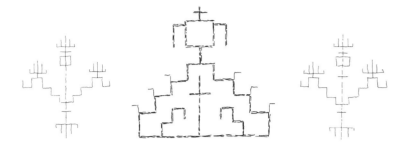

goddesses, but the ancient version of the tree of life in the form of confronting birds, perched on a branch or around a pillar. 8227/1 and 8227/2, the dingy bits of paper said, so obviously they belonged together.

The custodian was a young man, smartly dressed in a suit, and anxious to help. No, they had no idea where they were from, nor how old they were, no information at all. Only that they had been bought from a Jewish merchant in Cairo called Tanu for £2 in 1929. They could perhaps be Fatimid or from the Ayyubid dynasty that followed it, he didn't know. I felt it was impossible to assign them categorically to Egypt. They looked East European or even Russian, except that the colour was wrong. They were blue and in Europe would probably have been red. Nothing was solved, it was still not possible to come to any conclusions about Egypt and its linen, and any goddess figures that might have been worked on it, and to know whether Europe owed any debt to Egypt.

I headed on towards Europe, to Alexandria, a city that turned its back on desert and Nile, and faced the Mediterranean. A city of Greek and Roman domination, a city of classical antiquity that owed nothing to Africa, except perhaps trade. And not even Cleopatra.

Alexandria

The young French archaeologist sat in the garden of the Graeco-Roman Museum piecing together the skeletons of two women aged about thirty to forty five, found in a single urn. 'They must to be two women,' he said, 'because two examples of same part of masher.' 'Jaw,'

I corrected. He kept pinching himself, he continued in French, as he just couldn't believe he was sitting here in the sun at this, the most exciting time in Alexandria's modern history. Only last week a Greek diver had dredged up another sphinx from the newly-discovered Cleopatra's palace.

The seediness of present-day Alexandria – the anarchic traffic and scavanging cats, the hurdles of rubble on every pavement, the smells of spicy frying – merely scabs the living presence of the city's past. Each era can be peeled away, not in neat order, like the layers of an onion that shape the whole, but arbitrarily, as if in the tortured geology of volcanic disturbance . Every so often bits of glorious history erupt: when a block of flats is being built, a garage or warehouse demolished. This time it was the murky waters of the eastern harbour that had yielded slabs of marble floors, hunks of red granite, and water-eroded statues, that had revealed the whereabouts of the royal city of Antony and Cleopatra.

Alexandria was founded on the site of a fishing village by Alexander in 331 BC on his return from Siwa. Here he had had the oracle of Amun recognize him as the son of God and therefore Pharaoh, a situation the Egyptians readily accepted. He intended the city to be Greek, and laid it out as such, with Jews, Egyptians and the dead kept to their own defined quarters. When Alexander died in Babylon in 323 BC one of his principal generals, Ptolemy, became ruler of Egypt: the Ptolemaic dynasty was to last for three hundred years and to build Alexandria into a major port on the trade routes between Europe and Asia. Throughout their rule they remained Greek, most of the pharaohs marrying their sisters. The last of their dynasty was Cleopatra and their rule finally ended with a Roman takeover and an asp sting.

Alexandria was the most learned and wealthy city of the Graeco-Roman world, a city even more magnificent than Athens or Rome. Its library was the greatest of the ancient world, the Pharos lighthouse that guarded its harbour, one of the Seven Wonders.

The precise location of the lighthouse, that fell in an earthquake in the fourteenth century, and the royal city of Antony and Cleopatra, that was destroyed by an earthquake followed by a tidal wave in AD 335, were not recorded. Only some clues from Strabo, the Greek geographer who visited in 25 BC, could guide modern marine exploration.

Now two rival Frenchmen were glowering at each other across the harbour. A year or two ago the archaeologist Jean-Yves Empereur ('a name

which reads like a vocation,' 'the man of the moment,' his supporters
remarked) had suggested that the fallen blocks of stone his divers had
found in the sea around the Qait Bey fort at the western end of the
harbour were from the Pharos lighthouse. 'Entirely wrong,' the flam-
boyant Frenchman, marine archaeologist Franck Goddio, was saying.
Goddio, after years of searching, claimed to have located the royal city
of Antony and Cleopatra across the other side of the harbour, to the east.
The earthquake and tidal wave had toppled the harbour-front palaces
and temples into the sea, and they were still where they fell, on top of
the limestone paving that had been in front of them. They lay now in
murky water, but if the Alexandria governate carried out its plan to divert
the city's sewage away from the harbour, a future underwater museum
viewed from glass-bottomed boats or through transparent walkways
was a possibility.

Meanwhile, the jaws of two young women were being carefully pieced
together to be added to the museum collections.

The museum was an imposing neo-classical building approached up
a flight of stairs through a pedimented portico inscribed in Greek:
ΜΟΥΣΕΙΟΝ. The only time it ever closed was for Friday prayers. It was
a traditional, fusty place, unchanged since it was founded in 1892. The
collections were magnificent and among its treasures were plenty of
linen mummy wrappings and innumerable amulets, mostly scarabs and
realistic gods and goddesses. Even little statuettes who 'replied for the
deceased and worked for him when he was required to do work in the
Elysian Fields'.

The only item of relevance to my task was a Coptic funerary stele decorated with the Egyptian sign of life, the Ankh, which, with added lines,
turned into a branch-bearing goddess. It probably came from a monastery
near Alexandria, but there was no record and no one really knew.

I called at a scruffy little laundry shop in a back street on the way to
my room, to hand in my two shirts. The old man refused to take them
and an interpreter was found. 'He's very sorry, but he can't accept these.
He'd never be able to get them clean.' I had been travelling for too long.

Alexandria is strung out along the seafront, twenty kilometres long and
only two deep, with canals, lakes and desert behind. A spit linking the
coast to Pharos island splits the harbour in two, and it was from the western side that boats left for Heraklion with connections to Greece. But
first, way at the eastern end, there was still the jewellery museum to see

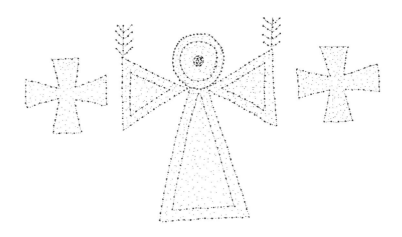

– perhaps amuletic triangles of gold?

The royal jewellery collection was housed in just one of King Farouk's many palaces. Some schoolgirl visitors were wearing sunglasses. Against the glare and dazzle of the diamonds, they joked. Diamonds were everywhere. Every possible object was encrusted and studded with them: coffee-cup holders, field glasses, letter openers, desk sets, cigarette boxes, garden tools, chess sets, a baby's rattle (the balls inside were, of course, of solid gold, the label assured us). The real McCoy that merely reduced everything to a bauble. There were tiaras of two thousand and eleven diamonds, and bracelets to match, that once adorned the pudgy white arms of Queen Nariman, King Farouk's second amour.

The Revolution came on 23rd July 1952.

And in the port the maritime officer was quite categorical: there have been no boats to Heraklion for several years. No boats go anywhere from Alexandria.

BULGARIA

GREECE

THRACE

TURKEY

Burs

ATHENS

Piraeus

CYCLADES

RHODES

Diafani

Olympos

KARPATHOS

Chania

HERAKLION

Sfakia

CRETE

At Sea

On the sea voyage between Alexandria and Greece, inescapably an imaginary one, it was time to sort out my baggage and throw some excess overboard.

First the jinn. As Islamic influence waned along this fault line north into Europe, and that of the Orthodox Church increased, these creatures would fade away. When propitiated, they are friendly to the human race and, as they live near the lowest heaven, they can hear the conversation of the angels and are happy to pass on to men the valuable information they glean. However, not all are so benign in nature, some having the reputation of nudging in on the sexual act if the man forgets to mention Allah, and thus creating children who tend to be 'effete'.

Made, as Allah assures us, from the fire of hot wind, the jinn are of three types: 'one flies through the air, one consists of snakes and dogs. A third is based in one place, but travels about'. Though they are found mostly in deserts, rivers, dunghills, bathrooms and graveyards – and I had frequented many of those on my travels – I was not aware of ever having been in the presence of one of these creatures, not even in the form of a snarling dog. A legion of amulets had protected me, but now that I was going where nymphs and naiads haunted streams and wells, and goddesses dwelt in birch trees and at crossroads, my amulets needed tidying up. Seven-foot scrolls petitioning Ab-Besma Ab-Besma Wold and One God, rolled into python skin, were out. So too were mullahs' prayers and extracts from the Koran encased in scraps of fabric or tucked into silver pendants. Cowrie shells would probably remain. Fulgurite, cloves and broken needles too. Garlic and red thread certainly. Red thread on linen shifts and on ritual towels in particular.

Linen – and flax and hemp – were still with me. Though Egypt's fine linen of ancient times seemed now to have boiled down to a few old people twisting ropes, in Europe linen had until recent times even been considered magical. In Bulgaria, for example, until a white linen shift, usually bordered in red, had been put on a new-born child, that child was not considered human and had no name. And merely the linen shift a man or woman was buried in served to identify them as human when they reached the next world.

Flax, *linum usitatissimum*, is a tall, skinny plant about four foot high with thin dark leaves and blue flowers, probably first cultivated for its seeds rather than its fibre. It is believed to have originated in south west Asia, but was already grown in Egypt in neolithic times: seeds and coarse linen fibre have been found there dating from 4500 BC. Though the wild variety is a common weed around the eastern Mediterranean, the Romans planted it throughout their empire, so that it reached even the north of Europe, where it thrived. The name flax comes from the Old English *flaex*.

Hemp, *cannibis sativa*, is a different beast, the word deriving from the Old English *henep*. A tall plant, about ten foot high, with stiff, upright stem, divided serrated leaves and glandular hairs, it originated in central Asia and was already used for its fibre across Asia and mid-Europe in the fifth millennium BC. To create hemp cloth the fibres were processed in the same way as flax, hempen garments being generally for the poor, and fine linen for the rich. But from about the first millennium BC the variety *cannibis sativa indica* is known to have been used by the steppe nomads for its narcotic effect. Scythian hashish. The Scythians are recorded by Herodotus as having made sealed tents of felt which they placed over a bowl of red-hot stones. They then threw hemp seeds on to the stones and rushed around screaming with joy as they inhaled the narcotic fumes. Herodotus's description was confirmed by the felted tents, stones and seeds found in 1929 in the frozen tombs of Pazyryk in the Altai mountains of southern Siberia.

But, in contrast to the Scythians, the Thracians, Herodotus also recounts, were only known to use hemp as a fibre, and I was headed for Thrace. And also Macedonia. Perhaps I should keep the link of Alexander the Great. In Siwa it was as if he had been around only yesterday, and in my wanderings through Asia on the same search I had often crossed his path. Maybe he would surface again in Macedonia.

The Ottoman Empire and Turkic influence would stay with me till the end, overlaying the beliefs of Old Europe, the region I was now entering. By the fifth millennium BC, the civilization of Old Europe had developed to the same high level as that of Egypt. It had been unique in character, with no ties to east or south. Goddess figures on embroideries still remain today from its matriarchal society and can be found not only on the mainland of Greece, but to an even greater extent on the islands.

I could, of course, spend several months at least zig-zagging around those islands instead of keeping to my diagonal line, but the embroidery of the Greek islands is comprehensively recorded and of their amulets I already had some knowledge: for example, the triangles of silk stuffed with bits of fishing net and umbilical cord, flowers from the epitaphios and garlic, that I had found in Karpathos. And J. Theodore had carefully recorded others: on Sikinos 'a good thing for everybody to wear round their necks is a three-cornered amulet with salt, coal and garlic inside'.

It would be wisest, I felt, to leave information on the islands to Mr and Mrs Bent as, travelling a hundred years ago, they had a better chance of finding ancient traditions and beliefs still intact. Even then, they had decided that the islands offered the best scope for the study of Hellenic folklore, as they remained untouched away from the coasts, whereas the mainland had been overrun by barbaric tribes, and the Ionian islands thoroughly Italianized.

Mr & Mrs Bent

'My husband headed the party, looking very tall and slim, with his legs outlined against the sky.' J. Theodore at the time was digging a mound near Bahrain – watched by Mrs Bent – and was so tall that, throughout their travels in the Middle East, a suitable donkey or horse could never be found for him and he had perforce always to ride a camel.

Since treading in J. Theodore's footsteps at Axum I had begun to revise my opinion of him. That he was a Victorian in the Superior British mould, of that there was no doubt. Dhofar in Oman he compared, stretching his imagination considerably, to the Isle of Wight 'not much bigger, and in its physical appearance not unlike it, cut off from the rest of the world by a desert behind, and an ocean in front' – perhaps the wastes of the New Forest and the vast horizons of the northern reaches of the English Channel. And of Derbat: 'if ever this tract of country comes into the hands of a civilised nation, it will be capable of great and useful development.' Worse, in Africa he referred to the 'niggers and their dancing, the chief art in which consisted in wagging their elastic tails with an energy which mortals further removed from monkey origin could never hope to approach.' As for his pomposity, that idea was somewhat shattered when I learnt that he took with him on his travels in the Greek islands – 'to amuse the natives' – a toy like a bread roll that a mouse jumped out of each time it was opened.

He was tough. In their two winters in the Cyclades, he and Mrs Bent slept under umbrellas in windowless flooded rooms, on mattresses that felt as if they were made of walnuts. Though enduring stoically such deprivations, he was somewhat disturbed by the lack, or eccentric quality, of the wine. He remarked that the Greeks cracked their walnuts and munched their almonds with nothing to wash them down, and when he was in fact offered wine, lunching at a remote spot, he commented that 'it came out of dried goats' skins, with the hair left on and turned inside; this gives it a strong flavour, suggestive of goats.'

He made detailed notes on the local costumes and customs, recording that on many islands, to cure the sick, bits of their clothes would be left near stones, so that the disease would be drawn into a stone. Everywhere he found stories of the evil eye and of harpies in the streams. Of Paros he comments: 'Witches they have in quantities among them, which haunt the caves and rocks on the mountain side: they are old men or women, past a hundred... not unlike the Harpies of old, for they can turn into birds at will, and sometimes have women's heads and the bodies of birds,' a depiction of the goddess that dates back to the neolithic society of Old Europe. For these harpies, 'unbaptized babies are their favourite food, and for this reason children wear phylacteries round their necks'. Babies had charms against the evil eye hung around them as soon as they were born, J. Theodore observed as he followed Mrs Gamp, the island midwife on Ios, to swaddle a new baby and baptize it.

Visiting a monastery during Lent, he took along his own supply of fat lamb and caviar, only to note that his ecclesiastical host partook of some of it himself 'for it is the same in Greece as it is all the world over – the women are supposed to do the greater part of the fasting and church-going.'

His bed there was in a damp cell and had no sheets but only coarse home-spun rugs dripping with wet. He attended Matins at four in the morning, standing for hours in a bone-searing chill. 'I even felt relieved when I found that by no manner of means could we wash ourselves that morning; there is a time when cold water may be repugnant even to an Englishman.'

In contrast to the cold and wet that he and Mrs Bent endured during these Greek island winters, in their later travels in the Middle East they were subjected to intense heat: the infernal fires of Aden, and the scorching furnace of Oman, which gave, in the words of a Persian poet, 'to the panting sinner a lively anticipation of his future destiny'. They were everywhere subjected to abuse and innumerable squabbles over dollars. They were threatened and harrassed by their guides, who often had never been to the place they claimed to know well, and led the Bents just anywhere.

They survived rough, uncharted terrain and sea voyages with no navigation, they suffered intense hunger and thirst, with nothing but dirty water, and were everywhere surrounded by filth.

Yet every year they left their home in Great Cumberland Place to escape the rigours of the English winter and proceed to a more genial clime. While J. Theodore's purpose was archeological research, Mrs Bent was merely his companion. To follow her husband, she undoubtedly dressed in corsets, ruffled blouse and long skirt, crushed hat, lace-up boots and gloves. She was everywhere stared at relentlessly.

On one occasion Mrs Bent even found a scorpion in her glove and on another, in Yemen, the ladies of the Wali's harem took off her gloves to see her hands, removed her hat and took down her hair, examined her shoes, turned up her gaiters, stuck their fingers down her collar and tried to undress her. They then brought her gifts of food, and substances to dye her teeth red.

The admirable Mrs Bent spent her time reading, doing needlework, developing photographs and treating the sick.

On their final trip, to Southern Arabia in 1897, both J. Theodore and Mrs Bent contracted malaria. Even when lying in a fever on cinder-like sand, waiting on the beach for a boat to take them to Aden, they could still comment: 'they send sharks' fins to China from here, as well as from Sokotra and the Somali coast. This is probably Ptolemy's Agmanisphe Kome.'

James Theodore Bent died four days after reaching home, at the age of forty five. At a meeting at the Royal Geographical Society on the 10th May 1897, the President spoke of J. Theodore as a charming companion, and a true friend, commenting that his wife, Mrs Bent, always accompanied him in his journeys and shared all his hardships and dangers. Mrs Bent survived him by thirty years and her name finally surfaced. It was Mabel, and before marriage Mabel Virginia Anna Hall-Dare.

The Bents had proved something of a red herring, but there remained still their contribution to the world of embroidery – the seven only known early 19th century dresses they collected in Karpathos. J. Theodore had given his three to the V&A during his lifetime. The fate of the other four was sealed only in 1930 after they had been 'knocking about in Mrs Bent's house in London for many years'.

Professor A. J. B. Wace, director of the British School of Archeology in Athens, where J. Theodore had worked some twenty years before, called on Mrs Bent at her home in Great Cumberland Place on the 4th April 1913 and borrowed the dresses to photograph for the exhibition he was mounting at the Burlington Fine Arts Club, and for the book he and Professor Dawkins were writing.

They next surface in July 1929, when Mabel's niece, Mrs Swiney, who had inherited them, tried to sell them and suggested that 'the Greek collector' – this was Mr Benaki, who was then setting up his museum – might like to look at them. After some acrimonious correspondence she eventually offered the dresses to Benaki for £600, but he refused to buy. She then approached Liberty's, who bought the dresses, cleaned them and kept three for Benaki, the other one being bought by a Mr Pratt of New York for the Metropolitan Museum.

Later, at the Benaki Museum in Athens, I was able to see the Bents' dresses. Two were being restored, the other I was allowed to handle. The cut of the dress resembled that of the Muslim women of Harar in Ethiopia in that it was immensely long, but whereas the Harar dresses are looped over a sash at the waist, the Karpathos dress had a tuck of sixty centimetres actually sewn into it, a feature accentuated by stitching in red floss silk.

The dress was scrunchingly embroidered in alternating red, green, red and blue blocks in which a pattern of the tree of life could be discerned from the change of direction of the stitching. There were also, down the front and over the sleeves, square patterns quartered by lines, as are found painted on Minoan pots. Below the front neck slit was a line of small bands of alternating colours with just one white band, which looked amuletic. It was difficult to discern whether the fabric was linen or cotton, but the dress was clearly a display of wealth, and pretty well impossible to wear.

J. Theodore and Mrs Bent would have handled it over a hundred years ago when they bought it on Karpathos. I touched it and thought back to my encounters with their memory in Massawa and Debre Bizen and Axum.

And whereas the Bents had ended their journeys by going east to Southern Arabia, I had already returned on track to my diagonal fault line, scuffing the toe of western Crete.

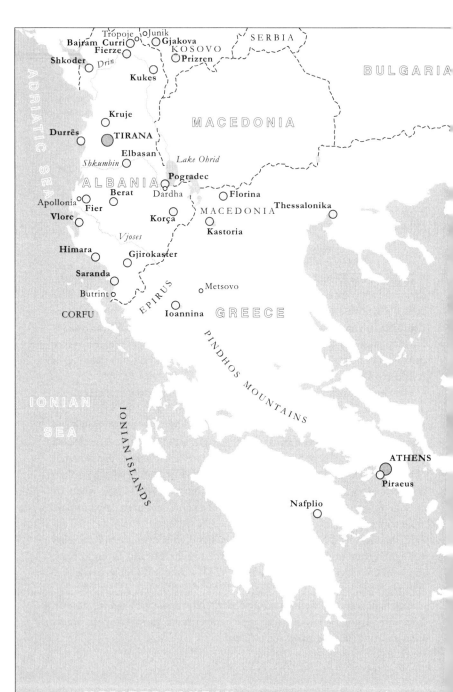

Greece

Western Crete

The only minaret in Chania was crumbling and whiskered with weeds, squashed in a side road not far from the cathedral, whose cheerful bells woke the populace at seven each morning. Christianity had been brought to Crete by the apostle Titus and had woven like a darning thread through the vicissitudes of conquest, to emerge as the dominant religion at the end of Ottoman rule in 1898.

The control of Crete by Byzantium had been interrupted by the Arabs for just over a hundred years from the early ninth century and then ended by the Venetians at the beginning of the thirteenth, though the region of Chania had taken several decades longer to succumb than the rest of Crete. The inhabitants continued to resist and to persist in their own traditions until the threat of the marauding Turks drew Venice and her Orthodox subjects closer together. When the town was conquered by the Turks in 1645 its churches were converted into mosques, only to revert eventually to Christian edifices, or be turned into heritage museums.

Centuries of occupation and oppression served only to hone the Cretans' dogged power of resistance, which never left them. 'The story of El Alamein would have been very different,' said Costas, 'if the Cretans – the shepherds and monks – and the British, hadn't tied up the Germans in these Skafian mountains. People still speak of the war.'

German bombing had badly damaged Chania, destroying its harbour, but the ravages of tourism had been worse. Now just a string of seedy tavernas semi-circled the water's edge, and the twisting streets mazed behind them were full simply of twee stalls selling fridge magnets of sharp-blue and ice-white island houses, phoney nautical jumpers and Superfast ferry tickets. What hope was there here of finding any trace of an embroidery tradition which was known to have died out at least a hundred years ago?

The embroideries on which the Cretan reputation rests are cotton skirt-chemises, rare survivors of an Aegean costume of the time of the Frankish occupation in the first half of the thirteenth century. They are gathered above the breasts on shoulder straps and worked at the hem with a deep band of patterns of the Italian Renaissance and Byzantium, in thick floss silk of gorgeous colours, and were worn with an under-chemise decorated with helmeted warrior women who have definite feet and look more like brides or Amazons than goddesses.

It is a common element of all embroidery of peasant or tribal origin that its source or survival will be localised, and these skirts could not have come from just anywhere in Crete. The only place suggested – by the daughter of Thomas Sandwith, British Consul at Chania from 1870 to 1885, who collected many – was Skafia in the south.

Olive and orange grove, confined vineyard, scrub of thyme and sage, gave way to a rough terrain of dry mountain where only stones and goats prevailed. Bijou white shrines along the winding roadside commemorated with gratitude accidents that had resulted only in injury and not in death. 'We Cretans believe too much in God,' said Costas. The stony range piled on and up until at the southern coast the road snaked steeply down and the mountains dropped almost straight into the sea, leaving just a narrow fertile plain to the east, where the ruins of the Venetian fortress of Frangokastello stood.

The goddesses of Cretan embroidery are not the seductive Minoan creatures – bare-breasted, wielding snakes, their skirts tiered into a triangle. They are instead the gorgon, the two-tailed mermaid, the Great Mother in her terrible and destructive aspect, legs splayed, genitals exposed. Female figures in this stance are common in all primitive art and have filtered through Renaissance pattern into the decorative arts of Europe, to be found frequently carved – sometimes with a male face – on the fountains of Venice and Rome.

But in Skafia there were no fountains. It was a tiny place, dead. 'Maybe there were a thousand people once, now two hundred,' said Costas. Cats marauded. Old stone houses lay in ruins, suffocated by white concrete hotels built on the slopes above their roofs. Overgrown gardens tangled between the bars of rusty gates. Tavernas boarded-up for the winter huddled around one of the village's two harbours. The mountains rose sheer behind the hotels to a hinterland that must always have been almost entirely cut off from the fishing port. How could this place ever have produced the wealth for the embroideries, made from at least the seventeenth century through to the end of the nineteenth?

'Very rich place,' said Costas. 'Very rich. They have many goats.'

Goats? It wasn't enough. The explanation perhaps was that the men of Skafia were prosperous sea merchants, building their boats from the pines of the mountains, fiercely safeguarding their independence from Arabs, Venetians and Turks. And then from the Germans.

The search for anything left of embroidery was futile, but at least I could ask Costas about the amulet. Yes, he knew it, a triangle of cloth, but it has something inside. 'What?' I expected the usual ragbag of potency – garlic, bits of fishing net, broken needles, cloves, flowers from the epitaphios, maybe even a prayer.

'Dung,' he said. 'Dung of those black animals that fly only at night and don't touch anything.' Bats. Bat droppings. Another smell, along with garlic and cloves, that evil spirits are deemed to find offensive. Then it hit me. The Church. The power of the Church again. No doubt priests busied themselves scraping the floors of belfries, just as mullahs industriously transcribed prayers from the Koran, and the priests of Lalibela scooped up their 'holy soil' to sell to lepers, all to promote the power of good over evil and make a few pennies for themselves.

I was back on track, and set off for mainland Greece.

Nafplio

The workshop of the *komboloi* maker of Nafplio formed the corner, below street level, of two narrow lanes of small, shuttered, Venetian houses. Their carved balconies jutted out so closely across the street that plants had swung like lianas to form arches of foliage. To step down from the paving into the tiny workshop was like stepping into a jewel box ablaze with the reds and golds of rubies, topazes, ambers, cornelians and garnets. Hanging on the walls all around were komboloi, the Greek version of prayer beads and rosaries, but used just as worry beads.

Up the little wooden staircase, the top floor – again just one room –

had been turned into a museum of the history of the komboloi from the eighteenth century on. There were Buddhist and Hindu chains of a hundred and eight beads, used as an aid to counting the prayers that those religions required. They were made of holy wood, bone, sandalwood, silver, agate and walnut shells. One was even the backbone of a snake. There were Chinese beads of engraved ivory. There were Muslim chains of the ninety nine identities of Allah, or of thirty three beads to be counted three times. They were made of amber, black coral, ebony, olive kernels, mother-of-pearl, ivory, bone, and faturon, a blend of amber powder and other resins, such as bakelite, which to the amateur was indistinguishable from pure amber.

It was from the Muslim prayer beads that the Catholic rosary derived, brought to Europe by the Crusaders and developed by St. Dominicus into a chain of five groups of ten beads, each separated by a larger one. These were of olive, bone, wood, glass, pearl and mother-of-pearl, and most ended in a cross or crucifix.

As for the Greek komboloi, they were taken from the Turks but were simply a length of beads that fitted gently round the hand. They were the only ones from any country not used for prayer and were almost always in amber, pure amber being preferred for its sensuous feel and delicate fragrance, for, when rubbed, true amber gives off a pungent smell and almost electrical impulses.

And was there any sign of the fulgurite I was looking for in all this? None. None whatsoever.

The komboloi maker sat in the corner of his workshop deep in threads and beads. The atmosphere was so medieval he should have been a wizened toymaker of some sort, creating his Pinocchio. Instead he was a young man. Komboloi means a knot that speaks to you, he explained. It has nothing to do with the Church, the Church makes *komboskini*, those bracelets of knotted rope that not only protect you, but also help with your prayers. And the Church, or at least the monks of Macedonia, make most of the amulets. He had a lot for sale – 'they're very important for the Greeks,' he said. There were triangles of fabric embroidered with the cross, little rectangles of sparkly brocade and of beading, all with something inside. 'They're for babies, and just stuffed with card, except the beaded ones that have something better inside.' He took a while to think what. 'Earth from the church,' he suggested.

Each colour had a special power. Blue against the evil eye, orange for health and vitality, green for prosperity and success, red for power and glory. And there was St. Christopher for travellers. A blue azurite cross came from Tilos – a remote island, he mentioned vaguely – and he had scarabs from Egypt. 'This shop is for Greeks,' he said. 'Greeks who don't travel don't know the scarab is Egyptian. We're very close to Egypt.' And the truly Egyptian amulets he had in his stock, decorated with the snake, the eye and the falcon's wing, were powerful enough to avert every kind of evil.

Alexandria seemed very close and the linen goddess receded further and further north. But of goddesses in general there would be ample evidence.

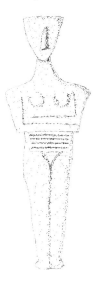

Athens

The Cycladic figurine, before which the Sudanese glass amulet hanging round my neck mysteriously fell and shattered, stood in the display case, arms folded, almost human in height. 'What are these figures?' the label read. 'Figures of the Great Mother, goddess of fertility, apotropaic figures, psychopompoi, nymphs, heroes, revered ancestors, divine nursemaids?' One, from around 2800 BC and nicknamed 'After Delivery', had what appeared to be stomach stretch marks, though to me they suggested not childbirth but a ritualistic belt or apron. Still, they gave her a distinctly human aspect.

Almost a thousand years after these Cycladic figurines, with their
severe purity of line, came the snake goddesses of the Minoan civilisa-
tion. Then there were the goddesses of the Mycenaean, from around 1500
BC. Rendered in clay, they have been found in large numbers at archaeological sites, especially in children's graves or at shrines. Though thought
to be goddesses or nursemaids, their true purpose is not known. Their
shape is a rounded lozenge pierced by perky breasts, on a stem repre-
senting legs, and topped by a bird-like face and flat cap, the *stephane*.

Others are embossed on gold plaques and are shaped like the Minoan
– bare-breasted, arms raised, tiered triangular skirts – or like the Cycladic
with arms clasped, or they are stylized into an oval surmounted by arms
raised in a complete circle above their heads. Then almost a thousand
years later again, in the period of Archaic Greece, came the plank
figurines of Boeotia whose heads were quite definitely those of a bird.

But the oldest of all were talismanic goddesses of the late neolithic, dating from some time between 4500 and 3200 BC and probably coming from Thessaly. Made of marble or stone, they had a hole in the back enabling them to be worn as a pendant, and thus were certainly amulets.

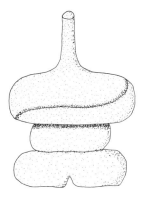

All these goddesses derived from the matriarchal society of Old Europe of the sixth millennium BC, and all were in museums.

The goddess of the streets of Athens was the Virgin Mary.

Averting one's eyes from the pornographic postcards in the tourist shops of the Plaka – the 'love-life of the Ancient Greeks', showing buggery, and huge erect penises – it would be impossible to miss the Virgin Mary, let alone the garlic and the blue eyes.

Blue as a celestial colour, as associated with Mary as the queen of heaven, and with the mother goddess in the same guise, plays no role in these street displays. The blue is without contention the eye against the evil eye. Round eye after round eye hangs beside the komboloi set up for sale, each string of beads centred by a metallic plaque depicting the Madonna, or St. Christopher, and surmounted always by an additional blue bead to make the purpose clear. Komboskini bracelets are displayed for sale, a tiny Madonna flanked by blue beads forming their clasp. Bulbs of garlic, made of white ceramic, dangle below blue eyes coiffed with blue ribbon. The tourists walk by and buy the postcards.

Who then are these amulets for?

'All Greeks buy them,' said the shopkeeper. 'They hang them in their houses, in their cars.'

I showed him the embroidered triangle with tasselled pendants from Karakalpakstan that I was still wearing. Yes, he knew it. He had one in the pocket of his jacket at home. His mother had bought it for him when he was a small boy and told him always to keep it in his pocket. Where had she bought it? At church, on a pilgrimage on the 15th August. Churches sell that sort of thing then – the 15th August is the Feast of the Assumption of the Virgin Mary.

There were other amulets that hedged every bet, like a blue bead tied on a string with a hank of red thread, a horseshoe, and a four-leaf clover. But I never saw any Greek wearing any of these amulets, at least not on their person.

Only, at five in the morning at the bus station of Nafplio, a bouncing, friendly dog, cream and fluffy and beautiful, and so a potential victim of the jealous evil eye, had worn the Virgin Mary in a blue glass bead hanging from his collar. Then, as I left Athens, a Rottweiler snarled at my passage and, as he bared his fangs, I noted that his collar bore a protective blue bead. A superfluous kindness, I thought, especially as he might himself have been a jinn in disguise.

Amulets were everywhere, but in a welter of blue beads, garlic and Madonnas, the triangle had vanished. Goddesses were everywhere as well, especially on old embroideries, but none bore any resemblance to the linen version, stylized into a triangle, that I was looking for.

The most significant embroideries of Greece for goddess figures are the shifts of Attica, made in villages that were settled in the fourteenth century by Albanians. American researchers working there in the early 1980s were told by old women who remembered making their bridal shifts at the turn of the century, that the figures they worked on the hems represented the family they would be acquiring on marriage, while the row of little stylized figures along the top were 'dolls' that expressed their hope for a lot of children. These skirts were usually of heavy cotton, rather than linen, and were worn until the birth of the first child.

The women surely spoke the truth, so the concept of the goddess had already disappeared more than a hundred years ago, and just as the Virgin Mary had taken over her role in religion, in the embroidery of Attica the mother-in-law had done the same.

Then there was the well-known embroidery of Arachova, a village near

Delphi, depicting a row of anthropomorphic figures, with triangular skirts, nine pendants, all that I required, but unfortunately they were set in a neat row below large brigandly figures of Turks waving swords, and so in no way represented goddesses, but more the victim about to be raped, or the poor little woman left behind at home.

Others resembled dancers, while another on a bridal cushion from the Ionian island of Lefkada, surrounded by small figures, wore earrings with three pendants, and a circular medallion decorated with two crosses and a diamond. But it seems she is known as 'the good fairy' and is claimed to be sheltering bride and groom.

If all that were left of goddesses were mothers-in-law, little women, dancers and good fairies, what of the triangle? Especially the triangle with three pendants.

Only the aprons of the Sarakatsani were embroidered with such a motif. The Sarakatsani – and the Vlachs – were once the nomadic and semi-nomadic shepherds of Greece. I headed north to find what traces remained of them.

The North 1: Sarakatsani

The true nomads had been the Sarakatsani. Believed originally to have come from the Pindhos mountains, they wandered over most of the Balkans through Albania, Bulgaria and Serbia, and from the Adriatic to the Aegean, even into the heart of Cappadocia, until borders devised by politicians caged them in. When the northern limits of Greek territory were set in 1923, their migrations ceased and they remained within Greece.

They moved between winter pastures hidden in deep ravines of remote valleys, and summer meadows high on untrodden mountain slopes. The transience of their passage set them apart from villager and farmer and imbued them with an aura of mystery, which their strange homes and dress served only to enhance.

They clustered together in *tseligata*, groups of related families and a sprinkling of non-kinsmen, building small beehive huts of wicker and rush, overlapping like the skirt of the Minoan snake goddess, and topped by a tuft and a wooden cross. Their society was patriarchal and dominated by the care of their flocks, whose grazing must have encircled the flimsy huddle of their dwellings with a melodious jangling and tinkling, for each animal's bell was chosen by the shepherd to harmonise. The melody came from the resonance of varying metals – the bells of the sheep, bulbous in shape, were made of beaten copper and those of the goats of cast bronze – and from graded size. The heaviest bell hung round the neck of the bellwether, who thus acted as a kind of orchestral leader as the flock grazed.

The Sarakatsani moved in this romantic, ephemeral setting like toy soldiers, in stiff, scratchy, unbending clothing. Men's legs were swathed in bands of blanketing under heavy pleated kilts of white wool, and thick jackets of black goats' hair, covered by crow-black cloaks so dense they almost stood on their own. The women looked like cut-out dolls in layers of medieval tabards, their rigid, homespun costume as austerely black and white as their menfolk's, but made even stranger by incongruous frivolities: black, gold and silver threads twisted into zigzags, haberdashers' ribbons in gold and silver, Viking-like buckles and pectorals, and pompoms. Though migrations brought variety into the costume of each region, it remained, like their lives, outside that of the everyday people around them.

All their patterns, whether embroidered on the women's chemises and aprons, on their horse blankets, bread-bags and marriage banners, or woven into their rugs, or knitted into their socks, had their origin in magic. They resembled, too, those on the pottery of the Geometric period from about 1000 BC, placing the origin of the Sarakatsani in Greece perhaps at least as early as that.

The pattern of the triangle with three pendants that I had seen on one of their aprons turned out to be an isolated example – they did not believe in the Trinity. Their favourite motifs were the cross, the sun in its various manifestations and the fertile field. This last, carved on the bellies of the goddesses of neolithic Europe, may point to even earlier origins.

The apron was the most significant item of the women's clothing. Aprons sent messages of age and status: brighter for the young and unmarried, sombre for the mother. There were even special ones to say you were feeling lonely, or to mark some public dishonour (black and no sequins), or to wear when moving from one pasture to another. A girl had to make twenty five to thirty for her dowry, to cover every eventuality, and still I only ever saw one with the triangle. There were no goddesses anywhere, not even stylized.

In the 1940s the Sarakatsani vanished. Their death knell was the Second World War, the German and Italian occupation and the Greek civil war immediately afterwards. Patrick Leigh Fermor's memorable meeting with a wild horseman with matted hair riding down the main street of Alexandroupolis, 'as inappropriate in these tame surroundings as a wolf in the heart of Athens', must remain one of the last recorded contacts anyone would have with these people. Though their true origin remains unknown, their own legends claim them as Hellenes 'taller than oaks and as strong, they spanned wide rivers at a single pace and strode from peak to peak. They never fell ill, they died suddenly and often broke their necks by falling down cliffs...' And in a way that is what happened. They simply and suddenly vanished. Not by falling down cliffs, but by giving up their nomadic life completely and melting into the sedentary Greek population.

'They're just like you and me now. No different,' said the swarthy baker, handing me a spinach pie. 'Businessmen, politicians, lawyers even.'

But in Macedonia they still gather once a year for a cultural evening singing old revolutionary songs at the Achilles tavern halfway between Drama and Kalambakiou.

The North II: The Vlachs

The way north from Athens to Macedonia had been along a rain-lashed highway flanked entirely by showrooms of Japanese cars or wedding-dresses, swanky banks, scrap metal dealers, hoardings, bedding shops, waste lots, pallet dumps and lavatory pan factories. The man beside me on the bus read a Russian newspaper. It hardly seemed like Greece, and when I arrived in Thessaloniki and asked for directions, the reply was in Russian. They'd come, the women said, through Bulgaria. That was the way they all got in.

The gold of Macedonia and Thrace was the source of Alexander's power. It lay in river sediments or in underground deposits of copper and iron. The miners, working in cramped galleries propped up by wooden sticks, were war captives, criminals, or those thrown arbitrarily into prison, and often their relatives too. All were naked, it was claimed, and left digging away until they died.

What of the objects fashioned from this gold? Was a gold triangle with three pendants – after all, a common form of jewellery in much of Asia and the Middle East – possibly something that Alexander took on his conquests? Would such a shape perhaps have gone from west to east, rather than vice versa?

Most of the gold on display in Thessaloniki predated Alexander by two or three hundred years. There were all the symbols still common in embroidery and jewellery throughout the lands of Alexander's journeys: solar double axes, as on the dresses of Siwa, solar rosettes, the eight pointed star – or sixteen, emblem of the Macedonian dynasty – pomegranates for fertility, necklaces of wheat seeds with the same purpose, spirals, horns, zigzags for power, even pyramids that looked like those of Meroë, and plaques like the hair ornaments of Eritrea. Triangles there were too, gold ones around the hem of a woman's dress, dating from the late sixth century BC, but they pointed downwards.

As for amulets, people in Thessaloniki denied any knowledge of them, except one man. Yes, he knew the triangle, but not embroidered, just plain. It had bones inside. 'Bones?' 'Yes, bones of those birds that eat blood.' 'Birds that eat blood?' 'Yes, birds with no wings. Membranes.' Bats. I looked at him quizzically. 'Where are you from?' I asked. Crete. There are more than two thousand caves on Crete, and they were always a refuge in times of conflict. The theory of priests scraping the floor of belfries flew out of the window. This was a much older, more primeval, sanctuary, a protection known to prehistoric man.

The region to the north west of Thessaloniki, home to the Vlachs, was one of the last remaining areas in Greece where traditional costume was still being worn as late as the 1970s. Though it differed from village to village, it was mostly gloomy – black homespun woollen overgarments, white shifts, knitted socks and large black aprons – jollied up with coins. The shapes and patterns had come via Byzantium from central Asia – Macedonia had remained Ottoman much longer than the rest of the country – but the Vlachs were from the west. As a semi-nomadic race, living on the edge of society like the Sarakatsani, they might have retained ancient patterns and beliefs. Some I already knew from Vlach shepherds in the hills of Slovakia, but they were believed to have originated in Romania, from where they had begun their nomadic life through eastern Europe. Their language, unwritten, was a remote derivation of Romanian, and a few years ago the Romanians had claimed the Vlachs as theirs and tried to set up schools in Macedonia and Epirus, but no one wanted them.

It seemed that the town of Florina could be a base from which to explore the Vlach villages, but no buses went there from Thessaloniki, only a slow train that dumped its few passengers at a small snowbound junction in the mountains halfway there. The door of the waiting room wouldn't close and the windows were broken. An old man in a tweed hat, rubbing his hands, led everyone to the small stove where Turkish coffee was served. It felt like the end of the line, bitterly cold, abandoned.

The whole region felt the same. The steep slopes were covered in dense, silent forest, concealing half deserted villages. A second toy train trundled its four remaining passengers past them and on to Florina.

The town's pretty name belied the reality. The teeming rain sliced into the cascades of flood water that buried pavements and roads under their hurrying torrents. Even their speed failed to shift the dirty crusts of lingering snow that blotched the pavestones and clung to the curbs.

The town was a morgue of hoarded-up shops, shuttered bars, jettisoned buses with missing tyres, hulks of rusting cars. A rushing brown river ran through the centre, its rasping sound like the sharpening of knives, dividing the town into a block of modern concrete monoliths on one side, and on the other a desolate waste of old Balkan homes. There, small brick houses were coated in peeling ochre plaster, the white marble of their coping stones and pediments deeply pocked, their wrought-iron balconies cankered brown, their shutters gaping and their walls graffiti-sprayed: 'Listen to the Beat'. 'Funky Shit'. 'Joseph', they said. The white and purple church, like most others, stood padlocked against the local populace. One music shop selling xylophones, drums and guitars, also displayed in its windows catapults, massive rifles and pistols: Beretta, Browning, Breda, L.Franchi, Marsberg, Maverick, Remington. It seemed irresponsible, so close to the Balkan conflict. Men shouted and argued aggressively, an Albanian trait, I was later to discover.

The town was sheathed by wooded, snow-capped peaks, on the top of one of which stood a huge Christian cross. It was a region of lakes and mountains backing up against closed frontiers, effectively a dead end since the disintegration of Yugoslavia had caused the town's decline. Its neighbour was now a new country known as FYROM, an acronym that attempted to bury the acrimony surrounding the name 'Macedonia'. The Germans and Austrians no longer came through on their way to the south and the sun, and there was virtually no one left in the area to come and shop. And no buses would run to the villages until the winter snow had cleared. The only escape was by the roundabout route to Kastoria, a snow-ploughed road snaking up the mountain pass to the south of Florina.

Kastoria's signposting was in Cyrillic, aimed it seemed at the Russian mafiosi rather than illegal immigrants. For they come here to buy fur. Kastoria lies on a peninsular jutting into a motionless steel-grey lake, its old Turkish houses and tiny Byzantine churches built daringly on sheer rock, while modern concrete flats lazily hug the flatter lake shore. The prosperity of Kastoria is based on the fur trade, though the local beavers, from where the town gets its name, were hunted to extinction by the nineteenth century. Now scraps of fur, bits of ears and paws, snippets of underbelly, imported from Canada and Scandinavia, are made up into everything conceivable to sell to the Russians and tourists. Fur is everywhere. There are key rings with what look like possum tails swinging from them, there are slippers and stuffed dogs made of cut-offs of rabbit and mink, there are coats contrived out of shaggy patches and leather ones with whiskery fluff from the reverse escaping at the seams.

I asked about amulets, there being nothing else in the town of any use to me, as the museums and churches were all closed. Old people still wear them, I was told. They have a splinter of the church cross inside them, and earth from the Holy Land. And then also the ashes of the dead beloved. It was only in Kastoria that I came across such a custom - perhaps dealing all their lives with fur, the people are less squeamish than most.

West from Kastoria into Epirus the bus trundles through grass uplands into the magnificent scenery of the deep Pindhos range. The lower slopes are shawled in beech trees, whose dead cinnamon-coloured leaves shiver and crackle in the light winds. Above them hang icicled waterfalls and, still higher, stand dark, brooding pines heavy with snow. The Pindhos forms an impenetrable barrier that virtually isolates Epirus from mainland Greece and turns her towards the Ionian islands.

If the barrier was geographical, on that day it was also physical: a huge Bulgarian lorry had turned turtle and lay across the road like a giant dead woodlouse, its serried rows of wheels pointing heavenward. It was impossible to pass. The road had seemed a far byway of outer Europe, cutting through remote scarps, but in the hours it was blocked it snarled up an extraordinary assortment of vehicles from every EU fringe and aspirant member. The temperature was below freezing, I had lost my gloves, and we were there for four hours.

It was a useful occasion to check on the amulets hanging from rear mirrors. In view of the variety of vehicles and the length of time we were there, it would seem to represent a fair cross-section of the transport amulets of a wider Europe. There were no triangles at all – so common in Asia and the Middle East – but instead almost nothing but Madonnas, or Madonnas with crosses. There was the odd stuffed teddy or nodding dog, and a number of green cardboard trees, which I had thought to represent the tree of life, but which turned out to be air fresheners.

We finally pulled into the bus station of Ioannina. The first cheap hotel room was windowless, the second boasted a slit overlooking a rubbish tip. The local café offered boiled goat at 500 drachmas, or boiled goat at 1200, or even more expensive Snitcheld wiener at 1500 drs. 'Frozen octopus vinegar', 'loaf of cheese in small frying pan', 'sausage-like stuffed with cheese' were the alternatives. Such culinary gaffes can be amusing to the tourist, but not when frozen and hungry.

Looking for amulets and embroidery is much like diamond mining: just as to locate one small gem means crushing thousands of tons of kimberlite, so to locate one snippet of information – let alone actually to see an amulet – requires endless hours of tedious journeying on buses, trains and ferries, hanging around ill-frequented bus stations at dawn, consuming boring meals and appalling red wine sold by the kilo, or making do with cheap cheese and spinach pies shared with the town cats. Then there is the hassle of finding a different roof almost every night, and always the dreary trawl through provincial museums full of stuffed buzzards, dusty flints and shepherds' lutes.

What would Ioannina offer?

The town promised well. Ottoman since 1430 and centre of Epirus, whose offshore islands were Venetian, it was at the meeting point of east and west. Some of its embroideries were the closest anywhere to those of central Asia, in particular to the *suzanis* of Bukhara, and the costume of the court of Ali Pasha was purely Turkish in style: goldwork on velvet, fine white muslin, none of the homespun wool and symbolic aprons of the villages around. And the silverwork for which the town was famous blended Byzantine, Venetian and Islamic motifs.

Ali Pasha governed Epirus from Ioannina as his own personal fiefdom from 1788 until he was deposed in 1820. His rule was both barbarous and cultured, renowned for tolerance towards Christianity. Now his citadel, its soaring minaret dominating the lakeside, was slowly crumbling, its wooden jalousies smashed and askew . A short ferry ride away across the lake, the tiny monasteries on the nearby island of Nissi were all under restoration, boasting blue and yellow signs of EU funding, and were closed. The lake was polluted and, as each ferry docked, the locals greeted the passengers with tanks of swirling carp, bloated goldfish and eels they would never risk eating themselves.

Buses to the Vlach villages around left before dawn, their only role in winter being to transport schoolchildren from mountain villages to small local towns. After catching them at Ioannina bus station, the only passenger, and then being dumped, before the villagers awoke, in dark, deserted streets, ankle deep in snow and spattered by sleet, I abandoned such forays and went instead to stay in Metsovo, one of the last remaining towns in Greece where traditional costume is still worn.

Metsovo, a Vlach stronghold famous for its beauty, its benefactors and weavings, guards the only pass over the Pindhos mountains. It stands high on steep slopes, some gleaming black like petrified coal dumps, others made of boulders of striated marble, or of stone pushed into vertical slices by some cataclysmic geological fiesta. Peaks even higher surround it, and forests where wolves and bears still roam.

The town's twisting alleyways, steps and dead ends, its dense small spaces, are all of rough-hewn stones sprouting with unkempt grass. Enclosing them are rambling houses, some converted into museums and art galleries, all built of the same stones, their roofs of grey-green schist shimmering under the snow, their balconies of pine and oak jutting over passers-by. Women, dumpy in their black Vlach costume of full skirt, and apron of wool embroidered with bright flowers, walk along the narrow paths carrying home-made wooden beehives, chickens pecking around their feet. The descent of the town into tweeness is almost inevitable. In the summer it must be intolerably overrun, in winter, though devoid of tourists, it resembles a Mary Poppins alpine stage set.

The small hotel near the main square was built by the owner's grandfather in Bavarian style, heavy with lugubrious wood. The family was Vlach, he explained, like everyone else here. But not all had stayed. Some had left for America or Alexandria and sent back the money that had changed their home village into a pastiche of the one they remembered with such affection. Those that had stayed were, in a way, still semi-nomadic, 'unlike the Sarakatsani,' he added, with a certain bite.

The Vlachs spend the summer months here with their flocks, though there were now only about twenty thousand sheep instead of the several million they used to own. Then in the winter they go down to the plains of Thessaly, but it isn't like the old days. The wives and families stay behind as the men can always hop in the car and drive back to see them. As for the sheep, no longer does some seasoned drover herd them south along ancient trackways, they are simply loaded into articulated lorries and driven there.

All there was to be seen of the flocks around Metsovo were a few goats scrimping a subsistence from frozen leaves, watched over by a couple of surly dogs and a Vlach goatherd, dressed in something Greek and woolly, but glimpsed too fleetingly on high slopes to be able to determine exactly what he wore. In the town itself, old costumes were being chopped up to make bags and cushion covers for the tourists, or expensively copied to send to California. The motifs were almost entirely floral.

Though here in Greece I had considered goddesses, Cycladic, Minoan and Mycenean, I had now lost the trail completely. Like a desert river that slivers into rivulets and peters out in the sand long before reaching the sea, I had floundered in a morass of blue beads, Madonnas and garlic, and was not one whit nearer achieving my goal of finding the source of the triangle and the locations of its metamorphosis into a goddess figure.

There was still Albania, sliding into anarchy, without food, without light, without heat. I would wait until the snows had melted.

Albania

Gjirokaster

Before leaving home, I invested a very small amount of money in an Albanian/English, English/Albanian phrase book. It was published by Birmingham City Council, clearly to help bewildered refugees from Kosovo and the strained employees of the benefits office. I jettisoned immediately the Albanian/English section, focussing as it did on: 'how do I get social security? how much furniture can I have?', and kept only part 2, Albanian for English speakers. Even this was somewhat slanted towards the requirements of the council, rather than those of a lone wanderer in Albania. 'You must change trains at Crewe – 'ju duhet te nderroni trenin ne Crewe' – was going to be of little use in finding my way to Gjirokaster, and most questions were designed to help importuned officials: 'has your... been stolen?' 'a te kane vjedhur..?', rather than the victim which, from all accounts, I was more likely to be. At least the word for 'stolen' would undoubtedly prove useful.

I plodded on. 'Can I introduce Winston?' (surely that should be 'may'?) – 'mund t'ju njoh me Winston?' and then finally gave up trying to learn anything at all at the useful addendum on the next line: 'this is Winston' – 'ky eshte Winston'. I wasn't taking anyone with me, let alone a bulldog. But I did slip the book into my travel bag.

I thought the most logical way to go to Albania was to return to Athens and then pick up my trail where I had left it, in Ioannina. I checked into the same small hotel in Athens as before, where from the shower, and from the shower alone, there was a spectacular view of the Parthenon, and set off to queue for a ticket on that night's bus to Tirana. I stood behind two portly Bulgarian women in print floral

dresses, and was immediately mobbed by a clattering gaggle of rapscal-
lion young men, their tousled hair and taut aquiline faces reminding me
of nothing more than the Rashaida in the market of Kassala. They
shared the same certain loucheness that makes you hang on to your bag
a little more tightly.

'One way ticket to Gjirokaster.' The Albanians pressed around more
closely to watch the ticket seller. He exploded. 'The town is not
Gjirokaster, it's Greek and it's Argirokastro. One way ticket to Argirokastro.' He slammed down the change. The Albanians mobbed forward.

Gjirokaster was once the second town of Epirus, ruled too by Ali Pasha.
The entire region of northern Epirus and southern Albania has always
been an ethnic mix of Greek and Albanian, swinging, with international
decisions made by distant bureaucrats, from one country to the other.
In 1941 the Greeks captured Gjirokaster and, though post-war borders
placed it in Albania, it was still thought of, at least in Greece, as emotion-
ally Greek, and its loss still riled.

I spent the day before leaving trawling again the tacky half-mile of the
Plaka souvenir shops, chatting about amulets. It was over the last ten years
that the street had changed so much, the antique dealer said, nothing but
tourist rubbish now. His stock was the real stuff: genuine Phoenician
beads, antique carvings of Cycladic origin, vases of ancient Attica whose
broken bits lay beside them on the dusty shelves. Father and son cared
little for dusters, but sat reading the paper in their gloomy shop, which
in its confined intimacy reminded me of the komboloi museum in
Nafplio. The son twiddled in his fingers a shiny silver komboloi. 'I bought
it over the road, at one of those tourist shops,' he confided. I asked him
why he didn't have a real one, a good one. It would wear out, he replied.
Amber is fragile. He denied that his figurines were goddesses or even
amulets. 'Too old,' he said. Only his scarabs were against the evil eye, but
they were from Egypt, not Greece. He regretted he had nothing else
against any kind of evil spirits, and suggested I try the tourist shops.

White elephants had suddenly appeared among the blue eyes, strings
of them interspersed by blue beads, topped by a blue ribbon and hung
with a bell. 'Elephants good animals,' said the stallholder. 'So bring luck,
and white better than blue against evil eye. And the bell is the power of
the church, it sings of the church. Keeps evil away.'

'So if these elephants are so good at protecting, why have so many of
them got a broken leg or trunk?'

'They are glass, they are of glass. Glass is real. Evil eye is other world. Elephants hang in car, and roads and traffic are real.'

There appeared to be some perverse logic in this argument, so I bought a string of broken white glass elephants for the real world of the night bus.

The hotel owner saw me off: 'take great care in Albania.'

'I will.'

'You need to. We had an Albanian working here. He just brushed past me one day and said "you've got two thousand drachmas in your pocket." I fetched out my money. It was three thousand. "Yes, but look. One's a very thin note. I missed it." I asked how he did it, and he said they were taught as children. They sit in the street and signal to each other. They'll never change. Aid to Albania is thrown away. The Serbs are different. They're honest, hard-working. The two will always clash. Take great care, Albania's dangerous. We want to see you back again.'

The bus passed through Ioannina in the small hours and arrived at the border as dawn broke. There were no cars, no tourists, just busloads of Albanians going both ways. Voices were raised, fists were shaken, armed police were everywhere. People thronged around, a few with round Mediterranean faces, but most thinner and pinched, with sharp noses and taut mouths. There were a surprising number of little blonde girls, and lovely young women, slim, high-breasted, a few dressed in casual Italian style, most in long dresses of glittery fabric.

Notices were pinned up of the visa charges for foreigners, a list of fees like school marks for the international behaviour of nations. Norwegians paid five dollars, French thirty seven and Americans forty, while the Brits alone were way ahead of anyone at fifty seven. I presumed this had something to do with our long-standing dispute over the shooting of two British ships in the Corfu channel in 1946, and Albania's refusal to pay compensation and Britain's to return the gold illegally seized in retribution. As the value of this was now about thirty million dollars, the odd fifty seven demanded of me seemed pettily vindictive, I thought, as I protestingly handed it over. It was something to do, the policeman countered, with the visa charge made in the UK for Albanians. The relative desirability of British tourists in Albania, and Albanian asylum seekers in Britain, did not enter into the equation.

Almost immediately after the border the road collapsed into nothing but a potholed cart track, the bus pitching and tossing, and veering off into fields when passage was impossible. Not into neat, tended fields, but unkempt ones, full of weeds, grasses, wild flowers, litter, and abandoned wrecked Mercedes. Gaunt, windowless, broken-down factories alternated with buildings that were destroyed or half-finished or half-begun or crumbling to pieces. And all the way along the road crouched Hoxha's concrete bunkers, every few yards, their horizontal gun slits like the watching eyes of squatting Daleks. All faced the road diagonally towards Greece and supposed attack from that direction, their backs to the mountains where most Balkan wars surely were waged. Gypsies walked by in flouncy skirts and gold glitter, shepherds led their flocks, men rode by on donkeys. There were no cars or anything that looked like the twentieth century, let alone the twenty-first.

Then abandoned vineyards, littered with bent and collapsed frames, gave way to rows of straight, firmly supported new vines, then to fields of maize, and the road was suddenly tarmacked. In the lee of the hills to the west lay a line of Greek minority villages. It was only later that I learned that the bus from Athens was always held up at gunpoint here and the passengers robbed, so the bus company had paid for a strip of new road past the villages in exchange for a moratorium on hold-ups. It was now safe to pass those villages, but not the others.

I was the only passenger getting off the bus at Gjirokaster, and so was dropped on the nearby highway. 'Be careful, just be careful,' one of the passengers, a young American-Albanian girl living in Boston, warned me. I stepped down into a quagmire of putrifying rubbish, just about exactly the spot where, in 1848, Edward Lear had painted in soft watercolours an Albanian in immaculate white robes and red fez sitting on the ground and gazing up at the romantic scene before him.

The old town of Gjirokaster shoulders up towards the citadel that dominates it from an eagle's eyrie of a hilltop, soaring even amid the pale circle of surrounding mountains. The first dwellings were built in the twelfth century within the precincts of the citadel and then others gradually crept over the surrounding slopes in the fourteenth, covering them in a beautiful shroud of grey slate and stone. The houses are small castles, their defensive walls of stone, their ground floors blanked and their living quarters set in the safety of upper storeys. Roofs are of slate or stone, crossed here and there by loose electric wires kinked to nefarious ends. The road between the top of the town and the citadel is of the same stone as the houses, chiselled by hand into paving that alternates black and white, polished by centuries of feet, hooves and wheels to a sunlit sheen. The centre of the town below is a small square dominated by the mosque whose recorded muezzin clanks into gear at one o'clock and five, to the general indifference of the populace. Opposite it stands the Greek consulate.

It was only in the mornings that the square, and the paved roads of little shops leading from it, came to life. Hordes of young men, vacant-eyed and curly-haired, hung around the consulate. Money changers sat on old wooden chairs outside the bars, holding fistfuls of leke and drachma. Then suddenly at twelve they all vanished. The police who had been controlling them went off to the shops to spend their loot on bottles of Red Label scotch. The bars jammed shut. There was no one. And even when the sun subsided and the temperature softened, the place was still deserted, only the evening cats slinking around, the shops shuttered, the cafés and bars closed. Not at any stage of the day was there again any life in the square. Though the muezzin sounded at five, it was of no consequence. Nobody came near the mosque and the crowds that in the morning had turned their backs on it, facing the Greek consulate, did not return to make amends. Not a single one of them. The opening hours of the Greek consulate were, it transpired, the mantra by which everyone lived. Every man wanted a visa to escape to Greece and every day they gathered. Greece was an open sesame to the rest of Europe and they would move ever westward. There were a few gypsies among them, the women in sparkly clothes, breast-feeding, the men of scurrilous bent. I hoped the officials at Dover would be vigilant.

It didn't take long to realize how badly destroyed Gjirokaster was, how many walls were rubble, how many windows void, how many roofs gashed. The houses' ancient defence of windowless stone walls allowing armed marauders no entry at road level, served little in the face of modern armaments.

And everywhere was buried in rubbish. The small stream at the top of the town no longer flowed, but was now a blocked effluent of blue plastic bags, tin cans, sodden paper and black muck. Just when the town seemed impossibly picturesque, eyes and nose were assailed by an ocean swell of decomposing litter. It was as if all the recycling boxes of the Home Counties had been joyously hurled along gutter, pavement, river bed. And then, in an ultimate moment of dustmen's delirium, the contents of a million dustbins had been chucked in for good measure.

It was only gradually that I became aware of the absolute anarchy that ruled Albania, an anarchy that made the idea of an organised system of refuse collection risible.

The evening passeggiata in the new town down by the highway, was uncannily like that of Asmara, the difference of black and white skins melting into irrelevance, as did the similar historical presence of the Italians. The young girls wore out-of-date Italian disco clothes, the men cheap T-shirts decorated with simple horizontal stripes and no word about saving whales or the environment emblazoned on them. Everyone strolled along, ignoring the barriers of broken concrete blocks, the dumped rubbish, the two-metre holes in the pavement down which they could easily have fallen. Not a car, not a bike, not even a donkey disturbed the quiet conversations and gentle footfalls. No older women took part. They were only to be seen earlier in the day humping and heaving their market purchases up the steep lanes, and were now at home cooking.

Very few women were dressed entirely in black, as I'd expected them to be. Most wore short floral dresses. Knowing that the majority of the population was Muslim – though under Hoxha Albania had been the only officially atheist country in the world – I had brought suitably concealing clothes. I had hoped to blend in, but merely stood out from the crowd in my general dowdiness.

Worse, without my consciously having met anyone, the whole town immediately knew I was English. After only one day strangers in the street greeted me cheerily: 'good morning, England'. At night, even in the dark, 'hello' rang out at my passage, when all that could be seen were exquisitely chiselled cobbles skidded by the glare of a few street lamps, and I had thought myself invisible. Late one night, making my way back up the steep, stone road to my room at the top of town, from the excellent Italian restaurant down near the highway, a woman rushed out of a building in the pitch dark, grabbed me, and took me to a side entrance. Here she removed my trekking sandals and replaced them with pink plastic flip-flops. She took me upstairs and showed me her pensione, palatial, empty. There were never any tourists now – though long ago some people had actually come from Alaska, she assured me – and her place was only fifteen dollars whereas she knew I was paying twenty at Hadji's, which was piccolo. She spoke only Italian, but her desperation would be clear in any language. She gave me a chocolate Bacio di Amore, as if it were a premium investment.

In the days when tourists used to come, Gjirokaster was described as a 'museum-town', which evokes an air of stultifying silence, of fossilized custodianship, of the rigidity of cold glass display cabinets. But Gjirokaster was a town that moved, everything about it was emerging, declining, swirling, evanescent. Nothing was static. Its houses crawled haphazardly up the mountainside of which they were made, up to the citadel. The cobblestones of its pathways twisted and turned, patterned in contrasted softness of tone that was neither completely black nor completely white, but which shifted at every step and every sheen of sun and rain. The schists of its roofs splintered into curving lines that jostled around each other, the walls of its houses blended from boulder to pebble, from rock to stone. Nowhere was there a straight line, a sharp corner, a peaked roof. Even the ground floors of the houses, which rose like vertical cliffs, defensive, inaccessible, slit only by an occasional grilled window before they opened into the crystal lightness of the living space above, were always more a pocked and raked natural cliff than a proud wall of neat masonry.

Wandering round the town I began to notice curious dolls and soft toys hanging on houses – woolly lambs, teddies and suchlike. Replies to my questions merely dismissed them as being where children lived, but this was obviously nonsense as almost every empty building under repair or construction had one. They turned out to be amulets against the evil eye, the modern equivalent of ancient figurines. They were best if they were red, I later learned, though a doll missing an arm or a leg, or even its head, was highly prized for its talismanic power. There were also a few animal skins, and horns fixed on walls or over doors to toss out spirits bringing disease and malevolence upon the household, as can be found anywhere between Afghanistan and Spain, though perhaps not in Düsseldorf or Tunbridge Wells. Here and there, even a horseshoe could be seen.

As for my other concern, that of embroidered costume, it had now vanished. It was still worn throughout most of Albania in the 1950s, though things had begun to change in the 1930s when King Zog ordered the unveiling of women and made covering the face a punishable offence. Then in 1967, Hoxha closed all the churches, which destroyed the social relevance of traditional costume, as it had dramatically in Hungary, when in 1924 in the town of Mezőkövesd the church elders banned gold decoration, so the women burned all their now useless costumes. In the same way, once costume in Albania no longer had any social status, it was kept only for the sham folk festivals beloved of the communist world.

Though everyone said the ethnographic museum had been looted and was empty, I wanted to see for myself anyway, to stand there and imagine the linen shifts, the *giubba* – the flared gold-embroidered coats of Epirus – the knitted socks, the white blouses with *oya* trimmings, that would once have filled it.

The ethnographic museum was housed in the lovely mansion that had been Enver Hoxha's birthplace and so was previously the Museum of the National Liberation War, until with the fall of communism all that had been consigned to the dustbin and replaced by the ethnographic heritage of Albania. It was a typical mansion of Gjirokaster, and old photos showed the spacious living room on the first floor furnished with a divan covered in a white filet cloth and white cushions embroidered with pink flowers. Draped pink curtains hung at the windows. Now all that, too, it seemed, had been destroyed.

The entrance to the museum was through a heavy wooden door locked by a thick wooden beam. The steep stone staircase inside was covered in rubble. With a huge iron key, Doshira opened the door to the storeroom at the top. The 'crazy people', the 'cattivi', the 'criminals', who in 1997 had wrecked the museum and begun to loot it, had taken several days to do so, she explained, rushing round the town pillaging wherever it took their fancy, so there had been time to hide some of the museum's possessions. The door cranked slowly open, revealing a higgledy-piggle of cobwebbed furniture, dirty clothes, wooden horses, cradles, leather trunks, a sort of down-market, jumble sale version of the disorder Carter found on opening Tutankhamun's grave.

Doshira unlocked a trunk. I waited in a state of great excitement, expecting her to bring out linen shifts embroidered with versions of the goddess, or with stylized renderings in cross stitch of symbols for the sun and moon, patterns of abstracted horns, diamonds and triangles, trees of life, all the panoply of symbolism I had been looking for. One after another Doshira brought out dresses that were purely Turkish in style. Made of crinkly silk, or a silk and cotton mix that she insisted was linen, they were embroidered in heavy gold plate in designs that were simply naturalistic flowers. Edgings were beautiful, fine narrow frills of the needlelace flowers called 'oya' in Turkey, 'bibila' in Greece, and 'oya' here. We might as well have been in Bursa.

The historical armaments museum in the battlemented castle of the citadel had also been looted. It was approached through a curved stone entranceway, speckled with grass and designed for a horse's foothold, cut through the citadel walls under heavy arches. The castle was just as it had been for centuries, entirely unspoilt: no notices, no souvenir kiosks, no son-et-lumière. The woman who looked after it did so with a heavy heart. She had been there for twenty seven years – she was in her mid-forties, she said – and in 1992 and '97 all the best stuff had been stolen. Weapons from prehistory, from the Stone Age, Iron Age, Bronze Age, and then later ones set in silver and gold. She named the man everyone thought responsible.

In '92 the border with Greece had been open, and it was easy to get things out. Greeks had come across with loudspeaker vans asking for silver, antiques, anything. The Albanians had no idea of values or of foreign currency and had sold all they had and all they could steal. In '97 it had been much worse.

She took me to see the prison, and the chamber where those awaiting execution by the Germans during the Second World War were tortured by freezing or boiling water. There were a lot of them crowded in there, she said, and the Germans (who also hung two young girls from the tree in the square down by the old hotels) poured cold water through the high barred window in winter and hot in summer. A stone step enclosing the room ensured that the level of the water was kept high. As I stood imagining the terror of the victims trying by their fingernails to cling to the dank stone walls above the water level, the horror of the scene was somewhat mitigated by the homely thrum of a washing machine in the next cell. The people at the castle were washing the shirts for the forthcoming folk festival to be held in its grounds. Some were already hanging on the line, and I noted with some cheer that they were white and had red machined zigzag stitching at the neck front and round the collar.

Life is very hard, the custodian said. No one has work and the women at home try to provide everything. They look years older than they are. The factories are all at a standstill. In 1991 they were 'privatised', which meant that the Democrats or Socialists 'sold' them to their cronies. As each man got a factory he closed it down, sold the machinery, or used it for something else. The one here used to make T-shirts, but the man who bought it now uses it just to repair car parts and doesn't give people work. Her husband has no job and she has two daughters. Her wages of sixty dollars a month are considered good. As I walked back down the hill, men sat by the roadside playing backgammon. They earned money like that – people can pay to watch and make bets, I was told. Derisive laughter greeted the suggestion that they might be better employed dealing with the litter.

I stayed on in Gjirokaster and began to ask questions about 1997, about people's lives and about the gleaming new Mercedes that were everywhere. The questions were easy, the answers less straightforward.

Mateos, who had just turned thirteen, spoke excellent English, and might be considered to represent the new Albania, was happy to give his opinions as he walked with me round Gjirokaster. He had the characteristic habit of stating something categorically that flew in the face of all evidence: 'there's no bell in that church,' 'the bus takes an hour,' 'there are always taxis there.' When the facts were pointed out to him, he merely repeated what he had said and refused to budge, or even listen. It seemed to be the same intransigence that formed the basis of political life here: shoot rather than listen and compromise. Mateos always knew best, and had the highest opinion of himself and his views.

The events of 1997 in Albania, the collapse of suspect pyramid savings schemes and the subsequent rioting, hit the international press, but I had had no idea of exactly what they entailed. I was to learn only gradually as I travelled through Albania and at first Mateos's explanations had to suffice. When I voiced surprise and considerable regret at the great number of memorials around the town and along the roadside to young men killed in 1997 – that were nostalgically reminiscent of those on walls around Paris commemorating the youth of the Resistance shot in the back by the Germans – he had his own unassailable theory. 'A man has a gun in his hand, it is something new, you have something new in your hand and you want to try it out. That's natural. But all those shot young men were a mistake. The guns shot at walls and when the bullets bounced back the men were in the way.' Nothing would shift him from this explanation, to which he added the gratuitous 'it's the same in your country.'

When I commented on the enormous number of big new Mercedes in such a small town, and asked how anyone had the money to buy them, 'people work,' he said. I remarked that there were virtually no jobs for the men, and that the vast majority of them hung around outside the

Greek consulate trying to escape – 'well, they get the money, they work.'
I asked where the cars came from. 'They are stolen from Germany,' he
said, 'so they are cheap because you can't take them outside Albania.' This
he found perfectly normal, and had nothing more to say on the subject.

In Circles 1: Butrint

I n the pyramid investment scam of 1997 most Albanians lost their life
savings, even their homes. When interest rates of up to 35% were
offered, they gullibly queued up to hand over everything they had,
their naivety born of fifty years of complete isolation from the world,
and the chaos and deprivation they had suffered since . Every town offered
a scheme and when the smaller ones began to be unable to meet interest payments, panic withdrawals were rapid and the whole scheme
collapsed like a toddler's building bricks. Revenge was vitriolic, mind-
less and self-mutilating. Believing the government to be responsible –
and, aided by the mafia, it was certainly involved – people smashed up
everything that belonged to the state: schools, hospitals, water supplies,
telephone lines, hotels, factories, banks. There was also in this reprisal
an element of the Albanian clan system, the fis, where if the supporters
of the government were of one fis and you of another, total destruction
was expected of you.

Corruption was endemic, so that arsenals were easily opened while the
military turned a blind eye. Most Albanian men – though none that I
ever spoke to – stole guns and went on a killing spree. Some were just
gratuitous shootings, others were the old vendettas and blood feuds
resurfacing.

So the Albania I travelled around might not that long ago have been
a landscape of spectacular untamed mountains. Now, though, where man
had been it was a wasteland of abandoned fields, windowless, vandalised
factories barricaded behind fences, wantonly wrecked schools and hospitals. And everywhere were the roadside graves I had first noticed around
Gjirokaster. 'It's easiest to take someone out on to a country road and
shoot them there,' I was told.

Where the mountains around Gjirokaster fall down to the coastal plain
in the west lies a tranquil region of lakes and wooded bluffs, of silted flats

and ruined castles. At its heart stands one of the greatest classical sites of the Mediterranean, Butrint. The circling sweep of its Roman theatre, the pillars of its baptistry, the walls of its sanctuary and sacred way, press against the rocks of the forested hillside on which it was built. The silence is absolute, save for the hum of cicadas. Butrint is one of those precious places of the world whose history is intense, but whose old stones shed the past in a simple emotional beauty.

Guarding as it did the once strategic straits of Corfu, it fell to one conqueror after another – Roman, Goth, Byzantine, Norman, Angevin, Venetian – until it lay forgotten in an obscure corner of the Ottoman empire, deep in the south west of Albania.

The peninsula on which Butrint stands is approached by a rough road from the small port of Saranda, leading through hillsides sliced with terracing where olives once grew. Most were cut down during the recent troubled years, felled after a thousand years for an evening's fuel. The road skirts the lake, whose silken waters are laced with lines of wooden frames, the delicate surface tracery of the mussel fishing below.

Butrint is virtually unknown, and is unmarred by souvenir kiosks, car parks and the usual trappings of tourism. Just a few youngsters, in T-shirts that proudly claim Butrint and its surroundings to be a World Heritage Site, volunteer to act as guides to the occasional coachload of visitors from Corfu.

The young Albanian in charge explains that they are trying to save Butrint and keep away any development, but the Institute of Monuments who are supposed to protect the site are corrupt. There are already problems – Butrint is one of the hundred world heritage sites most at risk. The water table is rising so that the steps of the amphitheatre look down on a pool instead of a stage. The museum set up in the 1960s in the restored acropolis, in the ruins of which Vlach shepherds once camped with their sheep, was looted in 1997 and is now empty and bolted. The fine mosaics of the baptistery are covered in sand to protect them.

The peninsula of Butrint juts out into the lake and is separated from the land opposite by the narrow Vivari channel. Around the end of the fifteenth century the Venetians built a triangular fortress on this further shore, and around it and its fisheries a small village grew up. Though a watercolour of 1820 by the English painter Henry Cook shows the fortress harbouring sailing ships, and linked to Butrint by rowing boats, it can now only be reached by a platform of roughly hewn wood planks winched across on chains and intended as a car ferry. I crossed on it to avoid the day's coachload of British holidaymakers from Corfu, and wandered round the ruins of the fortress, all that now remains of the settlement. No cars were making the return journey, so I was charged for the two it would have taken, and ferried across alone, sitting on the platform. It stopped dead four foot from the shore, the winch operator gesticulating from his cabin that I had to put more money down before he would pull it ashore.

A long time went by. I found myself humming a little ditty: 'oh, mister porter, what shall I do? I wanted to go to Albania and they've taken me on to Crewe'. After a few reprises this bored me, and another came to mind: 'for he's a jolly good fe-e-llow and Winston is his name'. However, this seemed to call for a raised glass and only increased my frustration. Finally, one of the T-shirted youngsters came into view, and as soon as I stood and hailed him, the platform moved sharply forward until it hit the bank.

I returned weeks later again to Butrint, but not to the fortress. It was the loveliness of the golden, unmortared stones, set in the peace of a gentle wilderness of woods and water, enlivened only by the ghosts of sailing ships and powerful men, that drew me back and set me journeying in circles round and round Albania, instead of travelling straight through, south to north.

There is a sharp division in Albania between south and north. The people south of the river Shkumbin are the Tosk, those to the north the Gheg.

The Tosks are mainly subsistence farmers, their society based on village life. There has always been a large presence of Greeks among them, and they were ruled from Ioannina, forming part of Ali Pasha's domain. The Tosks are mainly Orthodox Christian, their religion merely driven underground by the official atheism of Hoxha's period. The Ghegs in the north are a tribal society of closely-knit clans, Muslim and Catholic, hardly ruled from anywhere, but centred on Shkoder. It would be a while before I headed there.

In Circles II: The South East

Meanwhile, I left Gjirokaster on a shaky road across the mountains which followed the valley of the river Vjoses eastward. The first bridge over a gorge, a massive concoction of rusted struts and pinions, was so obviously strategic I wondered why it hadn't been blown up. The next one had.

As the bus climbed, loose shales spewed down adjacent precipices, and passengers vomited more and more exuberantly – every bus throughout Albania is provided with plastic bags that the driver hands out within a few minutes of leaving town. We saw one or two vehicles, driven with Toad-like bravado, but mainly we passed donkeys and mules, and horses lumbering under wooden saddles. People laboured in fields, with no sign of mechanised help. The men tended to be with horses, and the boys with sheep. The women attended to cattle or to crops, and wore big white poke bonnets and enveloping skirts. The corn had already been cut, undoubtedly by hand, so small sugar-loaf haystacks pimpled the landscape in little outbreaks. Everywhere slit-eyed bunkers watched our progress.

By Korça only two passengers were left, myself and one man. He cast a professional eye on the people milling around the bus stand. 'Have be care, have be care,' he whispered.

The main hotel in town had been blown up and was being repaired. I found another lesser version, then walked among the strolling citizens and bought a bottle of the local vodka for 30p. The market was in ruins and thronged with horses and carts. None wore amulets, though Edith Durham had said their harnesses were always hung with a blue bead. The old clothing was hardly even worth recycling, and included no embroidered linen shifts. There was absolutely nothing handmade for sale – just one little country family had a sheepskin, a hank of handspun wool and three pairs of handknitted socks. The woman chose the best for me to buy.

Hidden in an alleyway by the market was one of the oldest mosques in Albania, but Korça was obviously a Christian town. On the pavements, small shrines with painted icons aroused the weary passerby – fresh leaves and herbs had been offered and placed around them. A new Orthodox church, paid for with Greek money, dominated the main roundabout where the few paved streets met. Above the town, high on a hilltop, a huge cross looked partly towards Korça and partly south towards Greece. The town's proximity to Greece gave it an air of prosperity and buzz. There was even a post office selling phone cards, and in the main square, parked against the pavements like expensive yachts in a Riviera marina, were dozens of new Mercedes, every one registered in Korça. All through Albania, I was to find, most cars stayed in their home town and hardly ventured on the roads.

Korça was a town of easy emigration – to Greece and then America – so that money was trickling back in for building and repair. The new Orthodox church had been gutted in the recent troubled years, but plasterers and electricians were back at work. Still, nothing had yet been done about the two museums, both of which were empty and bolted. I left town on a Sunday, on a minibus – a *fugon* – taking day trippers north to the small resort of Pogradec, on the southern shore of lake Ohrid.

The road, potholed and nibbled at the edges, followed the strip of countryside that lay between the mountains, until it dropped down to the lakeside plain. Every small fertile patch was cultivated with strips of maize and tobacco. Hay was being scythed by hand, raked by hand, loaded on to horse and cart by hand.

Pogradec was virtually unspoilt, its long beach edged by a grassy promenade, behind which lay a street of small old houses, its low roofline snapped every so often by the insertion of a new hotel. Where now was grass along the shoreline, once had stood a row of lovely mansions. The communists had destroyed them, leaving just one as a museum of bourgeois decadence. That too had been looted and was now a bar. Beside it was a line of Hoxha's bunkers, cracked and overgrown with grass, their gun emplacements facing the lake. A woman sat by a pile of twenty bananas and five packets of crisps, embroidering a tablecloth in lazy daisy stitch with floral motifs that had nothing to do with the traditions of Albania, while she waited for custom.

It was on the fugon that I had met Gezim, taking his family on a day trip to Pogradec.

Gezim was so anxious to learn of the outside world, so profoundly aware that massive efforts had to be made to lift Albania into the twenty first century, and that most of his compatriots were unequal to the task, that he shouldered an almost impossible burden. As head of a primary school, and teacher of English to young adults, he stressed to his students that they were learning English to understand another culture, perhaps to be able to go abroad to study, but not to escape. They were always to come back to Albania to build the future of their country.

Gezim was in his early forties, his hair already completely grey. His wife, Natasha, was a sweet, smiling, slightly overweight woman, missing a front tooth. She taught Russian, but was now out of work as 'no one wants to learn Russian any more. The kids all want English.' They were embarrassingly hospitable. I was to return to Korça and stay with them. He would arrange a journey up to the mountain village of Dardha, where he knew old people still remembered their local costume. He would take me there and act as guide and interpreter.

I returned to Korça a few days later and called at his house, having carefully checked into a hotel first. The rules of hospitality were the same throughout Albania, I was to discover. Invited into a home, the guest was always sat down at a table on which was placed a glass of raki, a dish of sweets, a small saucer of plum jam with a teaspoon, a plate of Turkish delight and several serviettes arranged in a fan-shaped holder. The host and his family never partook, but just watched the guest eat – though I noticed Natasha later finished off the jam.

We spoke of the country's problems. When Albanians had first been allowed abroad, it was only nearby Macedonia that would accept them, and then only the inhabitants of Pogradec – a strong enclave of Orthodoxy – and then only for the day. Now it was easier. Gezim himself had been to Sweden, and the family took their holidays over the border in Greece. I asked about the crowds of young men outside the consulate in Gjirokaster, but he found that hard to understand. 'In Gjirokaster it's easy. They can walk to Greece over the mountains, get a job. I don't know why they need a visa.' But Gezim's feelings on emigration, especially illegal, were very strong. Albania would not survive unless people stayed, and he was devoting his life to help ensure that they did.

In 1997 the arsenals had been opened, he told me. Nobody knew how or why, and thousands of guns had been stolen. It was common to be robbed at gunpoint, and it was only now that it was safe for his family to go to Pogradec without being caught in somebody's crossfire. 'Crazy' people, 'cruel' people shooting each other were responsible for everything that had gone wrong since independence. And the politicians and leaders, of course. They needed new ones, not old ones who had just changed the name of their party. Like every other Albanian Gezim apportioned all the blame and responsibility elsewhere, though he was doing his best. He did not look in the least pleased with himself, but, as he sat comfortably in his acrylic upholstered chair, I thought I had never seen anyone whose expression was closer to the desperation of a drowning man.

If the Albanians of Boston and Phoenix put their money in Korça, it is to Dardha that they come on holiday. A tiny mountain village built around a spring of pure water, to those exiled – for ever, they presumed – it would epitomise all that was their homeland. Clinging to precarious slopes, a hidden refuge from the conquering Turks – its paths, walls and roofs merely stones cleft from the rocks that form its bed, its picket fences merely twigs from the forests that enclose it – its defensive poverty, its isolation and self-sufficiency mirror that of Albania itself. But change is coming. The spring, where the shepherd who discovered it first settled with his sheep, now feeds a small mineral water and orangeade factory. Most of the old stone houses have long been abandoned and have collapsed and then been left to rot.

From Dardha's heyday in the 1920s, when in a setting of breathtaking beauty the lives of the three thousand inhabitants fell deeper and deeper below subsistence level, a few houses had survived as Party holiday homes. Confiscated by the state, they were returned to their absent owners in 1991, and now these holidaying emigrants sat on white plastic chairs under vine-clad terraces, drinking the local raki, and thought about repairing them. The school had gone, the only permanent inhabitants now being a few old people. The five hotels had vanished long ago. The church that under the communists had been turned into a restaurant, its iconostasis hidden behind a screen and the icons removed by the villagers to their homes for safe-keeping, had now been reconsecrated.

Eight of us had gone from Korça to Dardha, piled in and on one small disintegrating car and an ancient ALCE motorbike, to a crumbling house recently restored to its rightful owner. Costanza was responsible for lunch, the traditional Albanian *burek*. She was insistent that I watch her every step, so that I could make it for my friends when I returned home. It was a leaden type of pizza, by which one pound of flour, one tomato and one onion, plus a smattering of butter and oil (which the shepherd's wife could omit if she didn't have it), fed eight people more than copiously. It took several hours to make, and the ratio of hard work to ingredients was disproportionate for the hostess of our little band of day trippers, let alone for a village woman who hauled water, carried wood, bore children, spun wool, wove and felted it, twisted braid and couched it into finery that would gain her a husband and a life, and still had to conjure meals from nothing.

There were no traditional costumes left in Dardha – most had been passed on to a daughter now living in Korça or Tirana. One old lady, sitting in her garden spinning, last wore hers in 1963. That year her husband died, and she never wore her costume again. Two women standing chatting on a steep stony path wore socks and aprons, and carried buckets and saucepans, but otherwise could have been in Korça.

When we returned there, I was given Gezim's young son to take on the bus with me to Elbasan and deliver to his uncles who had moved there. I hoped delivered safely as they were both money changers on the street, working the stretch between the hotel and the market. They spoke to me in French: in one of the bizarre twists of Balkan history Korça became a French republic in 1916 and remained under French military control until 1920.

In Circles III: Elbasan

In Elbasan, the old Turkish town of narrow streets and secretive houses still stood surrounded by its wall, and the ethnographic museum, housed in a beautiful villa, had survived unlooted. The men's reception room was palatial and carpeted, wide cushioned divans around the walls, the ceiling ornately carved. The women's was similar, just a few gold embroidered clothes hanging on the walls marking the difference. But it was the small attic room, with only a loom as furniture, that was unforgettable. Here, when a girl reached fourteen, she would be shut away until her marriage, required to spend all her days weaving and embroidering her dowry. Cotton scarves, shifts and towels, oya edgings, goldwork boleros and velvet dresses, aprons, floral brocades – her youth stolen in a prison that would ensure her future in another, that of marriage.

In the eight-storey hotel of Elbasan I was the only guest. The corridors rang hollow with my footsteps, the breakfast room had to be unlocked for me each morning.

In Circles IV: The Coast

F rom Elbasan I circled round and round the country, meeting no other
visitor. At ancient sites I was always the only person there, always
wandering alone. Among the ruins of Apollonia no one disturbed me.
Just the memories of Lear and of Byron followed me, even of Delacroix.
Apollonia was founded by the Corinthian Greeks and, like Butrint,
became an important Roman city on road and maritime routes. Now the
sea had receded, leaving the ruins of porticoes and theatres set on a beautiful hill of olive groves, overlooking a wide valley. The site had been
looted. Niches stood empty, headless statues lay around.

Apollonia can only be reached by taxi and I struck a deal with my driver
whereby the next day he would take me down the coastal road through
Vlore to Saranda. Eighty dollars for the two days. He took me to his
home, at least the home of his cousin who lives in America – he had lost
his own in the pyramid scam – and plied me with raki and sugar plums.
I was still happy with the deal.

The next day we drove past the calm waters of the Gulf of Vlore, boats
anchored in the stillness, faded baroque houses edging the waterfront.
Steep headlands encircled the gulf. We drove under one through a rough
unsurfaced tunnel of crude rock, hacked through the mountain, and
emerged on the coast road.

The terrain was wild.

'In Europe,' wrote Wadham Peacock in 1914, 'when a man speaks of a
road he means a more or less levelled surface, metalled and convenient for
motor, or at least for horse traffic. In Albania he means a track, or frequently
merely a direction, which he must adhere to in order to get from one place
to another.'

The road that follows the coast between Vlore and Saranda is such a
direction, lightly paved. It coils like a tight spring up the Çika mountains and twists open over crests to reveal valleys far below, their tiny green
fields and soft red roofs touched into life by the shafts of light that pierce
the high clouds. As the mountains plunge three thousand feet into the
Ionian Sea, another twist in the road lays open a panorama of misty peninsulas, distant mountains and a wooded coastal plain curving into limpid
pale grey water. It is a wild, untamed coastline, a tense clasping of
mountain and sea.

Just here and there the coastal plain spreads back into a valley clenched between steep scarps and set behind a deserted beach where the mountains dip to sea level. The road loops around the valley, the only signs of settlement perhaps a few olive groves and a small village of stone houses built defensively back from the sea, just a dozen of them in more than fifty miles. In some, especially in the little town of Himara, which Philip of Macedonia attacked in 214 BC, and where Ali Pasha massacred six thousand people in 1797, holiday homes and hotels are now slowly being developed.

In Circles v: Berat

Albania's history of brigandry and blood-feuds, of swirling white skirts and daggers – Byron's 'wild Albanian', kirtled to his knee – of romantic paintings steeped in the mystery of an orient not too distant but tinglingly threatening, had calcified over half a century or more into Hoxha's atheistic, suspicious, incarcerated cloud-cuckoo land. Only now was the country seeping out of its terrorised isolation, years behind the rest of the world, thrashing about, trying to find its role in a new century and a new Europe, still a tribal society, living in one of the most savage, raw wildernesses of mountain terrain in the world. An adulterated Eden littered with garbage and concrete bunkers.

The bunkers were everywhere, throughout the country, squatting like extraterrestrial slit-eyed beings about to advance. On the road up from Greece, they had had some kind of madman's logic to them, in that they lurked along the sides of the road, close to the shattered tarmac or in the scratchy bare hills above, their gun slits aimed in the direction of Greece. But travelling on through Albania it became more and more obvious that the concrete humps, peeping out under rampant grass, were the work of a complete lunatic. Sometimes they faced each other in rows across a field, so that they only had each other in their line of fire, sometimes they were clustered on some hillside that looked over nothing at all, sometimes there would be miles without a single one, and then, whoops, they were here again, dozens of them, lined up against each other on either side of a creek.

The gun slits never faced upwards so had any major world power been interested in bombing Albania it could simply have sent in a few out-of-date planes to deal with the bunkers – presuming they were manned throughout Hoxha's regime. And then in one or two remote areas it was clear that total dementia had set in, as little groups of them on obscure hillsides faced every which way. Like a small boy with games of soldiers, Hoxha seemed to have no concept of who he was ostensibly fighting or whether they knew they were in the game at all.

There were between seven hundred and fifty thousand and a million of these bunkers, I was told, though officially the number was closer to four hundred thousand. Each had cost the price of a large house. The essentials on which that money could have been spent – such as hospitals, roads, education – can never have been given priority. Yet literacy under Hoxha rose dramatically: an odd bedfellow with a bunker mentality.

The Albanians were unfathomable. They seemed incapable of talking without shouting, baring teeth and raising fists and picking up the nearest thing to hand – stone, branch – to attack the person they disagreed with. They would shoot each other, and strangers, with impunity, or offer raki and sticky plums. 'The Albanians are on a short fuse,' said the man at the British Embassy in Tirana, 'never argue with one.'

Though everywhere there was an underlying growl of danger, I met only kindness. 'Move, move, England!' the workmen in Saranda shouted as they were about to dynamite a building in my path. People directed me politely to looted, locked museums, wrecked churches, bolted shops, as if everything were still there and functioning as it should be. Or they would walk with me to show me where to go, rather than just tell me, and everywhere I rented a room the owner would carry my bag to the train or bus when I left. Always I was warned to take care.

I met Shkelqim on the fugon from Berat to Fier. He came from Berat, but was now studying medicine in Turkey and so felt he could see the problems of Albania from a detached, informed point of view. The pyramid scam was the fault of the Americans. 'They don't want to pay tax to their government, so they send this 'dirty money' to other places in the world to make 'clean money' out of it. First it was to Afghanistan, now Albania.' I asked about the graves by the roadsides. 'It's the best place to kill people,' he said. Some were blood feuds. He didn't use that word, but explained that if someone killed a man in your family, you had to find a man from his family to kill. Anyone would do, as long as they were male and older than seven. Then many of the graves were of men who had sent other men's sisters to Italy for prostitution, so the girls' fathers killed them.

There were not just graves along the roads, but whole new cemeteries, mostly of young men. It didn't seem possible that they were all killed in blood feuds. I suggested that maybe they had suddenly got hold of guns and rushed around shooting each other. He agreed that that was perhaps why, but then it was the fault of the people who gave them guns. I understood they stole them from the military arsenals, I replied. Then it was the fault of the people who let them into the arsenals. '1997 was not our fault,' he added.

He asked whether I liked Albania. I said I would love the place, but the crime and the litter got me down. 'In communist days,' said Shkelqim, 'we had clean-up days (I thought back to dear Eritrea), but when democracy came everyone understood they could do what they liked, so they throw rubbish everywhere and shoot each other.'

'And all these wrecked cars, abandoned factories and bunkers everywhere?' I asked.

'The wrecked cars are Italian. They don't survive more than a month here.' To my suggestion that it might have something to do with the terrible roads, 'no it's the fault of the cars. They are not new, they are secondhand.'

'And the factories?'

'Yes, we were wrong. When communism ended we destroyed all the factories, all the machinery, but we could have used them, used them to make other things. That was a mistake.'

I mentioned the men crowding round the Greek consulate in Gjirokaster when there was so much needing to be done to restore the town, even just to clean it up. 'Ah Greece,' he sighed. 'Greece owes everything to the Albanians. Its prosperity, its past, its future, everything is built on the Albanians.'

I sank into desolate silence, though I later learned there was a glimmer of truth in what he said.

'Here' – Shkelqim waved at the roadside and the four paltry trees beside it – 'here we had lovely trees every five metres.'

'Like France,' I commented, thinking of the destruction of the typhoon of 1999, but not mentioning it.

'Exactly, Enver Hoxha stayed in France and brought the idea here.' It was in fact King Zog who had lined the roads of Albania with shading elms.

'What happened to the trees?' I ventured to ask.

'I am shamed,' he said – the only time he used such a term – 'that we cut them all down and didn't replant them. So now there is nothing.'

I risked one last question. 'And the bunkers?'

'Oh, they would have been good in the time of the Second World War, the concrete was too thick for a bomb to go through, but, after, no use. One million of them.'

'It looks like the work of a little boy playing with soldiers,' I suggested. He nodded almost wearily and then sparked up again.

'Come to Kayseri.' He handed me his card. 'I will be there for four years.' While in Turkey he was a medical student, when he returned to Albania it was as a businessman with an ill-fitting suit and a serious brief-case, selling goods, though he did not specify what, together with his brother and nephew. Though anxious to be in time for an appointment, he found me a hotel, accompanied me there and carried my small bag. The next day there was a letter from him, hoping everything was alright. I felt fortunate to have fallen on a young man who epitomised everything Albanian.

Shkelqim's home town of Berat was the other museum-town of Albania, but whereas Gjirokaster was raw, rough, cut from and at one with the stone of its mountainside, Berat was neat. Its white, wide-windowed houses stood pinioned one above the other in an orderly gradient of Ottoman wealth and precision, serried up and up to the hand-hewn citadel at its crest.

The streets of this Muslim quarter were the width of a donkey, some stepped, some trapped by a blank stone wall until they twisted again. They wound in a maze of corners and slopes, the huge stones at their edges, painted white as the walls themselves, not a fallen part of the house but an outcrop of the mountainside. Rivulets ran down the centre as gutters, dark wooden arched doors broke the glare of white. The Christian town lay across the river, over a seven-arched stone bridge.

The citadel grew organically from the mountain top and the ancient Illyrian fortress that preceded it: there could not have been anything but a fortified refuge on such a commanding peak. It was entered by a massive stone gateway of the fourth century BC, unmarked by any trifles from succeeding centuries save the recent political graffiti PD-PD on each side of the portals. No tourist notices or souvenir kiosks marred its pristine strength. I was there alone.

Though there was no one around, the citadel was lived in. Washing hung on lines, the odd dog skulked in the shadows of the dry-stone walling. Everything was made by hand from the stones around, uncut, jammed together, rock and pebble, into a fluid village of pathway, wall and roof. The fourteenth century Byzantine church of the Holy Trinity clung to the mountainside, a soft building of walls first of unhewn stone, then more neatly layered with mortar, broken by arched windows of brown brick, and brooded over by the cluster of arches and domed tower that formed its roof, their pale pink tiles weathered greenish. Far below by the river lay the new town, and hills rolled away into the distance.

Miraculously, the icons in the citadel museum and the cathedral's exquisite carved iconostasis and high wooden pulpit decorated with snakes' heads had been neither damaged nor looted.

Nor had the ethnographic museum, an eighteenth century mansion in the town below, entered from a magnificent carpeted balcony, furnished with divans and commanding a view of the citadel. Here only men had been allowed. The women lived above in dark rooms, behind wood-barred windows, as in Elbasan. The costumes in the museum were of urban goldwork, Turkish in style, on velvet and silk. There were men's garments of fulled wool and goathair, decorated with braid. Only the village women's clothes, of white cotton and heavily embroidered, were of real interest. But there were no talismanic patterns, no triangles, no stylised goddesses. And there was nothing of linen. As more than three quarters of Albania is mountain, so was sheep-rearing the main activity, and so was there felt, knitting, weaving and fulled wool. Flax can only have been cultivated on the plains around the Roman settlements – Butrint, Apollonia, Durrës.

In Circles VI: Tirana

Tirana is approached from the south through mountainous terrain along a narrow hogback, whose sides fall steeply away into deep valleys crushed between high ranges, some wooded, some bare, that roll away, ridge after ridge, as far as the eye can see.

The city is bizarre: not one destroyed by war being busily rebuilt, but a city completely skewed. On the one hand it is a grandiose place of open squares and wide avenues, of buildings in a splayed-out townscape of Austro-Hungarian baroque, decorated in pink and yellow plaster, with pedimented windows and inlaid medallions, built in fact by the Italians. Then on the other hand, are narrow rubble-strewn lanes of sordid houses frequented by louche money changers and phone card sellers. Everywhere are half-started or half-finished, or never-to-be-finished, scaffolded incipient tower-block slums, and just here and there glitzy, newly completed buildings that stand alongside Soviet-inspired mono-liths decorated with 'Workers of the World Unite' – type paintings on their façades. People sit along the pavements, a dozen bananas laid out in front of them, individually priced, selling them one by one. Others are busy filling little paper flutes with sour cherries and plums.

The whiff of corruption is everywhere. There is no logic to anything, no sense of destruction and renovation, of slump and boom. Just a blank past on which banana sellers, property developers, kiddies' round-about operators, money changers and gunmen, chance their arm like poker players. Only the vagaries of a corrupt system could explain, or even just try to, the oddities of this capital city that is merely an overde-veloped village encircled by squatters.

In the National Museum there were cult goddess figures from 6000 BC, and a bronze amulet of indeterminate animal shape from about 1000 BC. I saw absolutely no one wearing any sort of amulet, nor any for sale in the market, but on the rear view mirrors of their cars they hung shiny CD discs and US one-dollar notes. Nor was anyone wearing anything embroidered. The style was more Bangkok Ralph Lauren, and T-shirts with silly slogans 'You on the Boulevard'.

I called at the British Embassy to find out about the north. It was halfway down a tree-lined avenue of embassies, guarded at each end to keep Albanians out since it was swamped in 1991 by people seeking asylum. There were no warning notices, as in Eritrea, but I was firmly told not to go to the north east, which was mined and where armed robbery was rife. The border into Montenegro had been reopened four months previously, but was now closed again. 'Never resist Albanian men,' I was told, 'just give them what they want. They're all armed, everyone's got a gun hidden under his clothes.'

As I strolled back into town I looked on the macho young hooligans in tight trousers and skimpy T-shirts with more benevolence, whereas their paunchy elders draped in baggy trousers and loose lurid shirts seemed eminently threatening.

I lodged with Nos, an 81-year old Italian speaker, his only other guest a young Norwegian lawyer taking lessons in Albanian. So many refugees had come into Norway that he could see a lucrative future in litigation, once he had mastered their language. The only other person in the house was Nos's wife, who never left the kitchen. Their walled garden of paving and plants was full of cats and bits of wool. Nos carded mattresses for a living.

Nos was a fervent believer in the benefits of communism. Then everything was secure and everyone worked. Now even the young have no jobs, especially as they wrecked the country in '97. It's all drugs and prostitution and crime. The Democratic Party are responsible for all that's gone wrong.

Gezim had remarked, I told him, that no one, not even any political party, could definitely be blamed for anything. No one had any idea what was really going on. They were all like wasps flying around in a cloud of smoke. And in any case, Gezim felt, no one had any real belief in any political party. It was all a question of vested interests, and that handled with circumspection.

I thought to ask Nos about amulets, seeing no one had commented on the Asian and African ones hanging round my neck, only on the Catholic medallion I had bought from a bus driver in Gjirokaster. At his age he would be sure to know of any tradition that once existed and might now have died out. He replied rather haughtily: 'we are the intelligentsia, we have no truck with such primitive beliefs,' this being a rendering in English of the more pithy Italian.

Kruje

The citadel of Kruje was, for twenty five years from 1443, the seat of the national hero of Albania, George Kastrioti, known as Skenderbeg. Here he fought off the Turks and established Albanian resistance to their rule, so that the citadel holds a special place in the people's hearts. It stands on a prominent ridge below commanding mountains, a huge blue Pepsi hoarding beside it brightening the majestic scene.

The town's hotel, predictably called the Skenderbeg, had been slumbering since communist times and its grimy, broken windows afforded a glimpse of a new one just built across the road. This offered a direct view across a deep valley of the Pepsi hoarding and the citadel, and was justly named the Panorama. The price was the same. No one else was staying there. The owner's mother fussed and brought a vase of plastic flowers into my room. She smiled, caressed my cheek and kept asking 'burre?' I shook my head. She patted me and walked out. I looked up burre in the Birmingham phrase book. 'Man' or 'husband' it meant, though it recalled the Spanish for 'donkey'. It was the same question asked wherever I travelled – 'where's your husband?' 'Son, then?'

From my room I could see in the valley between the hotel and the citadel a narrow stone street of stalls hung with old costumes, skirts from Shkoder, shifts embroidered in the style of the Catholic villages around Kruje, and objects of folk art less easily recognised from a distance. It was once the Turkish bazaar, built in the eighteenth century, destroyed and rebuilt as a quarter for artisans. I hurried down.

The short, steeply sloping street, was made of uneven rocks tumbled together, polished by hoof of horse and donkey. This was *kaldrmi*, that Edith Durham describes as '*large irregular stones jammed together to make a roadway. You cannot call it a pavement. There is no word in any other European language to express it. It is kaldrmi... no one ever thinks of driving or walking on it if there is any way of dodging it.*' Down its centre ran a gulley, presumably once carrying a stream or drainage, or even the rubbish that now was scattered more discreetly along the sides. Stalls of heavy, dark wood on a stone base were approached up high stone steps, fadingly whitewashed. Their deeply sloping roofs overhung so far that they almost touched across the lane. They, too, were of dark wood, topped with curved red tiles of Mediterranean style and carved below in zigzag patterns. The fronts of the stalls were completely covered by wooden shutters that lifted vertically on metal rods to expose the windows, and provide hooks on which goods could be displayed.

Though the stalls were supposed to be premises for working artisans, they had deteriorated into small shops, only two rug weavers still actually working. One looked at my goddess pattern and confirmed that it was a very common motif on Albanian rugs. But it didn't mean a thing.

Only the eagle was symbolic.

The market was presumably destined for tourists in the brief few
years when these had begun to filter in after the opening of the borders
in 1991 and the 'troubles' of '97. Now there was just an elderly French
couple. The woman wanted to buy a carved wooden cradle and had
plonked herself down outside the stall, spreading like lard across its stone
step. Her small anxious husband looked like Aznavour, and *'tu te laisses
aller'* hummed through my mind. 'Mais ça se demonte, Bernard.' Goats
and donkeys wandered by. He rubbed his hands in dismay. 'Mais nous
avons la voiture, Bernard.' This he was unable to contest in the face of
a lifetime of dismay.

Hanging from the hooks were red woollen bags worked with the
Albanian flag of the double eagle in black, leather belts, the black bell-
shaped woollen skirts of Shkoder, sheep's bells, tin pots, coats of white
fulled wool appliquéd in red braid and couched thread of yellow and white,
knitted socks, carved distaffs and cradles. It was a street of a myriad treasures, and was perhaps fifty metres long. I took four days to get down it.

One of the stalls was a restaurant, where I took my evening meals. The
same one, in fact, as they gave me far too much on the first night and
so, by mutual agreement, bits of the shish kebab and chips were fried
up again for me each time I called. The restaurant was small, dark, without electricity. The ceiling was of dark wood, the chairs and tables of dark

wood, laid with red check tablecloths like washing-up towels. It was like Germany a hundred years ago. There was no one else there. And when the electricity came back on, Tom Jones was belting out *Delilah*.

The food in Albania had turned out to be slightly monotonous, but rather good. Most things were deliciously organic – the butter crumbling and tasting of hot cow, the bread warmly baked, the eggs laid only yesterday but without the need of a stamp to say so, the fruit rotting before it reached the shops. In the markets, I noticed, fruit and vegetables were sold from pallets piled up on the mouldering refuse of the previous weeks.

Drink was slightly more problematic. It would be suspect vodka with Albanian lemonade, local rrushi raki with Greek peach juice or Yugoslavian slivovitz with Coke. And the restaurant in Kruje offered wine: 'Dry Red Wine of Korça region. Reserve 1998, gentle aroma and mild well-rounded taste. Best served chilled', which with any luck might disguise its acrid and overly tannic taste.

Kruje could almost have been the end of my travels, as it was there in the street of stalls that I found the amulet of a triangle with three pendants I had been searching for, this time carved on an old wooden distaff. The tools of spinning – spindles and distaffs – are a repository of ancient beliefs, fears and aspirations, carved with pagan symbolism. For women spinning share the same magical powers as blacksmiths and dyers in their ability to change a natural substance, powers that evoked fear of the supernatural in the plodding agricultural and shepherding societies in which they found themselves.

Women span whenever they could. On lonely vigils watching over cows and sheep, on quiet evenings together, when suitors might call presenting a distaff they had carved for the spinster they fancied. Special baskets, like knapsacks, were made to carry purchases home from market, leaving the woman's hands free to spin as she walked. Today in Albania – as in Ethiopia – women still stand in the fields, or in their gardens, spinning.

I bought a Vlach amulet in Kruje, too, a beaded version of the pagan solar motif of an eight-pointed star. The same pattern was the most common motif on the white shifts of the women from the mountain villages around Kruje. Though they were ostensibly Catholic, the women clung to pagan patterns that were mostly solar. The only motif remotely like a goddess was a simple triangle topped by a diamond, but with no arms and no pendants. And there was no sign of linen – their white shifts were now all of cotton.

I continued north to Shkoder. The cloaks of Catholic women there were embroidered with snakes and doves, claimed by Edith Durham to be symbols of the mother goddess worshipped at Knossos, and an important element in Egyptian mythology.

Shkoder

Photographs show Edith Durham as a slim young girl dressed in a smocked flowery dress with frilly white collar, her hair cut short and her eyes too intense for her pretty face. As a middle-aged woman she stands, stout and commanding, hand on hip, dressed in a no-nonsense long tweed skirt, buttoned-up blouse and shaggy hooded Albanian cloak. Her hair is still short. '*The Montenegrin proverb,*' she writes, '*says "long hair, short wits, a woman's head", and as I wore my hair short, an uncommon thing in those days, the simple folk accepted the fact that my wits must be long.*'

Mary Edith Durham, born in 1863, had no formal higher education save a training in drawing, but inherited the role of so many eldest daughters of Victorian families of eight siblings – that of looking after her parents. First her father, an eminent surgeon who became chronically sick, then her mother, no doubt a demanding and querulous patient. At thirty seven and still unmarried '*the future stretched before me in endless years of grey monotony, escape seemed hopeless.*' Her enlightened doctor, sensing depression, prescribed two months away every year: '*get right away, no matter where, so long as the change is complete.*' She took, in 1900 in the company of a friend, a trip on an Austrian Lloyd steamer along the Dalmatian coast, and her life changed forever.

It was first the embroidered costumes, particularly those of the men, that held her in thrall. From this her interest widened into the customs and beliefs of the Balkan people, of which of course the costumes were part. She returned every year, having learnt Serbian, and embarked on ever wilder and more dangerous travels. The Balkans became her purpose in life.

Though her interest in embroidery, and the anthropological and ethnographic lanes it led her down, remained always at the heart of her activities, it was in aid work and then in politics that she became more and more embroiled. The relevance of one to the other was clear to her: *'the vexed question of Balkan politics might be solved by studying the manners and customs of each district and so learning to whom each place should really belong.'*

She returned to the Balkans as a relief worker during the Macedonian uprising of 1903, and the Albanian tribal revolt of 1911 against the Ottoman, to give medical and humanitarian aid. During the Balkan wars she became the first woman war correspondent, and the most knowledgeable interpreter in England of Albanian affairs.

She worked tirelessly for recognition of Albania's right to independence, not endearing herself to the Foreign Office and British politicians: *'Miss Durham is a remarkable woman with a great command of strong language'*, *'an extremely unattractive manner'*, *'a difficult woman'*. She was considered wildly eccentric or even absolutely mad. But that was in Europe. In Albania she was respected and loved, and still is. There are streets named after her in almost every town, and in Shkoder even a small shop – *Artikuj: Kulture: Miss Edith Durham*. It was always closed. From the usual cack-handed manipulations of language, fortified by gesticulations, I learned from the neighbour that the owners were away at the seaside swimming.

It was to Shkoder that Durham first went, having discovered that the 'magnificently garbed' Albanian men she met in Montenegro came from there. Shkoder, then known by its Italian name of Scutari, is one of the oldest cities in Europe. It lies close to the strategic crossing of the Buna and Drin rivers and the ancient coastal route from Greece to Montenegro, where already in 500 BC an Illyrian fortress stood.

Shkoder has always been the centre of Catholicism in Albania. Albania was converted early to Christianity – Galerius is recorded as already persecuting the Thracian/Illyrian tribes in the early years of the fourth century, and by AD 387 Shkoder was the seat of an archbishopric. But Catholics, Franciscans and Jesuits are all established there, the Catholics faithful to the Pope, the Franciscans supported by Austria, and the Jesuits, in counterbalance, by Italy. Now in Gjirokaster nuns from Italy are trying to establish Catholicism there, Doshira had told me when I asked about the bells I heard, but Catholicism is the religion of the north. That of the south is Orthodoxy.

In Shkoder a new Orthodox church is being built, right next to the brand new, glitteringly kitsch mosque with pastel façade and silver domes. The competition between religions seems more an affair of politics than faith. Orthodoxy strengthens the position of Greece, and Catholicism that of Italy. As for Islam, its hold hardly warrants the brutality of ethnic cleansing by the Serbs, and the retaliatory militancy of the new Albanian National Liberation Army against its Christian neighbours: no woman is veiled, no one wears modest clothing – least of all the young – everyone drinks vodka and raki, no one mentions observing Ramadan or going on a Haj to Mecca. And it is always the church bells that ring louder than the muezzin.

I wandered round town. None of the houses or roads was being repaired. The town's rubbish lay in rotting piles delicately picked over by the fastidious paws of emaciated cats. At least, as in Tirana, it was heaped together instead of being hurled to the four winds as in the south, as if the citizens had tried to exercise some control.

The pretty gaslit street of wealthy mansions leading from the museum must have been one that Durham walked along and sketched. Most of the buildings are now gutted, the decorated pediments cracked, the wooden shutters hanging adrift. They look exactly like Durham's drawing of the sacristy in Shkoder after its bombardment in 1912. The museum has vanished and in its place a bar and restaurant, approached over an open trench, serve Coke and pizzas to the young. Along another of the roads radiating from the grass roundabout, grazed by horses, that forms a sort of town centre, all the buildings have been reduced to heaps of rubble.

The Catholic cathedral, turned into a palace of sports under communism and rededicated just before Pope Paul's visit in 1993, is locked. The imposing Franciscan church, turned into an auditorium under communism, and then back to a church displaying photographs of the priests of Shkoder who died in communist prisons, is freshly painted, washed in pale turquoise. The photographs have gone, only a tiny smudge of fresco has been left. At evening service the vast space held eight worshippers.

The undertaker's little shop lay suitably close to the Catholic cathedral, its windows decorated with a variety of crosses, and floral wreaths of tropically exuberant pink and red plastic flowers pimpled by phoney dewdrops. Among the larger crosses, which one could imagine a priest at the head of a funeral procession bearing aloft with dignity, were a few tiny ones made of wood, threaded on to a cord and clearly to be hung round the neck. I entered the shop. Much of its space was taken up by coffins, and the walls were lined with bigger and better plastic wreaths bizarrely oval in shape.

The elderly man stood up from his table and the usual stuttering conversation in several languages took place, aided by the accomplished gesture that I now presumed indicated to everyone else that I was talking about the evil eye. Were these amulets? The Birmingham booklet let me down again, as it already had that day when I wanted to enquire about the 'lake' of Shkoder, such a geographical feature presumably not being an important aspect of Albanian asylum seekers' needs in Birmingham. I tried again. 'Skumi pak,' the undertaker seemed to write, which had such connotations it would certainly not have appeared in the Birmingham booklet. 'Aufschreiben,' I contributed to the general malfunction of one language alone, 'Gegen il malocchio.' Fastidiously picking out, like the town cats, the words I understood, the rest, in Albanian, was lost on me, except that the word 'Christian' kept surfacing.

I bought one of his wooden crosses anyway as they were far less like a cross than an angel, indeed a flying angel, indeed a goddess. I forgot to ask whether it was made of hawthorn – and my faith in Birmingham had now entirely vanished – but I hung it round my neck along with the rest of the talismanic clutter I had by now acquired.

As for embroidery, the costume of Shkoder used to be one of the most decorative of Albania. The 'magnificent garb' that brought Durham here was that worn by the boatmen of Shkoder's port and described by Wadham Peacock in 1914:

> The small boats which take the passengers from the steamer to the pier were manned by boatmen whose appearance was that of brigands, and whose looks and gestures were those of all the ruffians of history and legend put together. These men were dressed in tight-fitting clothes of white felt embroidered with black; on their heads they wore white felt caps, in some cases bound round with a sort of turban of dirty white cotton; on their shoulders some of them wore a black sheepskin, and on their feet they wore raw hide sandals tied with leather straps. In their belts were arsenals of weapons, pistols and long knives, and with eyes flashing and moustaches bristling they argued at the top of their voices in guttural Albanian over the passengers, and seemed within

an ace of coming to blows with their primitive oars, or of drawing the vicious-looking knives and blades from their belts. The timid and unaccustomed travellers might be excused for hesitating to entrust themselves to such theatrical-looking brigands, but the officers of the ship evidently looked on them as quite normal persons, and occasionally addressed them with polite authority in Italian, which most of the boatmen could speak in moments of calm.

As for the women and girls, in the mountains around Shkoder, the heavy bell-shaped woollen skirts they wore, made from horizontal strips and believed to be of Illyrian origin, are unique in the world. And in the town of Shkoder itself, both Catholic and Muslim would wear indoors the giubba, a long sleeveless woollen coat embroidered with gold cord and deeply flared at the back, a shape deriving from ancient garments of the Tartars. The huge loose Turkish trousers, that look almost like a voluminous skirt, and which are still worn in Kosovo I was later to discover, Peacock also comments on. Those of the Muslims were made of silk, the Orthodox of gaily printed cloth and for the Catholics of 'horribly crackling glazed calico'. Out of doors, married Catholic women would wear the *japangi*, a red wool cloak with embroidered panels at neck and front. These were made by the men tailors, and their traditional pattern always included a bird, a snake, flowers and ears of corn. When Durham asked them why, they could only guess *'it must be some old tale, long forgotten.'* The japangi was given by the bridegroom to his bride and when he died she removed the embroidered panels and replaced them with black stripes. On this outfit Peacock comments that *'in fact no dress more absolutely unbecoming to women has ever been invented than that of the Latin women of Scodra. But in a few years' time it will no doubt have disappeared almost entirely.'*

And what is left of all this glorious costume? Traditional dress was still worn everywhere in the 1950s, and under the Chinese influence of Hoxha's years, silkworm production was set up in co-operatives around Shkoder to manufacture threads for the embroideries. The embroidered trousers were the first to go – the men of peasant societies always abandon local costume before the women, as they leave their villages to go off to fight. Indeed, Durham reports of a fiancée busily embroidering numbers of trousers for her prospective groom absent at war, only to be told on his return that he now wants western clothes. Find another fiancé who'd appreciate the trousers, was Durham's retort.

Women no longer wear the heavy woollen skirts and jackets. As the wool for all costume used to be felted in fulling mills worked by water power, where it was pounded for several days by heavy walnut wood hammers, it can be assumed that this industry died long ago. The white shirts, blouses and skirts always used to be made of linen, hand woven from hemp or flax, but linen is easily replaced by purchased cotton. So in Shkoder, and particularly in the villages around, some older women still dress in this way. They sit at the roadside, resting by their market purchases, their brown faces almost masculine, with sharp noses, and icy clear eyes that could easily conceal the malocchio. Their clothes are all handmade: white blouses embroidered in white satin stitch in diagonal patterns with small touches of red, and beautiful white needlelace on the shoulders; white trousers, white very full gathered skirt, blue apron, blue bolero and a striped belt wound round and round the waist with finely worked tassels hanging down the back. Perhaps even a gun tucked in it.

The night in Shkoder was fitful, any peace or hope of sleep shattered by the howling packs of prowling dogs and the disco marriage music that pulsated from the bar opposite the hotel, that had once been the gentle, instructive museum, nineteenth century palace home of an eccentric English aristocrat. This disco wailing became a frequent occurrence as it was by now August, and August is the best month for marriages: the first baby will be delivered in time for the woman to be set to work in the fields again for next year's harvest.

One version of Albanian history claims that in 1924 a fairly liberal government was set up by Fan Noli, but overthrown in the same year by the revolutionary Ahmet Zogu. Another that the revolutionary government of Fan Noli was ousted by the politician Ahmet Zogu, whose reign ensured years of political stability. What is certain is that he declared himself king, King Zog I, in 1928, and allied Albania with Italy. At the Italian invasion of 1939 he was forced to flee and, rifling the gold of the Albanian treasury, he settled in England, in a suite at the Ritz hotel, where his retinue was known to the Foreign Office as King Zog's Circus. His country home is just outside Shkoder.

I took a taxi ride outside town to the Rozafa fortress, founded by the Illyrians and rebuilt by Venetians and Turks, and on to Lake Shkoder to see Zog's local villa. A pink Italianate mansion on a hillside, approached by a once magnificent flight of steps, it commanded an impressive view of the lake and Yugoslavia beyond. It was completely trashed. Broken glass, bricks, plaster, ceiling mouldings lay smashed all over the floors that were gashed with so many holes they left only precarious walkways. Old mattresses, bits of their stuffing everywhere, remains of fires and blackened walls, scorched planks ripped from the wooden floors, horse shit, red beer cans and peach stones thrown around made it clear that the villa was camped in. A place of refuge where cicadas sang.

Every time Albania changes, the people rip up the past completely.

Though in Saranda I had hung around a yellow Land Rover Defender, painted with the insignia MERLIN, Medical Emergency Relief International, and with a no-guns sign like a no-smoking one, registered in England T193FXP, just in the hope of having someone to talk to, in the end the Westerners I met in all the time I was in Albania could almost be counted on one hand. There was Beryl, a sociologist from Newcastle working in Gjirokaster, there was a Belgian girl with an aid association in Korça, the Norwegian in Tirana, Bernard and his wife in Kruje, and there was a British policeman visiting Butrint who was working for MAPE – the Mission to Albania for Police Education. He had been sent for six months to train policemen in the ways of the west, and his wife had joined him on holiday – some places were better than others, Kukes was really bad, and he thought they were slowly making some progress, but corruption was an extra problem it was hard to deal with.

And that was it. No other. It was therefore all the more remarkable that, turning the corner by the Franciscan church in Shkoder, I should come face to face with four people who had all the air of being Brits, and that they should be Professor James Pettifer, expert on the Balkans and author of the Blue Guide to Albania, with his wife Sue and friends.

Consuls clearly have always erred on the side of over caution. When Durham travelled to Shkoder from Montenegro, the consul feared she would be molested, but far from that, she was given roses and coffee. In Tirana I'd been told to go nowhere near the north east – uncontrolled banditry, keep well away, you'll be fair game for armed robbery.

'They don't know,' said Pettifer. 'They never leave Tirana.'

In London, Foreign Office information for Albania, June 2000, was clear: *'Criminal activity and lawlessness remain common throughout the country. We advise against all but essential travel to the north east of Albania and against all travel to the area close to the border with Kosovo, especially Bajram Curri and Tropoje. In addition to the increased criminal activity in the area, there is also the possibility of unexploded ordnance along the Albanian/Kosovo border. The roads in the area are also in poor condition.'*

'You can get a ferry up the Drin,' said Pettifer. 'If you get stuck in Fierze or Bajram Curri, don't panic.'

'I never panic,' I said, with the confidence born of experience.

'On Wednesday mornings,' he continued, 'there's a market in Prizren and the women come down from the mountain villages in their costumes. They wear a funny sort of apron mounted on a wooden bar across the hips. It sticks out each side. For carrying babies and shopping. I don't think it exists anywhere else.'

Blood feuds and the way out

The most potent image of Albania's troubles, for the West, must be the television pictures in 1991 of twenty thousand young Albanian men, thin, ill-clad, bewildered, cramming the quayside of Brindisi, having stolen ships at Vlore and Durrës to get across the Adriatic. Some were allowed to stay, but when in 1992 another destitute ten thousand arrived, Italy was still trying to absorb those from the previous year, and sent them all back. In place of offering asylum, she instigated a food aid programme that saved Albania from mass starvation. But when later Italy sent $7million in humanitarian aid most of it was stolen. Perhaps by the Albanian mafia, perhaps by the Italian before it ever left.

The hostile mountainous terrain of Albania affords little fertile land – mainly the coastal plain and some inland valleys. The population was always small, but increased rapidly under Hoxha when both contraception and abortion were illegal, and the blood feuds, which killed many men, outlawed. Pressure on land and food intensified, so that the desire to escape was overwhelming once Albania's fifty-year isolation from the rest of the world ended in 1991, and people discovered that Hoxha's torture and repression had merely been replaced by total destruction of their environment. The refugee problem on Italy's doorstep hit the headlines.

To leave Albania without a visa by escaping by sea to Italy is now almost impossible, and over the mountains to Greece very difficult – in spite of the fact that border guards no longer face twenty years in prison if they let someone through – but via Corfu is a possibility, catching the ferry from Saranda to Corfu and from there the bus to Athens.

The Albanians sat at Corfu bus station waiting. They were easily recognized from their fair hair and hooked noses, their cheap clothes and worn, dusty shoes, and their general air of bemusement. They clung together in the café buying nothing. There was a glazed, disinterested look in their eyes as a young woman busied herself emptying the rubbish bins, tying the plastic bags, placing them on a trolley, replacing them with clean ones, as if they were watching some incomprehensible ritual. But they observed carefully, their hands behind their backs, rubbing their thumbs along the edge of their fingers, the baggage being loaded on the bus. They had no baggage.

The Albanians live by an ethic at odds with the rest of the world. It is called the *Kanun of Lek*. A code of honour, inherited probably from the Illyrians, it allows no place for honesty or responsibility or love of one's fellow men, nor for any of the virtues that might be believed to make society function. Instead, it is a scourge placed on the shoulders of every male, a tribal mafia based on revenge and protection, and designed to serve each *fis*, or clan, to the detriment of all others. Though the laws of the Kanun of Lek are known to most people only orally, they are part of every Albanian's moral heritage. They are the basis of the blood feuds. They centre on honour, honour that, if offended, must be avenged with blood. Revenge continues generation through generation – an offence, even seemingly trivial, even to a great-grandfather, can only be cleared by killing any male over the age of seven belonging to the fis of the offender. Blood feuds, the American Peace Corps noted, involved by the spring of 1996 sixty thousand people in northern Albania and there were nine hundred vendetta deaths that year. And that was before the feuds broke into the open again in 1997.

Women are exempt, not because they are held in any esteem, but because they are of no consequence, though if all the men in a family are killed, the eldest daughter must replace them, so becoming an eligible target. She must take on the debts of honour of the family, remain a virgin and live as a man. Other such virgins living as men, are girls betrothed as children who refuse the man chosen for them. They can belong to no other and have to assume the mantle and life of a man.

Women are generally expendable. If found on marriage not to be a virgin they can, under the laws of Lek, be killed by the husband. The bullet is supplied by the bride's father, so that no blame falls on the husband and no revenge is needed. Even today, I was assured.

But, in contrast, women are powerful in the world of superstition. The protective pagan devices that are shared by many societies are always in the hands of women, if not of shamans. Their menstruation and pregnancy are almost supernatural, their long hair must be kept hidden – even indoors – by a bonnet or scarf in fear of the tangible link it holds with the spirit world. Birds, too, have this function of a fleeting clasp on the world of men and that of spirits. Evil spirits lurk in dogs and in darkness, but the European fear of crossroads and groves of birch has no place among the winding goat tracks and bare crags of Albania.

But the devices known to protect against evil spirits, the evil eye, wolves and eerie manifestations of the night, are not expected to be efficacious in the face of a blood feud.

The Kanun of Lek has always been the way of life of Albania, particularly in the inaccessible mountains of the north beyond Ottoman control. It was confidently felt that King Zog would ban it, but he failed to do so. He made the veiling of women illegal, but left the blood feud alone. Hoxha outlawed it, replacing it with a regime of a different sort of terror, but it merely went underground and exploded again in 1991 and particularly in 1997, when even the south shed its veneer of western ideas and Greek influence, and the old mentality of Albania affected Tosk and Gheg alike. It is clan survival, but whereas the men used to hunt their presumed enemy with knives, now they have guns and all the scams of stolen Mercedes, drugs and prostitution bedevilling further what seems to the outside world a stone-age mentality. To the young Albanian male, emigration is the only escape from the burden of the blood feud.

Though revenge killings and armed robbery were here the norm, I glided innocently and trustingly above such things. I clambered on to old buses, wandering alone and carrying cash, there being no effective banking system, and was always looked after. The buses might amble past innumerable roadside shrines to those shot dead as their cars were stolen, I was only ever treated with total honesty and immense courtesy. For, if honour and blood feuds are at the heart of the Albanian's moral responsibility, so, too, is *besa*, the concept of the overriding importance of the unknown guest.

Responsibility towards a guest is well known as a major aspect of the Islamic and Arab world – in Albania it is a cornerstone of the Kanun of Lek. Once a guest enters the domain of a family, in any way whatsoever – let's say holding on to one of their goats, stepping on their path – he is to be honoured, even to the detriment of that family and its fis. Coffee and raki have to be offered: protection against harm as well. If a man of any family accompanies his guest on his way, he is then responsible for any dishonour that might befall him, and so would have to revenge him in blood. Once I knew this, the simple act of carrying my bag to the bus or station, that all the owners of the pensioni I had stayed at had done, acquired a tremendous significance. Until it occurred to me that, as I was a woman, they probably incurred little actual risk. Nevertheless, besa was there.

In so many respects the tribal life of the Albanians of the northern mountains is just like that of the high valleys of the Hindu Kush and western Himalaya where I began my travels in search of the triangular amulet. I had come full circle. The blood feuds, and the stone towers where men take refuge, sometimes even for years, are the same. The effect on the clan and family, where only the women are free to walk and work the fields, is the same: without the men there is no one to do the heavy work, the fields are left untended, the economy of the village slumps. And no children are born. In the valley of Palas in Indus Kohistan this was described as a way of 'population control'.

Then the people of the two mountain areas share the same precarious subsistence farming – a mangy, undernourished animal or two, a terrace or so of some poor crop of dwindling genetic strength. The snarling guard dogs that strain on their chains at night, their fangs splicing the dark with sharp spikes of witching gleam, are the same. They share the extreme isolation, even the primitive lighting of their fortress homes by burning resinous pine. There was so much in northern Albania that linked the beginning of my journeys with the end.

And where would that end be?

It should have been in the north, perhaps in the forgotten safe-haven of the Bosnian war, Banja Luka, where a watered-down version of the linen goddess could be found, or in Sarajevo, a town that no one forgets. The north I knew, but sadly when I travelled through Tito's Yugoslavia twenty years ago, I had no thought that anything would ever change, maybe just imagined that at best the hold of communism might one day gradually peter out. I never dreamt that the whole edifice would buckle precipitately under the truthful, penetrating gaze of Austrian and Italian TV. I simply made earnest notes on the embroideries, the linen shifts and bonnets belonging to a peasant life that had existed and would exist for millennia. I made no note of my surroundings, nor of the people I met, my interest always being in their textiles.

So that now only a few images, merely isolated wisps of images, were all I had left from those journeys: the stone-paved seafront of Zadar whipped by wind, totally empty, not a soul with the leisure to walk along its promenade of trees, no footfall, no laughter; the fjord coastline of Kotor, magnificent in the untouched majesty of its deep grey headlands slicing into pale grey sea; the rain-polished stones of Dubrovnik encircled by walls of mellow strength that separated domestic courtyards of cats and washing lines from a gently rolling sea; the canopied wooden stalls of the Turkish market in Sarajevo, where I had exchanged a bottle of whisky for an embroidered woollen waistcoat; and, most vividly, a peaceful farm landscape west of Novi Sad, that rumbled with menace, with insecurity, with an inexplicable sense of unrooted possession. And of Mostar, only the memory of a bridge, just an ancient arched stone bridge that had been and would be there for ever.

As for Cetinje – a miniscule Vienna of vanished splendours, waltzes and intrigues, home of the ambassadorial life of the whole of Europe at the collapse of the Ottoman and Austro-Hungarian empires, and dressed along its broken cobbled streets by the faded façades of toy embassy after toy embassy – all I recalled was that the shabby Intourist hotel was stratospherically expensive for foreigners and that I had billetted myself with a family of gypsies. Their little house was dark and insalubrious, my room approached up a concealed and rickety staircase, and I had slept on a mattress on the floor, divided by a makeshift curtain from the young men of the family who had listened clandestinely from early dawn to Radio France Deux.

In view of what had subsequently happened in this volatile corner of Europe – the killings of the Bosnian war, the siege and rocket assault of Zadar, the Croat destruction of the sixteenth-century Mostar bridge, the bombing of Dubrovnik – the idea of returning was tempered with foreboding. The green fields west of Novi Sad were now surely mined and ethnically cleansed.

Conflicts, minefields, terrorism had dogged my path from the Red Sea, and the aftermath of war sullied its beginning and its end. The silent streets of the Asmara I had left behind were no more. The renewed war with Ethiopia had filled them with the heavy vehicles of military personnel, aid workers and international observers. The Yugoslavia I remembered, which should have been at the end of my travels, was no more. The easy tourist destination of sixties and seventies northern Europe, offering cheap sun and sea, had exploded back into its ancient tribal territories.

Now, where Tito's Yugoslavia had been open and Hoxha's Albania closed, it was the reverse. The border from Albania to Kosovo was closed, I was told, Macedonia was closed, Montenegro was closed. But then so had been the borders between Eritrea and Sudan, and Sudan and Egypt.

I enquired further. The Hani I Hotit border post, the only one between Albania and Montenegro, had been opened only four months before, by mutual agreement between those two countries alone. Now that I was going there, it had closed again. Unilaterally by Belgrade. It was not a frontier of open countryside, albeit mined, like Eritrea, but a tarmacked road, bridged and hugged at the sides by a vice of solid buildings. Hellishly difficult to creep through. However, said Pettifer, though it was closed for Albanians, it was open for foreigners. 'But there's no public transport.' A pricey taxi would sort everything out. I felt inclined to stay with my memories.

The matter was clinched by the aprons. Instead of continuing north, I veered east. Heading towards Tropoje and Bajram Curri, the areas with the highest toll of blood feud murders in Albania, I left Shkoder before dawn, by fugon and then ferry.

Kosovo

The Border

I missed the ferry. It did arrive as I sat waiting on the narrow stone landing-stage at Kuman: a flimsy tug of the African Queen variety – a top deck ringed with a dozen wobbly metal chairs, a fragile hull below. Could this be the ferry to Fierze? No, no, I was told, another would come. After half an hour or so the boat blew its whistle and the four other people on the early morning fugon got on. I asked again but was told another ferry would come, that would be for me. I felt in my bones I should have caught this one, and so I should have done, but it popped off again, leaving me alone on the landing stage.

It may well have been a problem of language and gesture. Combined with the fact that 'yo' means 'no' when all it recalls is the German 'ja', and 'po' is 'yes' when it resembles the French 'pas', plus the nod meaning 'no' and the shake of the head meaning 'yes', all in all, I had little chance of understanding.

I sat and surveyed the beautiful sweep of the river upstream, trapped in a narrow curve between sheer mountain cliffs, but nothing came. Just a rowing boat over-loaded with a houseful of furniture.

After three hours, the only land approach to the river – a long, unlit tunnel chiselled into slabs of rock – suddenly jammed with vehicles, in anticipation of the large, decrepit car ferry steaming round the bend of the river towards them. Trucks and Mercedes tried to disembark, adding to the scrum. Wherever had they all come from, wherever were they all going? I hadn't seen so many vehicles in all the time I'd been in Albania. For hours the police stood ineffectually by, until an exasperated young driver finally sorted everyone out. Armed police joined the passengers.

The ferry followed the river Drin through the most magnificent mountain scenery, almost touching the soaring scarps and cliffs that rose sheer from the river banks on both sides. Some were softly wooded, most were barren, sharp and desolate, but all were utterly unspoilt, a primeval landscape with no sign of the hand of man. In two hours we saw no bridges, no other boats, no concrete bunkers, no villages, no habitation at all, apart from three tiny isolated homesteads. No movement, no sound, bar the lapping of water and the chug of the engine.

Half an hour before the ferry arrived at Fierze, it crashed deliberately into a wooded bank, and fourteen people got off. Some walked up the hillside, where one horse with a wooden saddle waited in the trees to shuttle them to some unseen and unimaginable settlement. Most went down to a rowing boat moored at the bank, where there was no cove or shelter.

The concern of the ferry passengers delivered me into the hands of a young, German-speaking Albanian, Max. His family came from Junik in Kosovo, but he had lived most of his life in Germany and had never seen his home town. This was the first time, and he was with a group of friends. He put me on a fugon to Bajram Curri and waved goodbye.

Bajram Curri was a desperate place, hardly deserving of the name of town. A wide cart track, dusty and deserted, flanked by wretched blocks of Stalinesque flats, led up towards the nearby mountains. Half a dozen fugon gathered where it joined the path to Kosovo, quickly disgorged the passengers they had picked up from the ferry and sped back. Among them was Max, who now had little choice but to climb with his friends into my fugon, the only one prepared to continue into Kosovo, the driver sensing a dollar fare.

We set off along a barely perceptible stony path, through farmland where children with old faces guarded a few cows. We backtracked, went round in circles, as craters barred our way and the few people we saw gave the driver conflicting directions. We followed grassy banks that were the sole indication of a track, we stopped at farm gates to ask the way yet again.

As we approached the border, four of the young men jumped out and disappeared. 'Gone for a picnic in the mountains,' the others joked. The track was closed off at each side by orange plastic tape tied to metal posts, on each side of which was the skull and crossbone insignia and the word MINA. The first border guards were Albanian police watched over by UN observers. 'This road is dangerous,' they said. 'It's safer ahead. Most of the criminals will be behind you soon.'

The second border was manned by Italian soldiers. They checked the remaining men's papers and ran metal detectors over bags, trousers, pockets, shoes. They enquired if there weren't more of us in the fugon and accepted a negative reply, though they must have known it wouldn't travel unless full. The Serbs won't give Albanian Kosovans passports, so the four young men had walked through the minefield to get home. The Italians knew this, Max said, but they felt sorry for them, so they let them get away with it. They accepted the bits of paper of the others, and the excuses for being without. Then they came to me.

The officer in charge dealt with me personally. He was a handsome, suave young man with an alert, intelligent face. His uniform was so smart it looked Armani-designed. He began questioning: 'Why are you going to Kosovo? Why are you crossing this mined border? What's your job?' I explained that I researched embroidery and traditional costumes, and was on my way to Prizren to see the aprons of the mountain women there. From my half-Italian granddaughters, I happened to know the rather obscure word for the little pinafores they had to wear to school – *grembiuli*. The women wear them to market, I explained, aprons stretched over wooden frames. 'It's very important for me to see this.'

The young man's thoughts moved visibly across his face: 'poor old dear. Absolutely barking, but probably harmless.' He asked to see my passport. Rather used, he remarked – all the gold had worn off – but perfectly in order. He handed it back to me. 'Bene,' he said. On you go. I thanked him. 'Grazie a te, signora,' he replied with a deep inclination of the head that was almost a kiss on the hand.

Kosovo for the Albanians is Kosova, and we crossed into it. At first the only people we saw were still little boys looking like old men, in charge of a few cows. Then, as we bumped along execrable paths beside wild flowers and weeds and smallholdings, we saw happier children. We passed one ruined building after another, bombed, blackened, annihilated. Was Serbia or Nato responsible? In the company of only Albanians, I didn't like to ask. Then among them were new houses of bright red brick, and the signboards and vehicles of aid agencies everywhere. Twice we negotiated road blocks of Italian tanks. We passed fields full of graves and a huge cemetery by the side of the road, solid with flowers both plastic and real, and with wreaths and people. Albanians murdered by the Serbs, the men said. At Junik my travelling companions left me.

Through this landscape, so painfully devastated by war that it seared the eyes, a chance assortment of buses took me in stages to the town of Gjakova, where the Serbs had firebombed the market and lacerated normal life. Then on to Prizren.

Prizren

Prizren was once a beautiful town. 'One of my dream cities,' said Durham. 'Best in the Balkans.' 'Still is,' had said Pettifer. It is built on a cleft in a hillside, a scramble of red-tiled Turkish houses and minarets jammed up a gradual slope each side of the Bistrica river. Channelled into a stone duct, the river must once have cascaded down from the mountains, but is now a slow gravelly stream. It is spanned midway by a fifteenth-century triple-arched stone bridge that leads from the new buildings of the town to the Gazi Mehmed mosque, where the black eagle on scarlet of the Albanian flag flies defiantly in all directions.

The town is surreal. Tanks are everywhere, manned by German soldiers finally allowed to take part in the military commitments of Europe. The newer bridge at the top of the town is lined with tanks, tanks wait outside churches. The streets are like a Paris Bastille Day parade of military hardware. Helicopters whizz over every half an hour. The electricity constantly fails, leaving the loud grinding of hundreds of private generators of a crudity more suitable for chopping up turnips. There are four hundred and fifty humanitarian agencies in Kosova and all are represented here. The fifty five nations of OCSE are here. Germans and Turks are the military presence – Germans sometimes also the police – the Italians are the border guards, and remote United Nations countries the peacekeepers and protectors. Swiss observers take breakfast on the hotel verandah at precisely the same hour each morning, eating precisely the same boiled eggs, toast and honey. Everything, even a loaf of bread, must be paid for in German marks.

The churches – but not the mosques – are all wrapped in barbed wire and festooned with warning notices: 'Kfor area: Danger Forbidden Area. Authorised use of firearms.' I thought to walk up to the white Orthodox church I could see among the trees on the hillside above

Prizren, but in a narrow street of town my way was immediately blocked. The two tanks were manned by German soldiers. Not allowed to walk up to the church, 'Verboten,' they said, 'Streng verboten.'

By day the young sit laughing and drinking coffee at the pavement cafés. In the evenings, the failure of electricity would pitch Prizren back to the beautiful town of a hundred years ago, were it not for the presence of foreigners wearing badges flaunting acronyms, and policemen in flared trousers lit by luminous yellow stripes. And those white plastic garden-centre chairs that have cloned a million others all over the world. Excitable men sit on them, bent over tiny cups of coffee and glasses of water and beer, in the candlelit squares.

Edith Durham commented that Prizren was highly picturesque but quite definitely a Moslem Albanian town and that of one thing the populace is determined; that is, that never again shall the land be Serb. Little would she have imagined to what lengths that determination had been pushed, almost a hundred years later, still to have found no concil-iation, and to have the troops of the world supporting it. Her sympathies at the time she was in Prizren lay discreetly with the Serbs, but she felt that the Serbian cause of regaining Prizren was as lost as England's claims to Calais and Bordeaux. She knew the Serbs well, and the ruth-lessness and bestiality of Slobavan Milosevic would hardly have surprised her. The Argentinians, Zimbabweans, and other United Nations person-nel on duty, would never have entered her horizon. The Turks and Austrians she would have expected to be here, but not in the roles of Red Cross workers and peacekeepers.

In Prizren, Durham knew, women spread out handwoven linen to bleach in the sun. The bazaar was a maze of 'long wooden tunnels, dark with hot, rich shadow, glowing with goods', and the gold embroidery there was the best to be found anywhere. She made no mention of aprons, but costume then was gorgeous – white shifts richly embroidered on the sleeves and bodices, headdresses and boleros hung with coins – and aprons hardly worth commenting on. It was only in the regions of Tropoje and Gjakove that they were curious: black and decorated with red crosses, but not stretched over wooden frames.

The Finnish woman, in her late fifties, was a forensic scientist and had been working in the Balkans since 1996, first in Bosnia and then here.

Her work was to follow up massacres, usually of Albanians by Serbs, and determine from the bodies whether their deaths were from warfare, or whether they had simply been murdered in cold blood. Her findings regularly led to indictment of the Serbs by the tribunal of the Hague. Had she ever had any threats against her? I asked. 'Ask me how many,' she shrugged. As Prizren is an Albanian town it is safer for her group to stay here, while they investigate the mass grave of forty five Albanians in the mixed village of Recak. 'I'm tired,' she sighed.

She spoke of her family in Finland, and then asked what I was doing. All my misgivings about being in such a place, among such worthwhile people as her, flooded back. 'I'm just superficial, trivial.' I explained about the aprons. She thought that was wonderful, it had such a touch of normality amid the horrors of her work. She had seen three women wearing them the day before, the first she had come across in all her years in the Balkans.

I felt slightly less superficial when I reached the market. The hot, rich shadows of Durham's wooden tunnels had gone, and flimsy constructions of tin and calico filtered the sunlight on to the crowds of women and girls who thronged round the embroidery stalls. It was clear that in the midst of war their solace was in embroidery.

The women were dressed in a far more Muslim way than in Albania itself. It was just one of the differences that seventy years of separation had brought about. While Albania had suffered enforced isolation and atheism, Kosova had remained open to the outside world, and predominantly Muslim. So most women wore headscarves, long coats – in spite of the heat – and huge harem trousers. These hung up for sale, at least six foot in width. For how much longer, I wondered, as the young were in jeans. Just a few men still wore the round white fez.

There was gold embroidery galore. On boleros and velvet coats, on white dresses, on sleeve bands. Women crowded round, girls tried on wedding boleros over their T-shirts. There were threads from Turkey and Bulgaria. There were women sitting making oya work edgings and wedding flowers. They sold blouses made of a coarse silk and nylon fabric woven in the villages, but they did their embroidery in the market for everyone to see. I bought a blouse decorated with oya pansies from Fahima, who smiled sweetly at having made a sale. The aid workers and UN military weren't very interested in oya pansies, she said. The woman stitching at the next stall was arguing with a customer. Her teeth were bared, the whites of her eyes shone, she missed a couching thread on her goldwork. 'The Albanians are too temperamentvoll,' Max had said.

As for the aprons, I found just four women from the village of Haas, but not together, clamped into their wooden frames that stuck out about a foot each side of their hips. The aprons were more like skirts, hanging both back and front. They made a lot of sense for women living on steep mountainsides, bent under loads of firewood, water and the latest baby. They supported the back and, in the town market, provided a ledge for carrying the shopping.

Disappointingly, they were merely woven in stripes and not embroidered. Weaving I always find rather boring, the woollen threads abandoned on the floor a Brazilian carnival of colour, the finished result on the loom a porridge of Harris tweed.

I was coming to the end of my travels – where then was the linen goddess?

I seemed to be finishing with merely a tangle, like a weaver's discarded wools. Linen first. I had seen none. Only the flax of the old rope spinners in Narya: the buckled women, the scutching and hackling, had long gone. It was easier to buy cotton in any market. And if anything glinted in the sun in the fields around Prizren it was smashed glass and not linen laid out to bleach.

Then the goddess. Almost nowhere throughout the regions I'd travelled in was she based on the shape of a triangle, adapted to linen and the mechanics of counting threads. That version, I presumed, was still to the north and east of me, in Ukraine and Russia.

When I began my search some ten years previously the alternatives had been simple. There was the triangle, hung with three pendants, made out of fabric, an actual object that was stuffed with something: from a dried umbilical cord or a sura from the Koran, to a bit of old cardboard. It was decorated, sometimes with a goddess motif, sometimes with rams' horns, sometimes not at all, and was always intended as an amulet to be worn round the neck or pinned on clothing.

Then there was the same triangle with three pendants, this time embroidered in silk as a motif on a dress or shawl, probably, but not certainly, still playing the role of an amulet.

Travelling westward from the mountain hub of central Asia, everything had become fragmented. What had I found of a goddess based on this triangle and embroidered on linen? And still amuletic? There had been plenty of goddesses, in all guises, bar the one I was looking for. Amulets had become as varied as a bag of liquorice allsorts: fulgurite had vanished, as had tangled fishing net; the jinn had reappeared, and together with them the Koran.

But it was the triangle that had remained the most potent symbol of protection. Even amid Madonnas, petitions to Ab-Besma ab-Besma Wold, rusty bits of iron, broken white glass elephants and a myriad blue beads, it had always been there.

And it was in the market of Prizren in 1908 that Edith Durham bought her amulet: a triangle of velvet with three pendants. Or so I was told. I set out to find it.

Halifax

E dward Akroyd grew up among the tall soot-blackened chimneys of
the wool mills of Halifax. Grimy back-to-back dwellings jostled
down steep paved streets that had once been open rolling moors. He lived,
not in such penury, but in a gritted mansion alongside his father's
worsted mill, together with his brother Henry and all the Victorian
encumbrance of a ramified family. In 1838, when he was twenty eight years
old and engaged to Elizabeth Fearby of York, he bought a rather
splendid house. Built on a slight rise overlooking the killing plumes of
smoke, the asthma and the pleurisy, it was grandly Italianate and clad
in fairfaced stone. The house was called Bankfield.

Over the years, as his life embraced politics, as well as the Church to
which he had always shown a deferential piety, he became a local bigwig
and embellished the house with chapel, library, ballroom, picture gallery,
smoking and billiard rooms, and a *porte-cochère* leading to a marbled
staircase decorated with frescoes of Pompeii and Herculaneum. All that
came up to the house from the infernal mills below was money and, it
was rumoured, ducted hot air to warm the baronial rooms.

The fate of almost all the buildings of northern England's Victorian
eminence – the cotton mills of Lancashire, the wool of Yorkshire – has
been to be rescued from derelict sites, heaven-sent for graffiti and skate-
boarding, to be turned into hands-on museums.

Bankfield was an early victim. In 1887, when Akroyd fell on hard
times, it was sold to Halifax Corporation and then turned into a
museum. Blackened now with grime so deeply ingrained a lottery wind-
fall would be needed to clean it, Bankfield broods on its windy hillock,
set slightly above the tribulations of Halifax, isolated almost. It houses
a major textile collection and boasts a gallery devoted entirely to Edith
Durham: Bread, Salt and our Hearts. Here are the costumes she collected,
the japangi, the giubba, the bright woolly socks, and the amulet she
bought in Prizren.

It is not clear why Edith Durham decided to leave the bulk of her
Balkan collection – beyond what had already gone to the Royal
Anthropological Institute – to Bankfield. It seems the curator at the time
was known to her, and respected. But Durham was born in Hanover
Square and spent her life between London and the Balkans. She knew
nothing of the world of broggers and staplers, of owlers and clothiers,

of tenters and mules, of shuttles and heddles, of woolhooks and teasels, of fulling and rowing. The mire on which Halifax was built.

Durham collected amulets for Sir William Ridgeway and seems to have bought two, not one, in Prizren market, perhaps both for him. The one on display, that I thought could have ended my quest beautifully, was indeed a triangle, but with the apex downward, and with no pendants. Of leather, it had three rows of punched holes all round it, filled with brass eyelets, and two pieces of wire at the top to hang it by. It was for a horse. The other was a necklace of three leather triangles decorated with sequins and white beads, each triangle separated by two blue glass rings. Also for a horse.

In the face of such a disappointing ending to years of travel, I asked permission to rummage through the drawers of Durham's other donations. In one was a pile of headscarves:

> *The woman who wove several of the head-dresses had a husband, born crippled, who begged in the streets of Scutari. They lived in a miserable one-roomed hovel, a large part of which was occupied by her loom, by means of which she supported herself, her husband and as many of her children as survived. (An addition came every year). The family slept in a heap on the ground by the loom on which she worked these gorgeous patterns.*

Among the headscarves was an embroidered one made of linen,

typical of those worn by the women of Prizren, which Durham had bought in the market there. All round the border, alternating with the motif of the tree of life, worked meticulously in counted thread in brown and pink silks, was a pattern 'like a fruit tree on a mound.' It was neither a fruit tree nor a mound, but a triangle surmounted by head and arms. It was the linen goddess.

I had been on the right track all along, just about a hundred years too late.

Bibliography

Allcock, John B. and Young, Antonia (eds), *Black Lambs & Grey Falcons, Women Travellers in the Balkans*, Bradford 1991

Andrews, Carol, *Amulets of Ancient Egypt*, London 1994

Ashour, Mustafa, *The Jinn In the Qur'an and the Sunna*, London 1989

Baines, Patricia, *Flax and Linen*, Shire 1985

Barber, Elizabeth Wayland, *Prehistoric Textiles*, Princeton 1991

Barber, Elizabeth Wayland, *Women's Work: The First 20,000 years*, New York 1995

Bent, J. Theodore, *The Cyclades or Life Among the Insular Greeks*, London 1885

Bent, J. Theodore, *The Sacred City of the Ethiopians*, London 1893

Bent, J. Theodore, *The Land of Frankincense and Myrrh, from the Nineteenth Century*, London 1895

Bent, J. Theodore and Bent, Mrs Theodore, *Southern Arabia*, London 1900

Bent, J. Theodore, "Obituary", *The Geographical Journal (Vol.IX, No.6)*, June 1897, pp. 670-1

Bouska, Vladimir and Bell, James F., "Assumptions about the presence of natural glasses on Mars", *Journal of Geophysical Research*, Washington 1993

Boustead, Col. Sir Hugh, *The Wind of Morning*, London 1971

Briggs, Philip, *Guide to Ethiopia*, Bradt 1995

Burton, Richard, *First Footsteps in East Africa*, London 1856

Charisis, Vassilis An., (transl. by Philip Ramp), *Greek Traditional Architecture: Metsovo*, Athens 1989

Ceka, Neritan, *Butrint: A guide to the city and its monuments*, London 1999

Crowfoot, Grace M., *Methods of Hand Spinning in Egypt and the Sudan*, Halifax 1931[1], Bedford 1974[2]

Charrière, Georges, *L'Art Barbare Scythe*, Paris 1971

Drake-Brockman, R.E., *British Somaliland*, London 1912

Dufalla, Hassan, *The Nubian Exodus*, London 1975

Durham, M. Edith, *High Albania*, London 1909

Durham, M. Edith, *Some Tribal Origins, Laws and Customs of the Balkans*, London 1928

Fakhry, Ahmed, *Siwa Oasis*, Cairo 1990

Fermor, Patrick Leigh, *Roumeli*, London 1966

Forbes, Duncan, *Rimbaud in Ethiopia*, Hythe 1979

Gervers, Veronica, *The Influence of Ottoman Turkish Textiles and Costume in Eastern Europe*, Toronto 1982

Gimbutas, Marija, *The Goddesses and Gods of Old Europe*, London (1974) 1982

Gjergji, A., Shkurti, S., Tirta, M. and Mitrushi, L., *Albanian Folk Costumes,* Tirana 1999

Hall, Rosalind*, Egyptian Textiles*, Shire 1986

Hatzimichali, Angeliki, *The Greek Folk Costume*, Athens 1977

Hill, Jeff, *Something New in Fulgurites, Rocks & Minerals*, Washington 1947

Hudhri, Ferid, *Albania and Albanians in World Art*, Athens 1990

Johnston, Dr Charles, *Travels in Abyssinia*, London 1841

Johnstone, Pauline, *A Guide to Greek Island Embroidery*, London 1972

Kadare, Ismail, *Gjirokaster: La ville de Pierre*, Paris 1997

Kelly, Mary, *Goddess Embroideries of the Balkan Lands and the Greek Islands*, New York 1999

Kendall, Timothy, "Le Djebel Barkal: Le Karnak de Koush", *Les Dossiers d'Archéologie (no.196)*, Sept. 1994, Dijon

Marcus, Harold G., *A History of Ethiopia*, California 1994

Moorehead, Alan, *The White Nile*, London 1960

Moorehead, Alan, *The Blue Nile*, London 1962

Nicholl, Charles, *Somebody Else: Arthur Rimbaud in Africa, 1880-1891*, London 1997

Paice, Edward, *Guide to Eritrea*, Bradt, 1994

Pankhurst, Richard, *The Medical History of Ethiopia*, Trenton N.J. 1990

Papantoniou, Ioanna, *Macedonian Costumes*, Nafplio 1992

Pereira, Benjamin, *Texteis: Tecnologia e Simbolismo*, Lisbon 1985

Pettifer, James, *Albania & Kosovo: The Blue Guide*, London 2001

217

Petzel, Florence Eloise, *Textiles of Ancient Mesopotamia, Persia & Egypt*,
  Oregon 1987
Philippidis, Eleni, *The Sarakatsan Apron in Thrace*, Athens n.d.
Plant, Ruth, *The Architecture of the Tigre*, London 1985
Sponholz, B., *Holocene fulgurite formation in the southern Central Sahara
  (Niger)*, Rotterdam 1993
Starkie, Enid, *Arthur Rimbaud in Abyssinia*, Oxford 1937
Start, Laura, *The Durham Collection*, Bankfield Museum Notes,
  Halifax 1977
Taylor, Roderick, *Embroideries of the Greek Islands*, N.Y and London 1998
Vallet, Odon, *Femmes et Religions*, Paris 1994
Vickers, Miranda, *The Albanians, A Modern History*,
  London and N.Y, 1995/97
Welters, Linda, *Women's Traditional Costume in Attica, Greece*,
  Nafplio 1986
Zali, Anne and Berthier, Annie, *L'Aventure des Ecritures*, exhibition
  catalogue, Bibliothèque Nationale de France, Paris 1998

Index

PALLAS EDITIONS

The Afghan Amulet
Travels from the Hindu Kush to Razgrad
Sheila Paine

Paine is in the direct line of intrepid English women travellers
International Herald Tribune

In 1990, armed with 'five kilos of baggage and a litre of vodka', Sheila Paine
set out for the high valleys of the Hindu Kush to seek out an intriguing embroidered amulet, her only clue beingthat it came from Kohistan – simply 'land
of mountains.'

   Undaunted by tales of terror her quest led her into increasingly dangerous
territories – alone. Frequently risking the dire penalties of Islamic Shari'a law,
this lone widow wandered around Pakistan and Iran, finding herself in situ-
ations which would terrify most of us. She was then smuggled into Afghanistan
– wearing a stifling *burqa* covering her from head to toe – where she was
surrounded by superstition, gunfire and Kalashnikov-toting *mujahedin*
making sexual advances to her. Continuing her journey through Iraq and Turkish Kurdistan she eventually reached the last link in the chain, the small
town of Razgrad in eastern Bulgaria.

   Sheila Paine has a quick and quirky eye for detail and vividly and humor-
ously captures the essence of the strange people and places she encountered
on her extraordinary adventures.

278 pp plus 48 pp colour plates   ISBN 1 873429 85 1   £14.99

PALLAS EDITIONS

The Golden Horde
Travels from the Himalaya to Karpathos
Sheila Paine

Every time she finds a sun-disc or a red-thread goddess... she is infused
with vitality – and you with her – and she has a lovely tenderness
towards those who made or make things
Veronica Horwell in The Guardian

In the second instalment of her trilogy, *Out of Central Asia*, Sheila Paine
describes the second, even more ambitious, phase of her quest. She visits the
remote, untamed valley of Palas in the Western Himalaya – previously closed
to her – and travels through the turbulent territories of the former Soviet
Union: from Arctic Russia through the lands of the Golden Horde and into
Soviet Central Asia. She ends up in the Carpathian mountains and on the Greek
island of Karpathos (whose similarity of names may be more than coincidence)
where women still wear the amulet to ward off evil spirits and where olive
branches from Palm Sunday are collected for their magical powers. A journey to the heart of a mystery which is also a tale of high adventure, full of
strange encounters with hippies, Orthodox pilgrims and a possible German
granddaughter of Lawrence of Arabia, this is travel writing at its most powerful, evocative and moving.

303 pp plus 48 pp colour plates   ISBN 1 873429 86 X   £14.99

PALLAS EDITIONS

The Light Garden of the Angel King
Travels in Afghanistan
with Bruce Chatwin
Peter Levi

This is a beautiful book, a poetic evocation and worthy of a place on the
shelf beside Kinglake's *Eothen* and Robert Byron's *Road to Oxiana*
John Morris in the *Sunday Times*

Rich in anecdote and general speculation
Simon Raven in the *Observer*

It has all the glamour of a revelation. I still turn to it for inspiration.
Stanley Stewart in the *Daily Telegraph*

From time immemorial Afghanistan has been a mountainous crossroads.
Through it have come merchants with indigo and Chinese silk, Alexander the
Great, nomads from the steppes, colonies of Buddhist monks, great Moghul
conquerors and the ill-fated armies of the British Raj.

In 1970 Peter Levi, classical scholar, archaeologist and later Professor of
Poetry at Oxford, set off with Bruce Chatwin to seek the clue which each
migration left. It is this quest that gives his fascinating book its theme. How
far east did Alexander really establish himself? Who built the great upland castle
that exists on no map? Could the sculptors of Athens really have influenced
the early Buddhist artists? In drawing back the curtain on Afghanistan, Levi
reveals not a rocky wilderness ranged over by plunderers, but, in the words
above Babur's tomb, 'a highway for archangels'.

First published in 1973, this account of Afghanistan is an acknowledged
classic of travel writing. It is now reissued with fresh photographs from the
Chatwin archives and a new introduction in which Peter Levi looks back on
a lost Afghanistan, 'an island in time, a ruined paradise', and on his friend-
ship with the young Chatwin.

234 pp plus 16 pp colour plates   ISBN 1 873429 35 5   £12.99

PALLAS EDITIONS

The Stones of Venice
John Ruskin
abridged by J.G. Links

It is a book for the lover of architecture, the lover of Venice, the lover of
lost causes... but, perhaps, above all, for the lover of fine writing.
J. G. Links, in his introduction

For fifty years, *The Stones of Venice* was read by all who went there and
thousands who could not; the sightseers whom the city captivates today
seldom have Venice's greatest guidebook with them.

The overwhelming clarity of Ruskin's vision, which would eventually lead
to his mental breakdown, makes him the most stimulating, entertaining,
aggravating and enlightening companion. At its best, his prose has a precision
and nobility that rank it with the greatest masters of the language.

His most influential book, *The Stones of Venice,* was written as part of an
impassioned polemic in favour of Gothic architecture. 'It is in Venice, and in
Venice only, that effectual blows can be struck at this pestilent art of the Renaissance.' This was Ruskin's war cry as he entered the now almost forgotten Battle
of the Styles on the side against 'the school which has conducted men's
inventive and constructional faculties from the Grand Canal to Gower Street.'

But first the reader must know the difference between right and wrong; he
must find out for himself the best way of doing everything. 'I shall give him
stones, and bricks, and straw, chisels and trowels and the ground, and then
ask him to build, only helping him if I find him puzzled.'

Unhappily, both these exciting objectives were attained only after the expen-
diture of nearly half a million words; glorious words, but too many. It is the
aim of this edition to remedy this and to put a fascinating book within reach
of those with limited resources of time. Much that was superfluous has been
omitted; what is left is the essence of a now most readable book.

272 pp plus many illustrations from the original editions
ISBN 1 873429 35 5   £12.99

PALLAS EDITIONS

Effie in Venice
Mrs. John Ruskin's letters home, 1849-52
Edited by *Mary Lutyens*

Even if these letters had not the special interest of being from John
Ruskin's wife, they would be absorbing in their picture of the social life
that dominated Venice at this particular period
Marghanita Laski in the *Observer*

A lively picture of the *ancien régime* re-establishing itself for its last fling.
Mary Lutyens has put so much into the narrative linking these hitherto
unpublished letters and is so at home with the vast cast of characters,
that the book is as much hers as Effie's. It is perhaps the most
radiant episode in Ruskin's life
The Times

Superbly edited by Mary Lutyens from the original letters discovered by her
untouched in the archives, Effie Ruskin's letters home from Venice give an
unparalleled view of Victorian travel and society through the eyes of a highly
intelligent and lively young woman. John Ruskin took his wife to Venice for
the first time in 1849, and while he worked on books that would define the
Victorian aesthetic ideal, Effie explored Venice with growing freedom and
independence of thought.
    Rightly considered a classic both of travel literature and of writing about
Victorian art and the milieu where much of it was made and appreciated,
Effie in Venice makes a welcome return to print.

368 pp plus 16 pp b/w plates   ISBN 1 873429 33 9   £12.99

PALLAS EDITIONS

The Generous Earth

*An account of life in the Dordogne Valley of France,
'the land of all Good Things'*

Philip Oyler

with a new introduction by Joy Law

In *The Generous Earth*, Philip Oyler 'describes a civilization which possesses a vitality and an integrity of which the excellence of its products is but an outward manifestation, and he describes from within, rather than as a mere detached observer.' So wrote Lord Northbourne in his foreword to this classic account of life in rural France, now reissued for the first time since 1961.

Philip Oyler, farmer and traveller, moved to the Dordogne after the First World War. There, in the district between the small market towns of St Céré and Sarlat, in the Dordogne valley about 100 miles east of Bordeaux, was a region completely unexploited by commerce or tourism.

He found a way of life that had hardly changed for centuries and is now no more. It was a world of true rural husbandry rooted in tradition and a beautiful countryside where the balance of nature had not been disturbed by man. The region was rich in real wealth – crops, vineyards, stock, timber, fruit and fish.

Anyone interested in travel, in France, in farming, good food. good wine, and sheer good living will enjoy this book.

192 pp plus 16 pp b/w plates   ISBN 1 873429 66 5   £12.99

PALLAS EDITIONS

The Surprise of Cremona
One Woman's Adventures in Cremona, Parma, Mantua,
Ravenna, Urbino and Arezzo
Edith Templeton

with a new introduction by Anita Brookner

A strip-tease Baedeker
Cyril Connolly

Mrs Edith Templeton...sojourned in old towns of North Italy
— Cremona, Parma, Mantua, Urbino and Arezzo.
None before her has been so frank, so robust, so comprehensive.
Tremendous fun... companionable, evocative and informing
Edith Shackleton in *The Lady*

A ruthless, ironic, exasperating,
immensely amusing companion
Sunday Times

Highly original, bald, assured...a virtuoso display of personality.
She makes the reader see through her eyes
— and sharp, ironic ones they are...
Pamela Hansford Johnson in *Bookman*

Edith Templeton, Bohemian aristocrat, accomplished novelist and widow of
the physician to the King of Nepal wrote this highly individual account of
her visit to six North Italian towns in the early fifties. Wonderfully evocative of the time and the places, her vintage narrative is a gem of travel literature
but has been unavailable for many years. An introduction by Anita Brookner
to this new edition gives a beautiful analysis of the astringent wit and classic
poise of Templeton's writing.

256 pp plus 16 pp b/w plates   ISBN 1 873429 65 7   £12.99

PALLAS EDITIONS

In the Glow of the Phantom Palace
From Granada to Timbuktu
Michael Jacobs

Jacobs is an engaging, wonderfully informative
and ever-surprising companion
Jan Morris

Funny, learned and beautifully written
New Statesman

He is the ideal companion we all dream of but rarely find: patient, lively
and endlessly generous with his encyclopaedic, cultivated mind
Irish Independent

The George Borrow of the High-Speed Train Era
ABC Madrid

In this new book, Michael Jacobs follows the trail of the Moors of Spain, exiled
from their last kingdom of Granada in 1492. This extraordinary journey takes
in ruins and discos in Andalucía, masseurs and literary lions in Morocco, before
finishing in the mud mosques of Timbuktu, where families still keep the key
to the house in Granada that they fled five hundred years ago.

On the way Jacobs conjures up a cast of irrepressibly alluring adulterers,
louche fixers, kings, professors, poets, cobblers and voyagers, in a kaleido-
scope of fiction, history, journey and imagination. How, Jacobs asks as he
journeys southwards, can we be sure who, where, or when we are?

Michael Jacobs is widely regarded as the leading Hispanist of his genera-
tion, and his books have been acclaimed both here and in Spain. *Andalucía,
The Road to Santiago* and *Madrid for Pleasure* have been published by Pallas
Athene. He is currently Fellow in Hispanic Studies at the University of
Glasgow.

224 pp, illustrated   ISBN 1 873429 36 3   £12.99

Cover *Rashaida woman and daughter, Massawa environs, Eritrea*
Half title: *Woman spinning outside her home in Axum, Ethiopia*
Title page and back flap: *Motif on the shawl bought by
Edith Durham in Prizren market, Kosovo*

If you would like further information
about titles published in the
Pallas Editions series,
please write to:
Pallas Athene
59 Linden Gardens
London W2 4HJ
or visit our website at
WWW.PALLASATHENE.CO.UK

Photographs by Sheila Paine
Illustrations by Imogen Paine
Maps by Ted Hammond

Series editor: Alexander Fyjis-Walker
Editorial assistant: Della Tsiftsopoulou
Series designer: James Sutton
Special thanks to Richard Fyjis-Walker,
Barbara Fyjis-Walker, Caroline Singer

First published by Pallas Editions
in conjunction with Ostara Publishing 2003

ISBN 1 873429 87 8

Printed on acid-free paper in Finland